# MEMORIALIZING the DEAD
# PREACHING to the LIVING

# MEMORIALIZING the DEAD PREACHING to the LIVING

## A Resource Manual for Christian Clergy

### JAMES SAXMAN

Pleasant Word

A Division of WINEPRESS PUBLISHING

Unless otherwise noted, all Scriptures are taken from the Holy Bible, New International Version, Copyright © 1973, 1978, 1984 by the International Bible Society. Used by permission of Zondervan Publishing House. The "NIV" and "New International Version" trademarks are registered in the United States Patent and Trademark Office by International Bible Society.

Scripture references marked KJV are taken from the King James Version of the Bible.

Scripture references marked NASB are taken from the New American Standard Bible, © 1960, 1963, 1968, 1971, 1972, 1973, 1975, 1977 by The Lockman Foundation. Used by permission.

NON SEQUITUR © 2001 Wiley Miller. Dist. by UNIVERSAL PRESS SYNDICATED. Reprinted with permission. All rights reserved.

B.C. Comics. Used by permission of Johnny Hart and Creators Syndicated, Inc.

FRANK & ERNEST reprinted by permission of Newspaper Enterprise Association, Inc.

Family Circus cartoon (6/21/01) © Bill Keane, Inc. Reprinted with Special Permission of King Features Syndicate.

Bizarro cartoon (12/6/95) © Dan Pirari. Reprinted with Special Permission of King Features Syndicate.

Quotes reprinted by permission from UNDERSTANDING MOURNING: A GUIDE FOR THOSE WHO GRIEVE by Glen W. Davidson, copyright © 1984 Augsburg Publishing House. Used by permission of Augsburg Fortress (www.augsburgfortress.org).

Worden: GRIEF COUNSELING AND GRIEF THERAPY 3E: Copyright © 2001 by Springer Publishing Company, Inc., New York 10012. Used by Permission.

Aquainted with Grief by Haven of Rest. Used by permission.

ISBN 1-4141-0012-4
Library of Congress Catalog Card Number: 2003109100

# To David Allison

By the end of life, all have a story to be told. To my knowledge, no one escapes unscathed. This would be a sad human epitaph were it not for the undeniable biblical revelation that the "downside of life" is the essence of the sanctification process in Christ.

'Tis mystery all, it is for our good. So too, is death. For the redeemed, the worst of all has been transformed into the glorious entrance into life eternal with Christ Jesus.

To know and believe this, and then to die well, is life.

This book is dedicated to my special friend, David Allison, who though being the recipient of a more-than-fair-share of God's mysterious providential "good chastenings," persevered unto the end to prove his calling (Hebrews 11:27). His journey directed him to the spiritual experience of finding New Covenant life and joy in Christ which releases the soul from bondage and gives ultimate meaning to an otherwise sin-tainted world, and then, to die well. Thank you, David, for taking the time to pass this on to me.

# Contents

# Preface

## MEET THE AUTHOR

### Credentials

If you want to make God laugh, tell Him your plans.

—Anonymous

*Some years ago I had a plan for my life. It hasn't gone as I thought it would. Not bad, just different. In college I had a good friend who could not wait to get to The Wharton School of Business in Philadelphia. He used to say that the clout which a post-graduate degree from that school carried was like nothing else in business. Today he is a seven-figure businessman working in Manhattan and living in pristine suburban Connecticut with his neighbor Keith Richards of the Rolling Stones. I guess he was right; credentials are important.*

*When I pick up a book to look it over, it is not long before I flip to the back jacket to see who the author is who is demanding my twenty dollars' worth of attention. A legitimate academic pedigree should mean that the author knows his subject. True enough, credentials say that we have paid our dues in the rigors of academia, written more papers than anyone would want to read, and tested well enough to satisfy the demands of formal education. But formal education without real life application is shallow at best. Degrees are only a part of the story.*

*What really rounds out the equation is, "On what road has God taken us to make theory reality? How successful have we been in life?" Here is my story.*

I was born and raised outside of Pittsburgh, Pennsylvania, and at an early age, developed a rather odd fascination and curiosity for the funeral industry and death and dying. It probably stemmed from two factors outside of my life that I believe were completely within God's directive hand.

Number one was that as a child I was taken to a funeral home to view the body of a family friend who had passed away. Subsequently, whether from fear of the dead or just plain weirdness, I do not know; but "funeralization" became something I wanted to know more about. Though uncomfortable with that initial experience, I think I was also struck by other issues: the preserving of the dead, the social necessity of the event, and moreover, the entire process of memorialization. I had many questions and this curiosity stuck with me for the days and years to come.

The second influence was when I worked one summer mowing grass in a nearby cemetery with the son of a local funeral director. During the monotony of mowing we memorized the names of long-time residents. There were a number of celebrities— Elizabeth Taylor, James Taylor, James Stewart; not the real ones, but our local versions. A lot of jokes and stories about the dead are shared when you work in a cemetery. It's boring work pushing a lawn mower past the same gravestones over and over. The mind wanders.

My friend lived with his family on the second floor of the funeral home. Eerie to some, but not to me. So in order to visit him, I needed to be in the funeral home. You are privileged to see and learn much about the dead when you hang around a mortuary. Later, I worked summers waxing cars, answering phones, going on removals, whatever needed to be done. They were good folks.

Because of these opportunities I was exposed more and more to the funeral industry. My fascination grew.

After receiving an undergraduate degree, I attended Pittsburgh Institute of Mortuary Science where I was an honors graduate in 1970. An apprenticeship followed, and, after successfully passing the National Board exam, I became a "Licensed Funeral Director and Embalmer in the State of Pennsylvania, being entitled to all the Rights, Privileges, Honors and Marks of Distinction thereto pertaining." Following my apprenticeship, I was employed for a time as a dienor (pathologist's assistant), assisting on post mortem examinations (autopsies) at the Milton Hershey Medical Center. This provided even more exposure to the dead, but from a very different perspective.

In 1975, as my mother put it, "I got religion." Via conversion and convinced of a divine call, I moved to the northwestern United States and attended seminary, graduating from Western Reformed Seminary in Tacoma, Washington. In 1982, while in seminary, I was employed by a rather large funeral home as a follow-up grief counselor heading up a biblically based program dealing with death, dying, and bereavement with family members who had lost loved ones. An unexpected by-product of this position was that I became the house chaplain for families who had no attachment to a local church and yet wanted a minister to officiate at their loved one's service.

Also, since I was working within the boundaries of funeral service, I came to know many of the local funeral directors. Understanding that I was working with the bereaved, they would often call me to officiate at services of their un-churched families as well. One minister calls it "preaching generic funerals." The result of all this was that since 1982 I have officiated at over twelve hundred memorial and funeral services. And while I will admit that I have come to embrace a somewhat repetitive general pattern for conducting these services, I have also learned that every service is unique in its individuality and its diversity. People live life differently from one another. People die for many different reasons and in varying situations.

Serving as an independent chaplain for people during the trial of a death experience has been one of the most rewarding experiences of my life. Because of that, I have written this book in an attempt to share what I have learned with others.

At times I have queried my friends, "What do you get if you cross a funeral director with a preacher?" And the answer: "You get a preacher who officiates at funerals." That is what I have become. It wasn't my original plan, but it seems to have been God's plan.

And so, I come before you as a funeral director/clergy person with a rich experience and perspective on a very practical issue that is constantly before us in ministry: *Memorializing the Dead and Preaching to the Living.*

# Introduction

## Why Read this Book?

Over the years of reading many books, I have formulated a simple rule: a book must make me read it. I will give nearly anything a try, but within about thirty pages or so, it must capture me. It must reach into my being and plead, "Read me, I have interest, I have value." I no longer feel obligated (as I once did) to painstakingly pore over a bad book until completion. The days of laboring out of dutiful devotion to some perceived principle of perseverance are behind me.

Now I admit that perhaps I've missed a few "late-bloomers" because of this rule.

It's like walking out of the ballpark in the seventh inning, trailing by five runs, and hearing on the car radio that the home team rallied to pull out a win. Sometimes it happens, but seldom. If you ask me how it is that I've come to this view, it is simple.

By and large it has been the axiom of Solomon, ". . . of the making of many books there is no end . . ." that has driven me to this position. So many books, and so little time. If you then are like me, you might be asking yourself the legitimate question, "Why should I read this one?"

The old maxim in book writing says: "If you want to be successful, write about something you know." Hear my confession. I do not consider myself to be a writer. A writer to me is a person who is gifted and passionate about the art of writing. He loves it; he lives for it. He does it nearly every day of his life. I cannot claim that. What I do claim is to have written this book, a book about something that I know.

My motive for writing grew out of the conviction that God had brought me on a path which, almost in spite of myself, had qualified me to tell others about that which I knew. I had come to the point of feeling a sense of duty to share some things that would be helpful to ministers and others who would want or need to read it. I would dare to call it the delightfully complex and unfathomable providence of God working on my conscience to cause me to forge ahead in compiling a resource tool for clergy.

O the depth of the riches both of the wisdom and the knowledge of God, how unsearchable are His judgements, and His ways past finding out!

—Romans 11:33

Since 1982 the over one thousand funeral/memorial services at which I have offici-ated have been quite varied: natural and unnatural causes, suicide, murder, AIDS, SIDS, Alzheimer's, Parkinson's, and cancer. For all types and ages: veterans, leukemic children, too-young tragedies, wealthy, poor, dearly loved and sadly forgotten. There are many different ways to die.

In 1997 I was encouraged by a friend (funeral director) that since I had "gotten good" at this thing (officiating at services), maybe I should write a book. At the same time it was occurring to me that I had arrived at a place where I actually did have something to say that would be helpful to others. I realized that in the midst of all these services, I had been forced to carve out a pattern for a service that would work for any situation, without compromising the principle duty of the servant of God, i.e. to advance the message of the gospel (a tension which I will address later in this book). Realizing that I had been fortu-nate to accumulate a great wealth of experience in these situations, and at the encourage-ment of my funeral director friends, I became smitten in conscience to make a disciplined effort to package this knowledge in order to help others.

For most of us, our theological academic experience was both challenging and thrill-ing. When we were turned loose into the real world, however, we found that there are some skills that can truly be learned only in the line of duty. Such is the case with our topic. Compare your experience with mine and consider these reasons for compiling this resource manual.

1. In a course on pastoral theology in seminary, only a small portion was devoted to "The Funeral." Most of my seminary friends can't remember much about any-

thing we covered in formal education in this area. Topics such as grief management, counseling in the context of terminal illness, is embalming necessary, cremation vs. earth burial, the value of viewing, and so on were never touched upon. These are the subjects on which people in churches will confront their pastors; the issues you "cut your teeth on" in the real world. We have to conclude that *our training in this area was perhaps insufficient.* And to constantly refresh ourselves in practical theology by way of new and challenging thoughts is always a healthy exercise.

2. *Our capabilities can be stretched by another's experiences.* Handling the funeral/memorialization process is a bit like parenting. By the time you get good at it, the kids have grown and are gone. In the average clergy career, a minister will conduct 100 services, more or less. But it generally takes an entire life to amass this number. We ask, "What can we do to cut down that learning curve?" Maybe a book would help?

   Also, we learn that although our ultimate message remains constant (gospel), the circumstances surrounding each individual's life are always different and multiple. For example, to officiate at the service of a thirty-year-old suicide in the context of AIDS is quite different from the death of a dear ninety-year-old praying saint of the church. God's Word assures us that as we are exposed to and share with one another our varied experiences, iron is sharpening iron. My hope is that my experiences may prove fruitful for all who digest this manual.

3. I am convinced that some ministers have not fully appreciated that, as in all areas of life, so too God, in death, allows us to see His hand open doors of *opportunity to advance His truth.* Death sometimes provides the opportune time to help people when they are most fragile and vulnerable and gives us the chance to win their hearts. Though not an absolute promise, it is not uncommon for people to seek God when they are in trials. As servants of God, we should be ready to be used— *carpe memento,* seize the moment!

4. Finally, it is my conviction that the clergy/funeral director alliance must constantly be viewed as a *cooperative effort* to serve the community. We are the team of professionals who are called upon to help people when they are truly in their greatest point of helplessness and pain. Shame on us if we do not work well together. I trust my book will enhance that union.

And so to answer the question, "Why should I read this book?" Simply put, the book has something to say which will have great practical value to those who choose to use it as a tool for their calling in serving people in the crisis of death. Some time ago I attended a symposium by a noted pastor/grief guru whose presentation disturbed me. He left us with four formidable challenges for the funeral industry in the days ahead. The second of those was "The Challenge of the Clergy," in which he outlined a need for a changing paradigm regarding memorialization. His premise was that since pastors as a whole have largely ignored the legitimate ministerial concerns of proper eulogy and bereavement care (especially to the non-churched), the funeral industry should reclaim the ground that was "given over" to the clergy. He actually made the statement, "We've handed it over to the clergy and they've ruined it; we need to take it back." He is now training funeral directors and independents to be lay ministers in funeral service. His attitude disturbed me because it seemed to me to be quite alarmist. I know that I (as with many of my colleagues) have not thrown in the towel in this area.

But as with most attacks, I have learned that there is usually a nugget of truth within. We may be hurt by criticism, but we're none the wiser if we do not listen carefully to the charge behind it. His personal frustrations had arisen because often the clergy have not met people's needs as they might have. And if true, that is a message we desperately need to hear and heed. I concluded that the difference between that speaker and me is that I have not given up on the clergy just yet. Hence, this book.

The topics that I have chosen to explore are death; theodicy, a biblical account of mourning, memorialization as opportunity, the visit/eulogy, the hope of resurrection, suggested scriptural texts, difficult services, clergy/funeral director relations, and an extensive selection of practical hands-on aids (hymns, poems, quips, stories).

I have written sparsely regarding the topics of "grief and grief management." In my estimation, those issues have been so extensively covered in volumes written by qualified professionals trained specifically in the counseling arena, that I refer the reader to those works. Also I have chosen not to include a chapter regarding the actual arranging or mechanics of a funeral service. The final orchestration of a service should be done by the Spirit of God and the minister, and to mechanize this effort seems a bit degrading to both the officiant and the Holy Spirit. Instead, what I have attempted to do is put a plethora of time-tested materials, tips, and aids into the hands of the minister.

Unapologetically, I have chosen not to be dogmatic in some of the areas of consideration treated in my book (for example, theodicy; burial vs. cremation). I have attempted to state the case well and give ample information regarding these somewhat mysterious and potentially controversial issues. It is my conviction that conscientious ministers must decide for themselves where to leave these topics.

Quotations in this manuscript represent my selection of the illustrations which best express my intent and content. Wherever possible, permission has been obtained to use them in this publication. If there has been any oversight regarding use infringement, I apologize to those offended and will make every effort to rectify the situation. To borrow the old maxim, "To steal from one person is plagiarism, to steal from many is research."

And so, we agree with King Solomon, "Of the making of books there *is* no end!"

My single intent is that the addition of this one to that endless collection will prove invaluable to all who minister in the difficult and tender task of death, dying, and the funeral/memorialization process.

God's blessing upon us all as we labor in His field.

James D. Saxman

# Death

## The Wisdom of Qoheleth

It is the same for all. There is one fate for the righteous and for the wicked; for the good, for the clean, and for the unclean; for the man who offers a sacrifice and for the one who does not sacrifice . . . furthermore, the hearts of the sons of men are full of evil, and insanity is in their hearts throughout their lives. Afterwards they go to the dead.

—Ecclesiastes 9:2–3

Everyone dies.

Along with the book of Job, Ecclesiastes reminds us that God is bigger and that our lives are more unpredictable than we might think. The problem with Ecclesiastes is that for those of us who require tidy answers to complex issues, this book leaves us a bit perplexed. The qoheleth, or teacher, represented the wise men of his day. These wise men studied closely the interworkings of creation (nature) and human experience. From their wisdom they made pronouncements regarding some of life's most perplexing issues. The qoheleth's message seems particularly aimed at the individual who would seek to find life's meaning outside of faith in God. Twenty-nine times the author uses the phrase "life under the sun" to designate life outside of God's control and goodness. He addresses some of life's most sensitive questions. One of these is the question, "How can understanding death bring meaning to life?"

Bill and Teresa Syrios, in their helpful study on Ecclesiastes, begin with a poignant illustration regarding the value that death has in bringing meaning to life.

A historical cemetery, which sits on the edge of the University of Oregon campus, has for years been eyed by the university officials as a highly desirable slice of real estate. Students think it is an inconvenient obstacle as they crisscross the campus. Someone once had even suggested they build a superstructure of above-ground buildings over the plots beneath. Mr. And Mrs. Syrios then suggest that all these objections notwith-standing, a cemetery within the view of college students is perhaps the best reminder for young people to seek to fashion their lives around lifelong values, since contempla-tion of death gives man the wisdom to live well. Would that there were more cemeteries to make us think.[1]

I read somewhere that John Wesley, the great circuit rider qoheleth (preacher, speaker, philosopher, teacher) of his day, was asked, "Mr. Wesley, if you knew that you were going to die tomorrow, what changes would you make for today?" His reply was, "I would do nothing different." Apparently his life was so caught up with the things of Christ that he did not feel the need to alter the events of his day. But I suppose most of us could not answer with the great Methodist. The fact is, the knowledge of the urgency of the inevi-tability of our deaths would likely make most of us restructure our days and lives in a radical way. This is one of the values of the knowledge of death.

Death then, is the great equalizer; it is the "common destiny" which awaits us all. Derek Kidner states, "Everything is vanity (empty) . . . moral or immoral, religious or profane, we are all mown down alike. In a hundred years, as we say, it will all come to the same thing. Yet death seems to say this—it has a way of getting the last word."[2] Dr. Walter Kaiser offers this thought: "Now Solomon does not level a charge against God when he labels what happens to good and evil men alike as an "evil" (9:3). His use of the term "evil," like his evaluation, is strictly from the human point of view and based on appearances. He has, for the moment, purposely left out all considerations of the divine perspective and revelational facts. Thus, so far as men can see, one "event," or "destiny," comes to all."[3]

Qoheleth tells us that there is one fate that awaits all. Righteous and wicked alike, all die. Jesus, in a similar way, explains that throughout life there will be evidence of God's common dealings with all men (Matthew 5:45). These reminders are to serve as wake-up calls on how to live in light of life's final event. Wise and foolish, righteous and wicked, clean and unclean, all will share this common experience. All die.

And so, what we discover is that qoheleth reminds us that a proper perspective on death will affect our priorities and values in life. If life is short, and death is an imminent absolute, then man must make certain that he has prioritized correctly. Redeem the life.

Jesus says, "Do not lay up treasures on earth, where moth and rust destroy, and where thieves break in and steal; but lay up for ourselves treasures in heaven where neither moth nor rust destroys, and where thieves do not break in and steal." In light of death, we learn that we must focus on things that have eternal value, such as service to God and service to our fellow man. Jesus said, "We must work the works of Him who sent Me, as long as it is day; night is coming, when no man can work" (John 9:4).

Finally, while death is arguably the greatest "known," at once it is still the greatest "unknown." We not only feel uneasy facing death, but just discussing death is a subject we avoid most of our days. And what is the reason for this discomfort? Most certainly it is because though death is thought of as a most "natural" part of the process of the life cycle, in fact the Bible tells us that it is not natural at all. Unlike Eastern cyclical philosophies, God's Word tells us that man was not originally created to die, but to live forever in perfect harmony with his God. Death, the result of sin, has come in as an unwanted alien, an intruder; and God's Word, our experience, and conscience all bear witness to this fact. It has taken us captive.

What then can man do to be set free from this life-long slavery, this fear of death (Hebrews 2:15)? God's answer: "For since by a man came death, by a man also came the resurrection of the dead. For as in Adam all die, so also, in Christ all shall be made alive" (1 Corinthians 15:21–22). This then is God's liberating message for mankind. To know the meaning of death is to know the meaning of life—eternal!

# DEATH

*Truly, there is no shortage of quotations surrounding the topic of death. The following is a collection of quotes from individuals whose diverse minds have influenced our times.*

*"Curiosity."*

## English and European Writers/Poets

Shakespeare was of us, Milton was for us,
Burns, Shelley, were with us—they watch from their graves!

I was ever a fighter, so-one fight more,
The best and the last!
I would hate that death bandaged my eyes, and for bore,
And bade me creep past.
No! Let me taste the whole of it,
Fare like my peers the heroes of old,
Bare the brunt, in a minute pay glad life's arrears.

—Robert Browning

Half our days we pass in the shadow of the earth;
and the brother of death exacts a third part of our lives.

Sleep is a death, O make me try,
By sleeping what it is to die.
And as gently lay my head
On my grave, as now my bed.

—Sir Thomas Browne

Straightway I was aware,
So weeping, how a mystic shape did move
And a voice said in mastery while I strove, . . .
"Guess now who holds thee?"—"Death", I said, but there
The silver answer rang . . . "Not Death, but Love."

—Elizabeth Barrett Browning


And when a beast is dead he has no pain;
But man after his death must weep and complain.

—Geoffrey Chaucer


Though nothing can bring back the hour
Of splendor in the grass, of glory in the flower;
We will grieve not, rather find
Strength in what remains behind;
In the primal sympathy
Which having been must ever be;
In the soothing thoughts that spring
Out of human suffering;
In the faith that looks through death,
In years that bring the philosophic mind.

—William Wordsworth


What I like about Clive
Is that he is no longer alive.
There is a great deal to be said
For being dead.

—Edmund Clerihew Bentley


Since every man who lives is born to die,
And none can boast sincere felicity,
With equal mind, what happens, let us bear,
Nor joy nor grieve too much for things beyond our care.
Like pilgrims to the appointed place we tend;
The world's an inn and death the journey's end.

—John Dryden

O death the poor man's dearest friend, the kindest and the best!

—Robert Burns

Is life a boon? If so, it must befall
That death, whene'er he call, must call too soon.

—Sir William Schwenck Gilbert

Death is still working like a mole,
And digs my grave at each remove.

—George Herbert

He lives, he wakes, 'Tis Death is dead, not he.

Death is the veil which those who live call life:
They sleep, and it is lifted.

How wonderful is death, death and his brother sleep.

I could lie down like a tired child,
And weep away the life of care
Which I have borne and yet must bear,
Til death like sleep might steal on me.

—Percy Bysshe Shelley

Sleep after toil, port after stormy seas,
Ease after war, death after life does greatly please

Death is the end of woes: die soon, O fairy's son.

—Edmund Spenser
The Faerie Queene

Life is the desert, life the solitude;
Death joins us to the great majority.

—Edward Young

Death is parting, 'Tis the last sad adieu 'twixt soul and body.

—Nicholas Rowe


For they're hangin' Danny Deever, you can hear the dead march play
And the regiment's in 'ollow square, they're hangin' him today;
They've taken of his buttons off and cut his stripes away,
And they're hangin' Danny Deever in the morning.


Yes, lad, I lie easy, I lie as lads would choose;
I cheer a dead man's sweetheart, never ask me whose.

—A.E. Housman


With proud thanksgiving, a mother for her children,
England mourns for her dead across the sea.

—Laurence Binyon


Take hold of the wings of the morning,
And flop round the earth til you're dead;
But you won't get away from the tune they play
To the bloomin' old rag overhead.

—Rudyard Kipling


And he that will his health deny,
Down among the dead men let him lie.

—John Dyer


Dead! And . . . never called me mother.

—Mrs. Henry Wood


That he who many a year with toil of breath
Found death in life, may here find life in death.


An orphan's curse would drag to hell
A spirit from on high;
But oh! More horrible than that
Is the curse in a dead man's eye.

—Samuel Taylor Coleridge

O me, why have they not buried me deep enough?
Is it kind to have made me a grave so rough,
Me, that was never a quiet sleeper?
Bury me, bury me . . . deeper, ever so deeper.

It seemed so hard at first mother, to leave the blessed sun
And now it seems as hard to stay, and yet His will be done!
But still I think it can't be long before I find release;
And that good man, the clergyman, has told me words of peace.

Authority forgets a dying king.

Come not when I am dead,
To drop thy foolish tears upon my grave,
To trample round my fallen head,
And vex the unhappy dust thou wouldst not save.

I held it truth, with him who sings, to one clear harp in divers tones
That men may rise on stepping-stones of their dead selves to
higher things.

God's finger touched him and he slept.

No life that breathes with human breath has ever truly longed for death.

Sweet is true love though given in vain, in vain;
And sweet is death who puts an end to pain.

—Alfred, Lord Tennyson

Death is the first breath which our souls draw when we enter life.

—Edwin Arnold

Naught broken save this body, lost but breath;
Nothing to shake the laughing heart's long piece there
But only agony, and that has ending;
And the worst friend and enemy is but death.

Blow out, you bugles, over the rich dead
There none of these so lonely and poor of old,
But, dying, has made us rarer gifts than gold.
These laid the world away; poured out the red
Sweet wine of youth; gave up the years to be
Of work and joy, and that unhoped serene,
That men call age; and those who would have been,
Their sons, they gave, their immortality.

—Rupert Brooke


And come he slow, or come he fast,
It is but death who comes at last.

His morning walk was beneath the elms in the churchyard;
"for death," he said, "had been his next door neighbor for so
many years, that he had no apology for dropping the acquaintance."
—Sir Walter Scott, *Legend of Montrose*


Death be not proud, though some have called thee mighty and dreadful, for, thou
art not so, for those, whom thou thinkest, thou dost overthrow, die not, poor death.
One short sleep is past, we wake eternally, and death shall be no more; death,
thou shalt die.

Any man's death diminishes me, because I am involved in mankind:
Therefore never send to know for whom the bell tolls: It tolls for thee.

Die not, poor death.

I shall not live 'till I see God; and when I have seen Him, I shall never die.

And what is so intricate, so entangling as death?
Who ever got out of a winding sheet.

O strong and long-lived death, how camest thou in?

I have a sin or fear that when I have spun my last thread, I shall perish on the shore; Swear by thyself that at my death, thy sun shall shine as it shines now, and heretofore; and having done that, thou hast done, I have no more.

—John Donne

Of man's first disobedience, and the fruit of that forbidden tree, whose mortal taste brought death into the world, and all our woe, with loss of Eden.

—John Milton

By turns we catch the fatal breath and die.

Tell me, my soul, can this be death?

—Alexander Pope

When beggars die, there are no comets seen;
The heavens themselves blaze forth the death of princes.
Cowards die many times before their deaths;
The valiant never taste of death but once.
Of all the wonders that I yet have heard,
It seems to me most strange that men should fear;
Seeing that death, a necessary end,
Will come when it will come.

The weariest and most loathed worldly life that age, ache,
penury, and imprisonment can lay on nature . . .
is a paradise to what we fear of death.

The worst is death, and death will have his day.

He that cuts off twenty years of life, cuts off so many years of fearing death.

The miserable have no other medicine but only hope:
I have hope to live, and am prepared to die.

Come away, come away, death, and in sad cypress let me be laid; fly away, fly
away, breath: I am slain by a fair cruel maid. My shroud of white, stuck all with
yew, o prepare it. My part of death no one so true did share it. Not a flower, not a
flower sweet, on my black coffin let there be strewn; Not a friend, not a friend
greet my poor course, where my bones shall be thrown. A thousand thousand
sighs to save, lay me o where sad true lover never find my grave, to weep there.

Be still prepared for death
And death or life shall thereby be the sweeter.

Golden lads and girls all must, as chimney-sweepers come to dust.

Look, here is the warrant, Claudio, for thy death:
'Tis now dead midnight, and by eight tomorrow thou
must be made immortal. A man that apprehends death
no more dreadfully but as a drunken sleep.

O death, a scent too faint for mortals to detect.

How oft when men are at the point of death have they been merry!
Which their keepers call a lightning before death.

This fell sergeant, death, is strict in his arrest.

—William Shakespeare

You'll look at least on love's remains,
A grave's one violet:
Your look?—that pays a thousand pains.
What's death? You'll love me yet.

A man can have but one life and one death, one heaven one hell.

—Robert Browning

Leaves have their time to fall,
And flowers to wither at the north wind's breath,
And stars to set—but all,
Thou has all seasons for thine own, o death!

—Felicia Dorothea Hemans


Life is a coquetry of death, which wearies me, too sure of the amour.

—Francis Thompson
To the dead Cardinal of Westminster


Dear, beauteous death! The jewel of the just, shining nowhere but in the dark;
what mysteries do lie beyond thy dust could man outlook that mark!

—Henry Vaughan


Underneath this sable hearse
Lies the subject of all verse,
Sidney's sister, Pembroke's mother;
Death! Ere thou hast slain another,
Fair and learned, and good as she,
Time shall throw a dart at thee.

—William Browne
Epitaph on the Countess of Pembroke


He did not wear his scarlet coat,
For blood and wine are red,
And blood and wine were on his hands
When they found him with the dead.

One can survive nowadays except death.

The Governor was strong upon the regulations act:
The doctor said that Death was but a scientific fact:
And twice a day the Chaplain called, and left a little tract.

—Oscar Wilde

Eat thou and drink; tomorrow thou shalt die.
They die not, for their life was death, but cease;
and round their narrow lips the mould falls close.
Think thou and act; tomorrow thou shalt die.

—Dante Gabriel Rossetti

Nor law, nor duty bade me fight,
Nor public men, nor cheering crowds,
A lonely impulse of delight,
Drove to this tumult in the clouds;
I balanced all, brought all to mind,
The years to come seemed waste of breath,
A waste of breath the years behind
In balance with this life, this death.

—William Butler Yeats
An Irish Airman foresees his death

Wild animals never kill for sport. Man is
the only one to whom the torture and death
of his fellow creatures is amusing in itself.

—James Anthony Froude

Faith of our Fathers, holy faith.
We will be true to thee til death

—Frederick William Faber

It irked him to be here, he could not rest.
He went; his piping took a troubled sound
Of storms that rage outside our happy ground;
He could not wait their passing, he is dead!

Strew on her roses, roses, and never a spray of yew.
In quiet she reposes: Ah! Would that I did too.
Her cabined ample spirit, it fluttered and failed for breath.
Tonight it doth inherit the vasty hall of death.

—Matthew Arnold

When death to either shall come,
I pray it be first to me, be happy as ever at home,
If so, as I wish, it be.

If thou canst death defy, if thy faith is entire,
Press onward, for thine eye shall see thy heart's desire.

—Robert Bridges

I am sure my bones would not rest in an English grave,
or my clay mix with the earth of that country. I believe the
thought would drive me mad on my death bed, could I suppose
that any of my friends would be base enough to convey my
carcass back to your soil.

—Lord Byron

O sing unto me roundelaie,
O drop the brynie tear with me,
Dance no more at hallie daie,
Like a reynynge river be;
My love is dead
Gone to his deathbed
All under the willow tree.

Minstrel song
—Thomas Chatterton

Can storied earn, or animated bust
Back to its mansion call the fleeting breath?
Can honor's voice provoke the silent dust,
Or flattery soothe the dull, cold ear of death?
The paths of glory lead but to the grave.

—Thomas Gray

Dying is a very dull, dreary affair. My advice to you
is to have nothing whatever to do with it.

—Somerset Maugham

To live in the hearts we leave behind, is not to die.

—Thomas Campbell

A man's dying is more the survivor's affair than his own.

—Thomas Mann

Death is not a journeying into an unknown land; it is
a voyage home. We are going not to a strange country,
but to our Father's house, and among our kith and kin.

—John Ruskin

Death is not death if it raises us in a moment from darkness
into light, from weakness into strength, from sinfulness into
holiness.

—Charles Kingsley

Death's but a path that must be trod,
If man would ever pass to God.

—Thomas Parnell

The crooked paths look straighter as we approach the end.

Each departed friend is a magnet that attracts us to the next world.
—Johann Paul Friedrich Richter

There are, aren't there, only three things we can do
about death: to desire it, to fear it, or to ignore it.

He who does not fear death has no fear of threats.

—Pierre Corneille

I acquiesce in my death with complete willingness,
uncolored by hesitation; how foolish to cling to life when
God has ordained otherwise!

—Jorge Manrique

I am afraid of dying—but being dead, oh yes,
that to me is often an appealing prospect.

—Kathe Schmidt Kollwitz

I am ready at any time. Do not keep me waiting.

—John Brown

I look upon life as a gift from God. I did nothing to earn it.
Now that the time is coming to give it back, I have no right to complain.

—Joyce Cary

Let me die. As the leaves die, gladly.

—D.C Claussen

The fear of death is worse than death.

—Robert Burton

The rich, the poor, the great, the small
are leveled. Death confounds 'em all.

—John Gay

When death, the great reconciler, has come, it is never
our tenderness that we regret, but our severity.

—George Eliot

I shall be like a tree, I shall die at the top.

—Jonathon Swift

How little room do we take up in death, that, living,
know no bounds?

—James Shirley

It is better to be a fool than to be dead.

—Robert Louis Stevenson

When I go down to the grave I can say, like so many others,
I have finished my work; but I cannot say I have finished my life.
My days work will begin the next morning. My tomb is not a blind
alley. It is a thoroughfare. It closes in the twilight to open in the dawn.

—Victor Hugo

## American Writers/Poets

A child said, "What is the grass?" fetching it to one with full hands;
Or I guess it is the handkerchief of the Lord,
A scented gift and remembrancer designedly dropt,
Bearing the owner's name someway in the corners,
That we may see and remark, and say "Whose?"
And now it seems to me the beautiful uncut hair of graves.

Come lovely and soothing death, undulate round the world,
serenely arriving, arriving, in the day, in the night, to all, to each,
sooner or later, delicate death.

Joy, shipmate, joy! (Pleased to my soul at death I cry,)
our life is closed, our life begins, the long anchorage we leave,
the ship is clear at last, she leaps! She swiftly courses from
the shore, Joy, shipmate, joy!

—Walt Whitman

He did not feel the drive of the whip; Nor the burning heat of day;
For Death had illumined the land of sleep,
And his lifeless body lay
A worn out fetter, that the soul
Had broken and thrown away.

There is a reaper whose name is Death,
And, with his sickle keen,
He reaps thee bearded grain at a breath,
And the flowers that grow between.

Emigravit is the inscription on the tombstone where he lies;
Dead he is not, but departed, for the artist never dies.

There is no death! What seems so is transition;
This life of mortal breath is but a suburb of the life elysian,
whose portal we call death.

—Henry Wadsworth Longfellow

The report of my death was an exaggeration.

Why is it that we rejoice at a birth and grieve at a funeral?
It is because we are not the person involved.

Whoever has lived long enough to find out what life is, knows how deep a debt of gratitude we owe to Adam, the first great benefactor of our race. He brought death into the world.

—Mark Twain

Anyone not coming to be a dead one before coming to be an old one
comes to be an old one and comes then to be a dead one as any old one
comes to be a dead one.

—Gertrude Stein

Death is the great adventure beside which moon
landings and space trips pale into insignificance.

—Joseph Bayly

I'm not afraid to die. I just don't want to be there when it happens.

—Woody Allen

Don't call this dying; I am just entering upon life.

—Henry James Sr.

If you treat your friend shabbily while he lives, you have no
right to try to even up matters by whining over him when he is dead.

—Joseph Berry

One consolation of death is that it is also the end of your taxes.

—Daniel Webster

So live, that when thy summons comes to join
The innumerable caravan, which moves
To that mysterious realm where each shall take
His chamber in the silent halls of death,
Thou go not, like the quarry-slave at night,
Scourged to his dungeon, but, sustained and soothed
By an unfaltering trust, approach thy grave
Like one who wraps thee drapery of his couch
About him, and lies down to pleasant dreams.

—Thanatopsis, William Cullen Bryant

There is no death. Only a change of worlds.

—Chief Seattle

The death of a child is an assault on our sense of future.

—Allan Wolfelt

If you submit to God's will, everything, including the
time of your death, is under God's supervision.

At death we cross from one territory to another, but we'll
have no trouble with visas. Our representative is already there,
preparing for our arrival. As citizens of heaven, our entrance
is incontestable.

—Erwin W. Lutzer

Art is long, and Time is fleeting,
And our hearts, though stout and brave,
Still, like muffled drums, are beating
Funeral marches to the grave.
Trust no future, however pleasant!
Let the dead past bury its dead!
Act, act in the living present!
Heart within, and God overhead.

Tell me not, in mournful numbers,
Life is but an empty dream!
For the soul is dead that slumbers,
And things are not what they seem.
Life is real! Life is earnest!
And the grave is not its goal;
Dust thou art, to dust returnest,
Was not spoken of the soul.

He is dead, the sweet musician
He the sweetest of all singers
He has gone from us forever,
He has moved a little nearer
To the Master of all music,
To the Master of all singing!
Oh my brother, Chibiabos!

Hiawatha's Lament
—Henry Wadsworth Longfellow

Death is not the greatest loss in life.
The greatest loss is what dies inside us while we live.

—Norman Cousins

There is one thing that keeps surprising you about
stormy old friends after they die—their silence.

—Ben Hecht

We are but tenants, and . . . shortly the great Landlord
will give us notice that our lease has expired.

—Joseph Jefferson

There is a strange beauty in Death's singular reliability as a
keeper of secrets, in the perfection of his cowled silence.

—Dean Koontz

Because I could not stop for death he kindly stopped for me;
The carriage held but just ourselves and immortality.

—Emily Dickinson

# Hymn Writers/Clergy/Religion

It is in dying that we are born to eternal life.

And thou, most kind and gentle death, waiting to hush our latest breath;
O Praise Him—Alleluia! Thou leadest home the child of God
And Christ our Lord the way hath trod.

—St. Francis of Assisi

Life is a great surprise. I do not see
why death should be an even greater one.

—Vladimir Nabokov

Death has an amazing power of altering what a man
desires because death profoundly affects his outlook.

—Oswald Chambers

It is only my body; all is right in my soul.

—Samuel Hopkins

Lord, grant that my last hour may be my best hour.

—Old English prayer

Lord, look out for me when I die. Make it a good
experience.

—St. Francis de Sales

Death is God's delightful way of giving us life.

Death has got something to be said for it;
There's no need to get out of bed for it;
Wherever you may be, they bring it to you free.

—Kingsley Amis

Could we but climb where Moses stood,
And view the landscape o'er;
Not Jordan's stream, nor death's cold flood,
Should fright us from the shore.

Death, like a narrow sea, divides
That heavenly land from ours.

—Isaac Watts

Death must be distinguished from dying,
with which it is often confused.

—Rev. Sidney Smith

God's eternity and man's mortality join to
persuade us that faith in Jesus Christ is not optional.

—A.W. Tozer

I fear no foe with Thee at hand to bless;
Ills have no weight, and tears no bitterness;
Where is death's sting? Where, grave, thy victory?
I triumph still, if Thou abide with me.
Hold Thou Thy cross before my closing eyes;
Shine through the gloom and point me to the skies;
Heaven's morning breaks, and earth's vain shadows flee;
In life, in death, O Lord, abide with me.

—Henry Frances Light, hymn writer

Day and moments quickly flying,
Blend the living with the dead;
Soon will you and I be lying
Each within our narrow bed.

—Rev. Edward Caswall

Every man must do two things alone; he must
do his own believing and his own dying.

—Martin Luther

Day by day remind yourself that you are going to die.

—The Rule of St. Benedict

I'm not afraid to die, honey. In fact, I'm kind of looking forward
to it . I know the Lord has His arms wrapped around this big,
fat sparrow.

—Ethel Waters

You can't die, for you are linked to the permanent
life of God through Jesus Christ.

—J.B. Phillips

Of course, I do not want to go—this is a mighty interesting world
and I'm having a mighty good time in it. But I am no more afraid of
going than of going through the door of this study. For I know that I
shall then have a spiritual body to do with as I please, and I won't have
to worry about the aches and pains of this poor physical body.

—Ozora S. Davis

Has this world been so kind to you that you would
leave it with regret? There are better things ahead
than any we leave behind.

—C.S. Lewis

I have talked to doctors and nurses who have held the hands
of dying people, and they say that there is as much difference
between the death of a Christian and a non-Christian as
there is between heaven and hell.

—Billy Graham

Fear not that your life shall come to an end,
but rather that it shall never have a beginning.

—Cardinal John Henry Newman

Nothing is so certain as death,
And nothing is so uncertain as the hour of death.

—St. Augustine of Hippo

Death, to a good man, is but passing through a dark
entry, out of one little dusky room of his Father's house
into another that is fair and large, lightsome and glorious,
and divinely entertaining.

—McDonald Clarke

A single death is a tragedy, a million deaths is a statistic.

—Anonymous

A sudden death is but a sudden joy.

—Anonymous

Take care of your life and the Lord will take care of your death.

—George Whitefield

Death is merely moving from one home to another.

—The Kotzker Rabbi

Teach me to live, that I may dread the grave as my little bed.

—Bishop Thomas Ken

How strange this fear of death is! We are never
frightened at a sunset.

—George MacDonald

No man ever repented of being a Christian on his death bed.

—Hannah More

Death to the Christian is the funeral of all his sorrows
and evils, and the resurrection of all his joys.

—Aughey

Whoso lives the holiest life is fittest far to die.

—Margaret Preston

You have laughed God out of your schools,
out of your books, and out of your life, but
you cannot laugh Him out of your death.

—Dagobert Runes

We go to the grave of a friend, saying, "A man is dead."
But angels throng about him, saying, "A man is born."

—Christian Shriver Gotthold

I have been shocked by the number of Christian men and
women who come to their deathbeds knowing nothing about
the God of love and mercy. They have known instead the Judge
of impossible standards, and they have been, naturally enough,
afraid to meet that God.

—Eve Kavanaugh

We understand death for the first time when
He puts his hand upon one whom we love.

—Anne-Louise Germaine De Stael

This world is the land of the dying;
The next is the land of the living.

One of the great lessons the fall of the leaf teaches is this:
Do your work well and then be ready to depart when God shall call.

—Tryon Edwards

Death is not the end; it is only a new beginning. Death is not
the master of the house; he is only the porter at the King's lodge,
appointed to open the gate and let the King's guests into the realm
of eternal day.

—John Henry Jowett

Nothing seems worse than a man's death,
And yet it may be the height of his good luck.

—Irish proverb

There is only one way to be born and a thousand ways to die.

—Serbian proverb

There is no dying by proxy.

—French proverb

Death is a camel that lies down at every door.

—Persian proverb

Death may be free—but it costs a life.

Every man knows he will die, but no one wants to believe it.

—Jewish proverb

Be happy while you're living, for you're a long time dead.

—Scottish proverb

To have and to hold from this day forward,
for better for worse, for richer for poorer, in sickness
and in health, to love and to cherish, til death us do part.

—Book of Common Prayer


May you be a long time in heaven before the devil knows you're dead

—O'Blarney's Pub

Scoffers/Atheists/Miscellaneous

Death: when man is put to bed with a shovel.

—Anonymous


I shall die, but that is all that I shall do for Death; I am not on his payroll.

Down you mongrel, death! Back into your kennel!

—Edna St. Vincent Millay


Death never takes the wise man by surprise;
he is always ready to go.

—Jean De La Fontaine


For each of us there comes a moment when death takes us
by the hand and says—it is time to rest, you are tired, lie down and sleep.

—Will Hay


But I had dreamed a dreary dream,
Beyond the Isle of Sky;
I saw a dead man win a fight,
And I think that man was I.

—Ballad


He who dies with the most toys is, nonetheless, still dead.

—Anonymous

Enjoy life, there's plenty of time to be dead.

—Anonymous

The ancients dreaded death: the Christian can only fear dying.

—Augustus William Hare

Don't take life seriously. It's not permanent.

—Inscription on a tee shirt

Now I know why the Spartans do not fear death.

—After tasting the dark broth served
in the barracks of the Greek army

I was kidding all along.

—The atheist

Going up?

—The elevator operator

I have no precedent for this.

—The judge

I pass.

—The bridge player

The end of the line.

—The railroad conductor

Who killed Cock Robin?
'I,' said the sparrow,
'With my bow and arrow,
I killed Cock Robin.'
All the birds of the air fell a-sighin' and a-sobbin
When they heard of the death of poor Cock Robin.

—Nursery rhyme

It's an old habit with theologians to beat the living with the bones of the dead.

—Robert G. Ingersoll

To fear love is to fear life, and those who fear life are already three parts dead.

—Bertrand Russell

Everybody wants to go to heaven, but nobody wants to die.

—Joe Louis

I know death has ten thousand several doors for men to take their exits.

—John Webster

One who longs for death is miserable,
But more miserable is he who fears it.

—Julius Wilhelm Zincgref

Though too much valour may our fortunes try,
To live in fear of death is many times to die.

—Lope De Vega

When our parents are living, we feel that they stand between us and death; when they go, we move to the edge of the unknown.

—R.I. Fitzhenry

There is no drinking after death.

—John Fletcher

Grass grows at last above all graves.

—Julia C.R. Dorr

I cannot forgive my friends for dying; I do not
find these vanishing acts of theirs at all amusing.

—Logan Pearsall Smith

Memorial service: Farewell party for someone who
has already left.

—Robert Byrne

Death is nature's way of telling you to slow down.

—Anonymous

Anything that kills you makes you . . . well, dead.

—Anonymous

Because through death alone we become liberated,
I say it is the best of all things created.

—Angelus Silesius

Death is but a sharp corner near the beginning
of life's procession down eternity.

—John Ayscough

"There's been an accident!" They said,
"Your servant's cut in half; he's dead!"
"Indeed!" Said Mr. Jones, "And please
Send me the half that's got my keys."

—Harry Graham

The newspaper does everything for us. It runs the
police force and the banks, commands the militia,
controls the legislature, baptizes the young, marries
the foolish, comforts the afflicted, afflicts the comfortable,
buries the dead and roasts them afterward.

—Finley Peter Dunne

Grandpa expired, maybe we can renew him?

—Anonymous

Getting eliminated from the World Series is an
emotional small taste of what death is like, only you
don't have to die.

—Anonymous

A steak a day, keeps the cows dead.

—Anonymous

If somebody has a bad heart, they can plug this jack in
at night as they go to bed and it will monitor their heart
throughout the night. And the next morning, when they
wake up dead, there'll be a record.

—Mark S. Fowler,
FCC Chairman

Dirty-Air Cities Far Deadlier than Clean Ones, Study Shows

—New York Times

Death is the ultimate statistic, it claims one out of every one.

—George Bernard Shaw

Death is the flowering of life, the consummation
of union with God.

—Anonymous

Death is the Liberator of him whom freedom cannot release,
the Physician of him whom medicine cannot cure, and the
Comforter of him whom time cannot console.

—Charles Caleb Colton

Death is the opening of a more subtle life. In the flower, it sets
free the perfume; in the chrysalis, the butterfly; in man, the soul.

—Juliette Adam

A direful death indeed they had
That would put any parent mad
But she was more than usual calm
She did not give a single damn.

—Marjorie Flemming

There's one good kind of writer—a dead one.

—James T. Farrell

Every day I thank the good Lord that I'm playing golf and
still on the right side of the divot.

—Lee Trevino

He's dead, Jim. You grab his wallet, I'll grab his tricorder.

—Gene Rodenberry, *Star Trek*

## Statesmen/Philosophers/Explorers

The angel of death has been abroad throughout the land:
you can almost hear the beating of his wings.

—John Bright

Death is psychologically as important as birth . . . shrinking away
from it is something unhealthy and abnormal which robs the second
half of life of its purpose.

—Carl Jung

Then out spake brave Horatius, the Captain of the Gate:
"To every man upon this earth, death cometh soon or late.
And how can man die better than facing fearful odds,
For the ashes of his fathers, and the temples of his gods?"

—Thomas Babington Macaulay

Death is not extinguishing the light; it is only putting
out the lamp because the dawn has come.

—Sir Rabindranath Tagore


Here's death, twitching my ear: "Live," says he, "for I'm coming."

—Virgil


We all labor against our own cure;
For death is the cure for all diseases.


For the world, I count it not an inn,
But a hospital and place not to love but to die in.

—Sir Thomas Browne


As to death, we can experience it but once and
are all apprentices when we come to it.


One must always have one's boots on and be ready to go.


All days travel toward death, the last one reaches it.

—Michel Eyquem DeMontaigne


Are we willing to not run away from the pain, to not get busy when
there is nothing to do and instead stand rather in the face of
death together with those who grieve?

—Henri J.M. Nouwen


As a well-spent day brings happy sleep,
so life well used brings happy death.

—Leonardo Da Vinci


Death is the end of labor, entry into rest.

—William Alexander, Earl of Sterling

Death and taxes are inevitable.

—Thomas Chandler Haliburton

I am ready to meet my Maker. Whether my Maker is prepared
for the great ordeal of meeting me is another matter.

—Winston Churchill

Death takes no bribes.

Three can keep a secret, if two are dead.

Death is as necessary to the constitution as sleep,
we shall rise refreshed in the morning.

—Benjamin Franklin

Death is the grand leveler.

—Sir Thomas Fuller

Death is an awfully big adventure.

—Sir James M. Barrie

Few die and none resign.

—Thomas Jefferson

Nearly all our best men are dead! Carlyle, Tennyson,
Browning, George Eliot! I'm not feeling very well myself.

—William Pulteney, Earl of Bath

Tyrawley and I have been dead these two years;
but we don't choose to have it known.

—Earl of Chesterfield

Revenge triumphs over death. Love slights it.
Honor aspires to it. Grief flies to it. Fear preoccupies it.

One of the fathers saith . . . that old men go to death,
And death comes to young men.

Men fear death as children fear to go in the dark;
And as that natural fear in children is increased
with tales, so is the other.
There is no passion in the mind of man so weak,
but it mates and masters the fear of death . . .
Revenge triumphs over death; love slights it;
honor aspires to it; grief flies to it.

—Francis Bacon

Let us not lament too much the passing of our friends.
They are not dead, but simply gone before us along the road
which all must travel.

—Antiphanes

It makes dying lose its customary aspect and begin to seem
merely a slight but universal weakness,
like catching a cold.

—Margaret Halsey, upon touring Salisbury
Cathedral and seeing all the tombstones

Oh well, no matter what happens, there is always death.

—Napoleon Bonaparte

Pale Death, with impartial step, knocks at the poor man's
cottage and at the palaces of kings.

—Horace

A man should be mourned at his birth, not at his death.

—Charles de Secondat Montesquieu

Death: a punishment to some, to some a gift, and to many a favor.

Wouldn't you think a man a prize fool if he burst into tears
because he didn't live a thousand years ago?
A man is as much a fool for shedding tears because he
isn't going to be alive a thousand years from now.
As the mother's womb holds us for nine months, making us ready,
not for the womb itself, but for life, just so, through our lives,
we are making ourselves ready for another birth.
Therefore, look forward without fear to that appointed hour—the last
hour of the body, but not of the soul . . . . That day,
which you fear as being the end of all things,
is the birthday of your eternity.

—Lucius Annaeus Seneca

## Scripture

A good name is better than precious ointment and the day of death
than the day of one's birth. It is better to go to the house of mourning,
than to go to the house of feasting.

—Ecclesiastes 7:2

The wages of sin is death.

—Romans 6:23

For since by man came death, by man came also
the resurrection of the dead.
For as in Adam all die, even so in Christ
shall all be made alive.

—1 Corinthians15:21

The last enemy that shall be destroyed is death.

—1 Corinthians 15:26

O wretched man that I am! Who shall deliver me from
the body of this death?

—Romans 7:24

I have set before you life and death, blessing and cursing:
therefore choose life, that both thou and thy seed may live.

—Moses, Deuteronomy 30:19

And in those days shall men seek death and shall not find it;
and shall desire to die, and death shall flee from them.

—Revelation 9:6

## Dying Last Words

Ah, Jesus!

—Charles V, King of France

Doctor, I die hard but I am not afraid to go.

—George Washington

Eighty-six years I have served him, and
He has done me no wrong.
How can I blaspheme my King
who has saved me?

—Saint Polycarp

I am not dying. I am entering into life.

—Therese of Lisieux

I have been dying for twenty years, now I am going to live.

—James Drummond Burns

I have been everything and everything is nothing.
A little urn will contain all that remains of one
for whom the whole world was too little.

—Lucius Septimius Severus

I shall hear in heaven.

—Ludwig Van Beethoven

I have lost a world of time! Had I one year more, it should
be spent in perusing David's Psalms and Paul's Epistles.
Mind the world less and God more.

—Claudius Salmasius

I surely must be going now, my strength sinks so fast.
What glory! The angels are waiting for me!

—Thomas Bateman

I will stick to Christ as a burr to a topcoat.

—Katie Luther

I would give worlds, if I had them, that "Age of Reason"
had not been published. O Lord help me! Christ help me!
O God what have I done to suffer so much? But there is no
God! But if there should be, what will become of me hereafter?
Stay with me, for God's sake! Send even a child to stay with me,
for it is hell to be alone. If ever the devil had an agent,
I have been that one.

—Thomas Paine

Like as thy arms, Lord Jesus Christ, were stretched out upon
the cross, even so receive me with the outstretched arms of
thy mercy.

—Mary Stuart

See how pure the sky is, there is not a single cloud.
Don't you see that God is waiting for me?

—Jean Jacques Rousseau

Standing as I do in view of God and eternity, I realize that
patriotism is not enough. I must have no hatred or bitterness
toward anyone.

—Edith Cavell

This is the last of earth! I am content.

—John Quincy Adams

Turn up the lights; I don't want to go home in the dark.

—O. Henry

Weep not for me, but for yourselves.

—John Bunyan

The last words of Noah Webster probably were:
zyme, zymosis, and zymurgy.

—Anonymous

What a beautiful day!

—Alexander, Emperor of Russia

What is life? It is the flash of a firefly in the night. It is the
breath of a buffalo in the wintertime. It is the little shadow which
runs across the grass and loses itself in the sunset.

—Crowfoot of the Blackfoot

Wonderful, wonderful, this death.

—William Etty

If Mr. Selwyn call again, show him up; If I am alive I shall
be delighted to see him: And if I am dead he
would like to see me.

—Henry Fox, First Baron of Holland

Why fear death? It is the most beautiful adventure in life.

—Charles Frohman; last words before
going down on the Lusitania May 7, 1915

Into Thy hands, O Lord, I commend my spirit.

—Christopher Columbus

I am about to take my last voyage, a great leap in the dark.

—Thomas Hobbes

I am going to seek a great perhaps. Bring down the
curtain, the farce is played out.

—Francois Rabelais

The hour of departure has arrived, and we go our ways;
I to die, and you to live. Which is better,
God only knows.

—Socrates (last words, Plato)

On the whole, I'd rather be in Philadelphia.

—W.C. Fields

Only one man understood me and he didn't understand me.

—Wilhelm Hegel

Die, my dear doctor? That's the last thing I shall do.

—Lord Palmerston

So little done, so much to do.

—Cecil Rhodes, builder

I believe we must adjourn this meeting to some other place.

—Adam Smith

It is finished.

—Jesus Christ

# CHAPTER TWO

# Theodicy

## IT'S ALL AROUND US

A caring minister must have a point of reference from which to begin. We have such a point in the Wisdom writings. Surely the unfolding drama of the patriarch Job is set before us because his is the common lot of man. A minister who has not diligently ploughed the field of God's Word in this arena of mystery cannot possibly be prepared regarding crisis counseling, in both what to say, and what not to say. Hence the value of beginning by studying theodicy.

I'm watching Marlin Perkins's Wild Kingdom show: it's a warm day on the savanna of Africa. A mother antelope is nursing her offspring. Birds are chirping. Other animals lie peacefully on the ground. All is well. Then, without hearing an audible sound, all ears go up, and the gathered antelopes begin to stir. As if in synchronization, all move suddenly as one. From the bushes a lion lurches and viciously sinks his powerful jaws into the young antelope's hindquarters. Fearful and confused, the mother runs away with the rest of the pack. The young one is left alone to be torn in pieces by the hungry carnivore. I sense that the cameraman wants to react, but true to his calling he stays steady on the scene before him. The animal is still alive and breathing while its entrails are torn from its body. It will be minutes until the antelope expires.

Showing no mercy, the lion enjoys his meal. And so it goes in the world. I say to myself, "I'll bet the young antelope didn't think that was fair." If an animal could reason, surely it would question the benevolence of God. I can reason, and I wonder why in God's providence "things happen." Is He there? Does He care? Sometimes it certainly does not seem fair.

And then there is young Mary Ingalls (*Little House on the Prairie*) who is mysteriously struck with blindness at the tender age of seven. She goes to her parson and church family and pleads, "What can I do? I'm helpless." The parson says, "Pray." A parishioner concludes, "God must have a real special plan why He would bring a seven-year-old girl through this, but is it right?" Confused, Mr. Ingalls replies, "How can it be right that God would make a seven-year-old girl blind?" Someone somewhat glibly quotes Romans 8:28.

On a lesser level, I'm writing my book. I've just spent around two hours on a rather difficult section. I'm making great progress. For no reason, the computer freezes up, and then goes blank. Immediately I realize I haven't saved this portion yet. It's lost. As the bumper sticker says, "Stuff happens."

Song lyrics echo this sentiment as well.


Life ain't got no reason and it sure don't rhyme
Don't let frustration get you boy—it happens every time
When life would be a song if you could write just one more line
Life ain't got no reason and it sure don't rhyme
                    —From the CD, *Along For The Ride*—J. Clarke Wilcox


To think that only yesterday
I was cheerful, bright and gay
Looking forward to, well, who wouldn't do
The role I was about to play?
But as if to knock me down
Reality came around
And without so much as a mere touch
Cut me into little pieces
Leaving me to doubt, talk about God in His mercy
Who, if He really does exist
Why did He desert me?
In my hour of need
I truly am indeed
Alone again, naturally.

                    *Alone Again Naturally,* Gilbert O'Sullivan

# Theodicy

It's called theodicy, from the Greek, "theos" (God) and "dike" (justice). *Webster's* defines it this way: "a system of natural theology aimed at seeking to vindicate divine justice in allowing evil to exist" or, why does God allow evil in His creation?

A successful theodicy resolves the problem of evil for a theological system and demonstrates that God is all-powerful, all-loving, and just, despite the existence of evil.

The problem of evil has been called the Achilles heel of Christianity, and it may be the most troublesome issue Christians face. The issue, as much of theology, is so simple and common that everyone knows about it and identifies with it, yet so complex that it rejects a simplistic black and white answer. It is with the issue of theodicy that most skeptics and critics level their charges because theodicy is an explanation of the character of God in the face of circumstances which don't seem consistent with His nature. Two considerations:

1. Theodicy has interest only to those who hold to a notion of God as being consistent, logical, omnipotent, and benevolent. In other words, God will always do consistent, logical, loving deeds according to His all knowledge. The skeptic says, "See, you don't know who God is. These don't match up." Hence, we protect God by preparing a theodicy or explanation for this seeming dilemma.

2. Theodicy implies moral agency, i.e. a man cannot be responsible for something about which he cannot do (acts of God).

Simply put, the problem is this, (assuming God's existence):

A.  If God is WILLING but UNABLE: He is impotent (He is not truly God).
B.  If God is UNWILLING but ABLE: He is evil.
C.  If God is WILLING and ABLE: WHY IS THERE EVIL?

Often the first word we utter when faced with a tragedy is, "Why?" This tells us at least two things. First, we consider unexpected blows to be unkind and unjust. When sorrow destroys our pursuit of happiness, we no longer understand life. Our basic concept of life is shattered. Second, obsessed with the sense of the necessity of fairness, we complain to Him who controls our fate because He has obviously failed. An interesting observation is that the very question, "Why" betrays the fact that a great many people start with an often unstated belief in a higher Being who is in fact in charge of life. In this "Why?" is hidden nothing less than the question of a higher Authority from whom we expect justice, indeed happiness. We feel abandoned by this One when we are in sorrow.

## Possible Solutions

In theology evil is referred to as "the mystery of inequity." Christianity admits that evil exists; indeed most religions admit to its existence, with the exception of a few which argue that evil is an illusion. Unfortunately, most theodicies that seek to explain the origin of evil raise more questions than they answer and leave us more theological problems than the problem of evil itself. And as the saying goes, "The cure is worse than the disease" (Dr. R.C. Sproul).

To address the issue of evil, one must ask the question about the nature of evil.

Theologians understand that biblically, evil is characteristically defined in negative terms: *unrighteousness, injustice, lawlessness, antichrist*. Sin is called *disobedience*. We cannot understand unrighteousness without the standard of righteousness. It is said that evil is parasitic; it cannot exist except as a privation or negation of the very good. Church father, Augustine, argued that evil depends upon the good for its very definition. We draw comfort from those who complain that evil is a problem because they can only do so once they have affirmed the existence of the good. If we insist that evil is real, then good must be real as well. If there is no God, then we must not only account for evil, but for the good as well.[1]

The philosopher Gottfried Leibniz constructed what has probably become the best known theodicy regarding the problem of evil. Leibniz, a rationalist, concluded that there are not only reasons that God does whatever He does, but such reasons are *necessary laws*. He begins with the proposition that God has, of necessity, created the best of all possible worlds. Considering that God could have chosen from many possible models when He undertook to create a world, this one which He ultimately chose would be according to His infinite wisdom, omniscience, and righteousness (any other possible model would have been rejected). If we perceive a better world, it is because we lack the eternal perspective necessary to make the final judgment only God is able to make.

Next, Leibniz argued that only God is perfect, and it would be impossible for God to create another God. If so, the second God would not be God, having been created.

Third, Leibniz made a distinction among three types of evil: *moral evil, physical evil, and metaphysical evil*. Moral evil has to do with volitional sins of humans. Physical evil refers to sickness or natural calamities such as earthquakes, volcanoes, floods, etc. Both of these moral and physical evils proceed from what he believed to be metaphysical evil, which has to do with *imperfect being*. It is related to finitude.

Anything that is finite is a lower order of being than the pure eternal and infinite being found in God. Since the finite being is a lower form of being than an infinite being, it is metaphysically impure or "evil." It lacks the perfection of a being found in God alone.

For Christians the problem with this schema is that it makes sin a necessary consequence of creation. This, of course, is contrary to the biblical prohibition of sin and God's promise to judge sin. If moral evil is a necessary consequence of metaphysical evil, then the question of culpability is raised, "Why then would man be responsible?"

Also the biblical record of creation does not say either man or cosmos *created* evil. Rather, the divine evaluation of the work of creation is that it is "good."

The Fall was a fall from original righteousness and is not viewed biblically as a necessary consequence of creation.

Other attempts of theodicy have been made. A common one is called *dualism*, which maintains the eternal co-existence of forces of good and evil. This view is prominent in Eastern philosophies and religions and sees two equal and opposite forces locked in an eternal cosmic struggle (light versus darkness, the ying and the yang). An evident problem with this to Christianity is that it depicts Satan as an evil being who is equal in power and eternality with God. It also, by implication, makes redemption an impossibility. If the two forces are equal and opposite, there is no hope of either one emerging triumphant. It is the death of monotheism as well because God is no longer ultimate since there exists two distinct deities.

More recently, *process theologians* have placed both good and evil into the nature of God Himself: God vacillating between the two poles. He then becomes like the Roman god Janus adorned with two faces. The problem with this theory is that God no longer can be considered absolutely holy, but contains a shadowy side to His character from which comes evil.

*Skeptics* conclude that the problem of evil is solved by realizing that evil really doesn't exist after all, but then neither does good. The view reduces to nihilism and the idea that we live in an amoral universe: there is neither good nor evil, only conventions and preferences. This view is related to a relativistic view of life which insists that there are no absolutes, except the absolute that there are absolutely no absolutes (which then makes them absolutist?).

Harold Kushner put forth the *deistic* approach to the problem of evil in his 1983 best-selling book, *When Bad Things Happen to Good People*. Rabbi Kushner, the father of a son with progeria (abnormal premature aging), speaks from his personal heart-wrenching experience. The philosophical definition of deism is: "A view which represents the universe as a self-sustained mechanism, from which God withdrew as soon as he had created it, and which He left to a process of self-development."[2]

Philosopher Ten Broeke posits, "Deism emphasizes the inviolability of natural law and holds to a very mechanical view of the world. Its God is a sort of Hindu Brahma, 'as idle as a painted ship upon a painted ocean'—mere being, without content or movement. God made the world so good at the first that the best he can do is to let it alone." This hands-off view of God naturally promotes a fatalistic view of theodicy. Rabbi Kushner summarizes this same abandon in his statement, "When considering the question of 'why,' we must simply conclude that apparently there are just some things which are too difficult even for God to handle."

We see then that all of man's efforts removed from revealed truth ultimately lead to despair in one form or another. Only Christianity offers a path of hope and purpose, a remedy to this despair.

Some time ago a theological pal and I were discussing this idea of the hopelessness of man's efforts (outside of revealed truth) to answer the "why" question. He passed on a powerful illustration. In Vietnam there is a deadly toxic snake called the two-step-viper. If an individual was bitten by it, the common practice among the people was to first be responsible for protecting others by killing the snake. Then, and only then, the individual would sit down and rather quickly and quietly die (take two steps and die). The GI's there had an anti-venom, but the nationals did not know about it. So even in the presence of U.S. forces, they silently accepted their fate, did their duty and died. It was the ultimate in resigning oneself to the fates. Sadly, such is the fate of the humanly contrived philosophical explanations of theodicy.

## The Christian Answer?

Unfortunately, what is often the easy answer of conservative Christianity poses its own problems as well. Most Christians quickly declare that evil originates in man's free will, but on closer investigation we are still faced with a major dilemma. This answer is not sufficient because it fails to get to the root of the problem. The Bible clearly reveals that man chose evil instead of good in the Garden of Eden. And there is no explanation for how a creature that was created good chose evil. Nor does it explain the role that Satan played in the choice. And if the old explanation of "the devil made me do it" is used, we still must answer the issue of culpability. If they were coerced into their decision, then the guilt would be Satan's, not theirs. They could not justly be held responsible for doing something they were forced to do by Satan. If Adam and Eve were totally deceived, they would have sinned in ignorance. On the other hand, the Bible teaches that to claim ignorance as an excuse was not an option for them either. They were told and told clearly what God commanded and what He forbade. They acted in the clear knowledge of these things. Therefore, one could not say that they were totally deceived.

So the question comes back to free will. We can grant that Adam and Eve freely willed to sin, but the deeper question still remains: Why? Did they sin because they wanted to sin; did they desire to sin? Did they commit an evil action out of an evil desire? Without the desire they could not sin. If they acted against their desire, then they would be acting against their own will, and the choice would not have been a free choice. If the act was truly free and according to their desire, then they must have had an evil desire to start with. But, from where did it come? Was it there from the beginning? Did God give them the evil desire? If so, how could He hold them responsible? And what would this say about the nature of a Holy God? If He didn't give it to them, where did it come from?

Man was created to be dependent upon God, and as such received truth in conjunction with his relationship with God, and therefore pleased God. Eve, however, accepted Satan's proposition of autonomy and independence. She then could speculate apart from and even against the revealed will of God and thus could no longer please God. She sought truth apart from God and thereby lost all foundation for truth.

Is there a solution to the problem of evil? Most of the theodicies do not fully satisfy the mind. They could never satisfy the mind which is not subjected to God and His Word. This does not mean the problem is either insoluble or should not draw our serious attention. We do conclude then that evil exists and is real. We also conclude that evil depends upon good for its very definition. Ultimately, it would seem that we must believe it is good that there is evil or else it would not exist. Yet to say that it is good that evil exists is not the same thing as saying that evil is good. Evil is evil. But we do conclude that God is good and that His providence extends to all things, which includes evil. Hence, Romans 8:28, ". . . all things work together for good . . ."

Evil is not, however, fatal to Christianity. What is known is that God is, and that He is good. We also know that we sin and that God has solved the problem of sin (evil) in Jesus Christ. Do we conclude that our pursuit takes us full circle to the strangely comforting verse of Deuteronomy 29:29? God tells us there "the secret things belong unto the LORD our God; but those things which are revealed belong unto us and to our children forever, that we may do all the words of this law." Isn't it all about faith anyway?

## Why Study Theodicy?

1. **Because truth matters.**
   All other systems of theodicy ultimately lead to some form of skepticism, cynicism, or hopelessness and despair. God in His Word does give us—though not complete—sufficient explanations in the face of the tribulations of life.
   We must answer man's criticisms and accusations of inconsistencies in Christianity. Our theology/theodicy incorporates particular views on God, evil and man's will. Working within the broad stream of Christian theism, we are defending God's name (the apologetics of 1 Peter 3:15), and at the same time testing our own understanding and faith of what we believe God reveals.

The ways of God are defensible against the charges of the skeptics who say theistic positions are hopelessly irrational. This striving toward intellectual clarity and consistency reminds us that we must seek to avoid a theological position that contains contradictions. The skeptic will be unmoved by anything less than this.

2. **Pastoral Implications**

We proceed from theory to practice. What we know and believe will mold our every action. To study theodicy is to constantly remind ourselves that Job was a man such as we. Theodicy takes place in life, not in theory, and suffering is common to all. The apostle Paul exhorts us to "weep with those who weep" (Romans 12:15). We need to take the explanations of theodicy out of the abstract and put them into practical use. Perhaps the prime biblical example of this is 2 Corinthians, chapter one where Paul was able to pass on comfort to others after having experienced it himself.

We (pastors) are the counselors people come to when they hurt. It is amazing how often people in the face of calamity will rest their confidence upon us to wave our biblical wands so that "all the waves will stand still." How we handle these situations, how we represent God, how we search for comfort, whether for others or for ourselves, will always proceed from what we believe to be true (theodicy).

The greatest portion of this book is about hands-on ministry, but without the solid foundation of theodicy first, we are left to fumble with repeated simplistic clichés in our own discomfort. When a pastor meets a mother and father at an emergency room after the death of their child, though they may never verbalize it in lofty theological terms, you can be sure that those parents are running theodicy through their minds and hearts. And like Job of old, the underlying struggle may really be (although legitimate) their personal anger with God. As pastors and counselors we must have thought through this difficult issue and, as the Boy Scouts say, "Be prepared."

## The Patience Of Job

There is a curious schemata which encompasses the entire life and history of the Patriarch Job. The account begins with his rich state and ends in an even more glorious state. That which transpires between the two is the account of the Divine dealings with the suffering servant in his humiliation. Forsaken by all, his at last is the victory because of the mighty dealings of an Almighty God. Truly, the parallel of this account to the wondrous plan of redemption in Christ decreed in eternity past, brought forth in time, and fulfilled eternally, can be no less than God's marvelous providential revealing of Himself and His wonderful story.

> . . . they lifted up their voice and wept; and they tore everyone his mantle, and sprinkled dust upon their heads toward heaven. So they sat down with him upon the ground seven days and seven nights, and none spake a word unto him: for they saw that his grief was very great.
>
> —Job 2:12–13

The book of Job is intensely practical. It throbs with moral, physical, and spiritual reality. Every one of us is Job. Many thematic issues are considered within its pages: prosperity, family, domestic relationship, righteousness, emotion, true friendship, confronting God, and of course the invisible war in the heavenlies, to name a few. For those reasons, Job makes for good preaching.

The book of Job is basically a book about God. It is about an all-wise God, who for His own reasons allows suffering and evil.

It is also about a man, who at least in the beginning and again at the end, had a large enough image of God to respond as he should. Job is best known for the drama of its star and his wrestlings with suffering, pain, and abandonment by God, all within the context of belief: **theodicy**. It is the preoccupation and stage-to-stage personal debate with God which gives Job's speeches their compelling fascination. Job does nothing less than charge God outright with immorality, while still believing that fellowship with Him is the highest good. He is able, therefore, to hold together incompatible concepts of God.

And yet, like Job, the reader is surprised that God does not explain to Job why he suffers, and especially why light is not thrown on the general problem of suffering. We discover that Job (and you and I) needs a sharp rebuke from God to drive away his presumptuous attack upon the Creator and to learn the true relation of God to man. The speech of Yahweh does not explain the origin of Job's suffering. It is not what God **says** that is all-important. Rather, it is the overwhelming impression made on Job by the vision of God that leaves him contrite and subdued. It is imperative that God leave Job in ignorance at the end, so he might learn to trust God, even if he does not understand the reason for God's actions. Job is a model and help to all who are confronted by the insoluble mystery of their own or the world's pain.

All of the Wisdom writings (in the Bible) are extremely practical and axiomatic. The Proverbs are formulae for success. We come away from them feeling that if we do well, all will go well and that evil is retribution for our failures. This was the reasoning of Job's friends when they confronted him. In fact, without the first two chapters of the book and the pronouncement of Job's righteousness, we would take our copy of the Proverbs and join Job's accusers on the dung heap. But God in His wisdom gives us this story to lay the axe to this simplistic teaching and demonstrate that the explanation for suffering is much more multiplex than that.

And so, while the final word on theodicy may not be extracted from the Old Testament patriarch, this much can be said:

1. **Job himself never is fully informed** about the big picture, though the reader from the beginning **is** allowed to see the entire drama unfold. Even when Job is restored in **this** life (which gives us hope), Job can only conclude that suffering, while inexplicable, can come full circle. One commentator suggests that this restoration was necessary in order to reconcile the reader to God.

2. **The argument of Job's accusers does little to convince Job or change his mind.** Unlike the comfort they were initially, his comforters become his antagonizers. This points out that an added dimension to suffering is often personal attack from acquaintances, when the sufferer himself knows that it is not personal sin which is at the root of the problem. Job's defense is that affliction is not always divine punishment; therefore, it is not necessarily a measure of sin. In this way Job (and we) discover that, for the reprobate, affliction is indeed punishment, but for the elect, it is chastisement.

3. **A remoteness of God** (Where is He?) often accompanies great suffering which can bring about confusion and deep depression which can then lead the most godly to accuse God and spew out sinful words. Moses faced the dark night of the soul when he cried out to God, "If you treat me like this, please kill me here and now, if I have found favor in your sight, and do not let me see my wretchedness!" (Numbers 11:15). Jeremiah expressed the same sentiment, "Cursed be the

day in which I was born! Let the day not be blessed in which my mother bore me!" (Jeremiah 20:14).

Danish philosopher Soren Kierkegaard in his theology of despair remarked that one of the worst states a human being can face is to want to die and not be allowed to. We are unable to force God to give us an answer. It is not ours to lay down the terms on which God must meet us. Our frustration brings us to the point of crying out at God. And while this emotional catharsis may be understandable, it comes with a high price. We are reminded of the old illustration encouraging the venting of anger: "It's okay, go ahead. God is big enough to take it." This indeed may be true, but it does not address the issue of whether man is big enough to continue in alienation from God.

4. **The only solution to theodicy** is found by leaving our narrow thoughts and consulting God for a fresh revelation of His sovereignty. This changing of perspective is what God does to Job. Job is reminded that man does not constitute the whole of God's animate creation and as he comes to a humbler view of his own importance, he learns that he must transcend his self-centered attitude if he is to judge the ways of God aright (chapters 38–41).

5. Job's condition ultimately is **restored by a right standing before God.** The actual blessing of God comes later, but it is while Job is still in pain that he is rejuvenated (Chapter 42:1–6).

6. To quote John Calvin, "In the entire dispute, it is patently put before us that Job maintains a good report, and his adversaries maintain a poor one." This (along with chapters one and two) demonstrates to us the idea of "**testimonial suffering**" in order to show that mortals can and do serve God out of pure love for His person and not because of what they can get out of it.[3]

## Old Testament Commentary

There is yet another key factor to consider when looking at the biblical record regarding the issue of theodicy. Walter Kaiser, in his book, *A Biblical Approach to Personal Suffering* (Commentary on Lamentations), shows clearly from the Old Testament that God documents suffering as **multiplex** in its causes, purposes, and explanations. All attempts to reduce the explanation to a single reason could earn the quick rebuke from God as it did for Job's three friends. One of the harshest acts we mortals inflict upon one another is the flippant way in which we automatically assume that any pain or suffering visited upon another person **must** be a result of that person's sin. Kaiser warns, "Let us be Biblically sensitive and spiritually alert to the wholeness of God's revelation, and let us be reticent to postulate total patterns based on the presence of a single swallow."

From the standpoint of theistic religion, the Old Testament gives us the most comprehensive survey found anywhere regarding the problem of suffering. It even exceeds our hope for guidance on this subject by indicating that our Lord also suffers along with us; indeed, He suffers just as much as we do.

Dr. Kaiser outlines eight basic kinds of suffering in the Old Testament. It is significant to note that each one has a very distinctive part to play in the program of God and in the formation of godliness in each believer.

They are:

1. **Retributive Suffering:** The most comprehensive kind, it is given great prominence in the Bible simply because it is one of the fundamental principles by which God governs His world. Simply stated: the basic choices of life are good or evil, life or death (Deuteronomy 30:19) when the sufferer has failed to live by the existing norms, whether they be of a ritual, ethical, social, or doctrinal nature. Often in this kind of suffering, the misfortune can be calculated from the very beginning of the indulgence in the sin that eventually must call down the judgment of God. When a criminal suffers for his crime, he may be distressed, but he has no reason to be perplexed. There is no surprise that punishment should be the consequence of his crime.

2. **Educational or Disciplinary Suffering:** God often afflicts His people for the purpose of teaching them. The man or woman whom God loves He chastens and corrects often through pain, suffering, and anguish (Proverbs 13:24, 13:5; Hebrews 12:7). The first epistle of Peter in the New Testament speaks of this "fruit" which appears from suffering (1 Peter 1:6–9). We are admonished by Scripture not to think that it is an unusual thing that we should suffer. Peter wrote, "Beloved, do not think it is strange concerning this fiery trial which is to try you, as though some strange thing has happened to you, but rejoice to the extent that you partake of

Christ's sufferings, that when His glory is revealed, you may also be glad with exceeding joy" (1 Peter 4:12–13).

3.  **Vicarious Suffering:** This begins to appear in the substitutionary nature of the Old Testament sacrifices, and becomes even more vivid in the "Suffering Servant" of Isaiah 42–53. The Servant suffers not for Himself, but for others: "He was wounded for our transgressions, He was bruised for our iniquities." The formula is of one suffering so that others may be forgiven and freed. Closely aligned here is the idea that suffering belongs to the discipline of all of Christ's followers (Colossians 1:24). This fellowship in suffering unites us with the saints of God in all times (James 5:10), and is indeed a fellowship with the Lord Himself (Phil. 3:10), who uses this discipline to mold us more and more according to His character.

4.  **Empathetic Suffering:** Grief oftentimes enters fully into the lives and feelings of those whom the sufferer loves or knows. It even affects our God. In Hosea 11:8 God spreads forth His hands as if He were a distraught parent and asks, "How can I give you up . . . ?" Likewise, we are to "weep with those who weep" (Romans 12:15) and share in others' afflictions as Paul did (2 Cor. 2:4).

5.  **Doxological Suffering:** This is the concept that we go through an experience in order that God's own glory and purpose might be worked out. Genesis chapter 45 and following, tells of the trials of Joseph whose suffering during those years of imprisonment had nothing to do with his own sin, his discipline, or educational growth; it was allowed solely for the glory of God: "You meant evil against me, but God meant it for good" (Genesis 50:20).

6.  **Testimonial or Evidential Suffering:** The first two chapters show that Job was clearly a test case to show Satan (and would-be mockers of true religion) that mortals do serve God out of love for His person. When the prophet Habakkuk complained to God about the alarming increase of evil without any apparent divine judgement, he was informed that retribution at the hands of the Babylonians was to come. A witness, a testimony with strong evidence, was given to the faithfulness of God: "The just shall live by faith."

In the New Testament Peter concludes: "Therefore let those who suffer according to the will of God commit their souls to Him in doing good, as to a faithful Creator" (1 Peter 4:19). In this conclusion, Peter erases all doubt about the question of whether it is ever the will of God that we should suffer. He speaks of those who suffer "according to the will of God." This text means that suffering itself is part of the sovereign will of God. First Peter 1:6–7 says that the proven faith is more precious than gold, and without fiery trials (intense suffering), there is no proven faith. Peter also clearly points out that to suffer as a Christian carries no shame.

7. **Revelational Suffering:** The lengthy story of Jeremiah's physical, spiritual, and mental sufferings is given, in part, so that all the more convincingly, he might know and describe by word and life the suffering Judah was causing for her rejected Lord. It is used to bring us into a deeper knowledge of our God and the special relationship He has to His own.

8. **Eschatological or Apocalyptic Suffering:** God will permit a period of intense suffering just before the end of this historical era. Just when it has grown the darkest, and men have despaired of all hope, then will God emerge in His most glorious moment in the universe (Isaiah 24–27 Jeremiah 30–33; Ezekiel 33–48; Daniel 2–12; Zechariah 12–14; Revelation).[4]

## Can Bad Be Good?

The following are short surveys of three authors who have made solid contributions to the study of suffering and pain. These works are recommended to those seeking a deeper understanding regarding the human experience.

## Paul Tournier

Physician and Christian counselor Paul Tournier in his book, *Creative Suffering*, explores the notion that: "If anything be certain, it is that every one of life's trials, if only because it breaks the hard crust of our physical and mental habits, creates, like the ploughing of a field, an empty space where a seed can be sown." His theory is that the proper inner attitude and personal response can help our suffering contribute to actual development, maturity, and fulfillment.

He blends his personal experience in over fifty years of counseling practice with the examples of the great thinkers and artists who have triumphed over tremendous personal anguish. Tournier suggests: "The encounter with bereavement, loss, and deprivation brings the need for, and room for, creative response. In any situation of deprivation/bereavement, infirmity, marital conflict, or the suffering of a dear one, the sufferer is concerned to find relief from his trouble, a cure for his depression, generally without suspecting that this will have a great effect on his evolution as a person. That which will stimulate the personal maturation, in fact, is the brutal confrontation with the existential problem that the individual is trying to remedy."

Suffering is never beneficial in itself and must always be fought against. What counts, however, is the way a person reacts in the face of suffering. That is the real test of the person: What is our personal attitude to life and its changes and chances? To miss this perspective—the positive in the negative—is to become the loser in the many growth phases of life. In trials and suffering, creativity awakens.[5]

## Viktor Frankl

The disciplinary explanation to suffering is closely aligned to the theory of "soul building" or "greater good." This is the idea that the inner being of man (soul) can only be exercised and matured through trials, and that though the trial itself can never be considered a good thing, there is a greater good which can be derived at the end of the process. Suffering, it is said, always produces something. Our reaction to it is what determines whether we grow or regress.

Viktor Frankl fathered the psychological/sociological theory of **logotherapy** primarily from his own personal experiences in the prisons of Auschwitz, Germany. In his book, *Man's Search For Meaning,* Frankl recounts the horrifying experiences of some fifteen hundred prisoners of war cooped up in a building made to hold two hundred. In an attempt to keep his mind occupied, which Frankl believed was a matter of life or death, he began to mentally document the different phases a man experienced which would ultimately lead to the death of the individual.

Phase one was shock and horror while still holding to the notion of a reprieve.

Phase two was a shift toward the hard reality of the condition. This was marked by apathy, lack of emotion, gradually becoming blunted to daily beatings, dreaming of old times and overall numbness to the life around them.

As the hope of their release decreased and dimmed, Frankl found that there was one thing which separated those who went on to the third phase and died, and those who were able to stay alive. Those who died tended to become occupied with retrospective thoughts. They sat with closed eyes living in the past since the present life held no meaning and no longer made sense (theodicy). This pattern became so strong that Frankl could nearly always read a starry-eyed trance-like demeanor, and it would then be just days until guards carried the person out to his/her grave. This self-absorbtion in the past, Frankl concluded, was a sure formula for death.

In contrast to that, he had been helped out early on in his experience by a man who had smuggled in a piece of broken glass and had the habit of "shaving at any cost." The man would look and feel fit for any work assignment he was given. Frankl believed there had to be meaning in suffering or else man becomes cynical, calloused, and defeated in life. While the physical wastes away, the spiritual and creative intensify. For Frankl, his reason to live was the future hope that he would go on to father his theory of logotherapy, a theory which holds that as long as man sees reason and/or purpose in pain and suffering, he can and will endure tremendous amounts of it. To lose this is to die.

Frankl concluded not only that there is meaning in suffering, but what is more, to go without suffering is to say that human life is incomplete. This thinking would seem to be endorsed by the apostle Paul for on an occasion in the city of Lystra (Acts 14:19–22), after having been stoned and left for dead, he amazingly returned to that same city and "confirmed the souls there and exhorted them to continue in the faith, for through much tribulation we enter into the kingdom of God," i.e. that suffering indeed has distinct (and eternal) meaning and purpose.[6]

## Phillip Yancey

A thorough and comprehensive work on theodicy is the book/study guide, *Where Is God When It Hurts?* by Phillip Yancey. Especially intriguing is Yancey's treatment of what he calls, "Pain, the gift nobody wants." A correct perspective of pain is to recognize that it is a good thing in the overall makeup of our bodies, for it acts as a warning device without which we cannot fully function. Like the disciplinary explanation of suffering, Yancey points out the example of childbirth as perhaps the greatest human experience which demonstrates the delicate balance between pain and pleasure. Other highlights of his work are the accounts of differing but valid Christian reactions to theodicy, demonstrated through the lives of pole-vaulter Brian Sternberg and artist Joni Erickson.[7]

## How Should We Then Think?

The beginning point for forming our understanding of good and evil (theodicy) then must be revealed truth. Though we all experience suffering (some more than others), experience alone is not a trustworthy foundation upon which to base our beliefs. It makes the judgment too subjective because our view of evil is shaded by our consciousness of evil. It is the slippery slope to skepticism and despair.

## Looking to the End/Claiming His Promises

The conclusion of the writers of Scripture regarding the good/evil tension is based upon their revealed knowledge of God and His past performances to the faithful. This is demonstrated in the Old Testament by what theologians classify as the Lament Psalms. The Lament Psalms are intended for those who are in a suffering mode. We identify with the author who finds himself in the thick of trials and the process of grief. In the midst of complaining to God, the inspired writer reflects on God's faithfulness and looks to the end.

Psalm 3 is such an example:

Oh LORD, how are they increased that trouble me!
Many are they that rise up against me.
Many are they that say of my soul, "There is no help for him in God."
But Thou, O LORD, art a shield for me;
My glory and the lifter of my head.

(1–3)

Arise, O LORD and save me, O my God:
For Thou hast smitten all mine enemies upon the cheekbone;
Thou hast broken the teeth of the ungodly.
Salvation belongeth unto the LORD;
Thy blessing is upon thy people.

(Selah) (7–8)

Complaining, crying out, finding confidence, and a victorious triumph are all consistent elements of these Psalms, which are intended to comfort those hurting while in the midst of trial. We remember God's promises and His previous consistent acts of salvation to His children, and we claim them for ourselves.

The apostle Paul picks up a similar theme in the New Testament Epistle to the Romans where he instructs the griever to consider that suffering is revealed to us as a vital part of God's program for the sanctification process of the believer. Theodicy (Paul would say) is to be metaphorically viewed as the painful part of the process of childbirth, which focuses upon the hope (birth and life of the child) which is to follow. It is an effective metaphor, for in real life there is nothing much more laborious and painful, and yet quickly and radically glorious, than birthing a child. Following the birth, in a moment, the mother completely forgets the long struggle leading up to the birth because of the exhilaration of the new life that comes forth.

> For I reckon that the sufferings of this present time are not worthy to be compared with the glory which shall be revealed in us. For we know that the whole creation groans and travails in pain together until now.
>
> —Romans 8:18,22

It is then the focusing on the goal that gives hope throughout the suffering experience. For the mother in the birthing experience, it is her child. For the believer, it is the final redemption and deliverance from the bondage of sin and suffering.

Paul says that it is ". . . the anxious longing of creation that was subjected to futility in hope of freedom from slavery to corruption . . . that causes the groaning of creation" (Romans 8:20–22). We await with eager anticipation the redemption that is yet to come. With this focus, Paul says that the comparison not only gives the endurance to persevere, but adds meaning and purpose to suffering.

## Enduring Suffering

The following excerpt is from an article which appeared in the *Acquainted With Grief* newsletter. It is written by Elder Earl Oliver of Fellowship Bible Church in Tacoma, Washington.

No normal person likes to suffer. Even Christ Himself manifested a reluctance as He faced the impending cross, though it is clear from Scripture that He came for this very purpose. We know as well that a part of our following Christ involves suffering. Paul, in a somewhat mysterious passage in Colossians 1:24, seems to indicate that his (our) suffering is in fact fulfilling the contribution to the total sufferings of Christ which will in the end be attributed to Him. Christ's afflictions have overflowed to us. Believers enter into the fellowship of Christ's sufferings by identification (possibility). If suffering then is inevitable (Phil. 1:29) and in fact ordained, the question people face is, "How can I survive it?" The answer is that we cannot without God's grace. That which makes suffering so difficult to endure before we have to face it is that God does not give grace to endure a hardship until He sees our response. This is a powerful truth. God gives grace to the humble (James 4:6).[8]

Regarding enduring suffering, the Scriptures give no better illustration than that of Christ's sufferings. Note the significance of the order of events of the account of Jesus' agonizing prayer at the Mount of Olives.

Luke 22:39–43 tells us:

1. It was common for Jesus to go to the mount to pray.
2. He exhorted His disciples to pray also.
3. He began praying.
4. His plea was coupled with an expression of total submission to the Father.
5. An angel came to strengthen Him.

It is when Jesus (we) responds in complete submission to the will of the sovereign and loving Lord, that He (we) is strengthened in His grace. In like manner, Paul prayed for his physical malady to depart from him (2 Corinthians 12:7–10), yet God told him that His grace was sufficient for him. As Paul submitted himself to God's will in this matter, he was empowered to do a great work for the Glory of God.

There is a Russian Proverb that speaks to the issue of positive submission to our sufferings:

Every one of us should take all of our pain and suffering and put it into a basket. Then we should go out and put our basket in the street with all of the other baskets of our family, friends and neighbors. All of us should then walk around and look into all of the baskets in the street. If we all did this, we would each return home with our own baskets, happy to take them with us.

This positive submission does not mean that suffering is not painful. Otherwise it would not be suffering. But throughout the trial, there is the resignation and settled assurance that God is good and righteous, sovereign in all His ways, and can do no wrong—strengthening me with all that I need as I humble myself before Him.

## Suffering and Comfort

When children cry out in pain, unless we are barbarians, we rush to their sides. Small children especially look to parents and others for support and comfort. We hold them, kiss their scrapes, and apply Band-aids. This is not exclusive to children. I have seen numerous times in the church when young mothers have gone through miscarriages that older women will rise up to give comfort through relating a similar story from their own unrevealed past.

Whenever we comfort one another we are, in reality, imitating our heavenly Father who is called the "God of all Comfort" (2 Corinthians 1:3). God, who is the Father of Mercies, comforts us in our afflictions out of His very nature. He can do no other.

The apostle Paul related to the Corinthian believers this truth which he learned first-hand while in Asia Minor. This experience (we do not know what) was so dire that he used language such as "burdened excessively, beyond our own strength, despaired for our life, had the sentence of death, we dare not trust in ourselves," to describe it. Paul literally believed that it was the end. However, this great peril had at least three positive effects upon him.

First, he tells us that this changed his perspective during the trial so profoundly that he had no choice but to seek the God of the supernatural (God who raises the dead) for deliverance, for nothing short of this would do. Not only did God deliver him, but Paul concludes that in accordance with God's nature, he could have the confidence to rest assured, knowing God would do the same in the future as well.

There was a second truth that Paul realized through this trial. He concluded that God's purpose in delivering him was so that he might be able to comfort others who were in affliction, with the comfort with which God had comforted him. Paul believed that his affliction was tied up with the comfort and salvation of others. So too, we are told that we share Christ's burdens, one another's burdens, and one another's comforts. And in doing so, God is glorified in the end.

The third truth that Paul realized was that the prayers of many for him in his trial had blessed him and had glorified God as well (2 Corinthians 1:11).

## Power in Suffering

In 2 Corinthians chapter twelve, Paul relates his discovery that God's power is best displayed in a way that is directly opposite of the natural mindset. God restrained Paul from boasting about his supernatural experience (being caught up into paradise?) by bringing him a thorn in the flesh. Like us, Paul assumed that God's power is best displayed by removing his affliction and suffering. Paul prayed three times that he might be delivered from his condition. But in contrast to Paul's reasoning, God revealed to him that His power would be perfected in Paul's weakness (suffering). Having his perspective changed, Paul concluded the unthinkable: that as the power of Christ dwelt within him, all of his sufferings for Christ's sake have become an exceedingly profitable experience, for in his weakness he had in fact, become strong. It demonstrates one of the great twists of the gospel and a key difference between God and natural man's thinking regarding suffering: "Not by might nor by power, but by my Spirit says the Lord Almighty." Once again, this explanation of good and evil is built upon God's revealed Word, for were it not, it would be the logic of a madman.

## Epilogue

The phone rings and you (pastor/caregiver) are summoned to take a key role in helping a family through the most difficult experience in all of life. Someone has died, and now you are asked to make the waves calm. Yes, there will be attention to details and arrangements. There will be interaction with others: musicians, caterers, and other professionals who also serve their community. But before all of that transpires, there is the issue of theodicy to settle.

Recently I sat at a restaurant collecting information in order to officiate at an upcoming memorial service. I was meeting with a Korean lady in her 60's who was the mother of a 40-year-old daughter who had died unexpectedly of an unidentified virus. The daughter was married and had two children, but none of them was at the meeting. The two boys (17 and 19) were too confused and grief stricken, and the father was content to let his wife's mother make all the arrangements. I found out later that he was estranged from his family, and because of aggravating habits over the years, was disliked by the rest of the family.

The young lady had essentially lived her days for her sons, and they had had a strong relationship. She had been the peacemaker many times for the children. She had gone the extra mile on numerous occasions, but now they would be with their father whom they could not tolerate. It was evident she had lived a life devoted to her family. The husband had not.

It is an unnatural occurrence to outlive your children, no matter what the age.

A wife who loses her husband is called a widow,
A husband who loses his wife is called a widower,
A child who loses his parent is called an orphan,
There is not a word for a parent who loses a child.

-Anonymous

The elderly Korean lady asked me point blank about theodicy. Oh, she didn't know the term, but she knew the concept. She said to me in broken English, "All my life I pray to God, and He never let me down, never once. But this time He didn't keep His word. It makes me wonder if He's really even there? It just doesn't seem fair."

Once upon a time a man named Job had a similar experience. I thought back to all the thinking and studying I had done in the area of theodicy. There was a lot I knew about and could say to her, but it was mostly very heavy theology, and I was not convinced that she could either handle it or wanted it. I knew that her comfort was in getting a better, more Biblical perspective of God and who He is, just like Job.

God makes it clear to us that suffering is within His plan and that He has not forgotten us. But the funny thing about theodicy is that while it is great to discuss with your theological friends, it probably doesn't go too far for individuals in the grip of actual suffering. At the time, though, this poor little lady was not concerned that trials are a vital part of the sanctification process. Maybe there would be a day when I could say more, and she would process it. All she knew was that her daughter had died an untimely death, and at the moment it didn't seem to be fair. I didn't say a great deal that afternoon. I held her hand. I listened. I prayed with her. And I read to her Deuteronomy 29:29.

## The Weaver

My life is but a weaving between the Lord and me
I may not choose the colors, He knows what they should be
For He can view the pattern upon the upper side
While I can see it only on this—the under side
Sometimes He weaves in sorrow, which seems so strange to me
But I will trust His judgment and work on faithfully
'Tis He who fills the shuttle, and He knows what is best
So I shall weave in earnest, leaving to Him the rest
Not 'til the loom is silent and the shuttles cease to fly
Shall God unroll the canvas and explain the reason why
The dark threads are as needed in the Weaver's skillful hand
As the threads of gold and silver in the pattern He has planned

# CHAPTER THREE

# The Bible and Mourning

## THE JUDEO PATTERN

### Grief/Mourning

And she said unto them, Call me not Naomi (pleasant), call me Mara (bitter) for the Almighty hath dealt very bitterly with me.

—Ruth 1:20

Mourning never ends, it only erupts less frequently.

—Dr. Allan Wolfelt

The Bible has a great deal to say regarding the topics of grief and mourning. There are some twenty Hebrew words translated in the King James Version of the Bible for some form of the word *grieve*: sorrow, complaint, fool's wrath, vexation, pain, hurt, suffering, bitterness, faint, weariness, to be vexed, to loath, to name a few.

In the New Testament the occurrences are more infrequent. This is significant because Christ came to "*comfort* all that mourn, to give a *garland* for ashes, the oil of *joy* for mourning, the garment of *praise* for the spirit of heaviness" (Isaiah 61:3). Christians, however, cannot but feel sorrow and be moved by grief, and it is interesting to note that in both the Old Testament and the New Testament, *God Himself is said to be susceptible to grief.*

A man of sorrows and acquainted with grief.

(Isaiah 53:3)

Then He [Jesus] said to them, "My soul is deeply grieved, to the point of death, remain here and keep watch with me"

(Matthew 26:38)

Much of the following information regarding the biblical and historical aspects of grief has been gleaned from the International Standard Bible Encyclopedia; Wm. B. Eerdmans Publishing Co., W. L. Walker, Author; James Orr, General Editor.[1]

## Why Do People Grieve?

In the biblical account, many situations cause grief and mourning: defection (1 Samuel 15:35), disobedience (Ezra 9:4–7), desolation (Joel 1:9–10), defeat (Revelation 18:11), discouragement (Psalm 42:9), disappointment (Lamentations 1:4), disease (Job 2:5–8), wicked rule (Proverbs 29:2), misinformation (Genesis 37:34), invasion (Joel 1:9), political failure (1 Samuel 16:1), reading of the law (Nehemiah 8:9), and the accompanying of end time judgment (Revelation 18:8). Ecclesiastes 3:4 tells us that there is a "time for mourning" appointed under heaven. The prophet Jeremiah says that in a certain day, the creation itself will mourn because of the destruction in the land (Jeremiah 4:28). And in one of the most poignant messianic prophesies in all of Scripture, the prophet Zechariah tells of a time when the inhabitants of Jerusalem will mourn for Messiah as one who mourns for a first-born son. As our own experience in life reinforces, so the Bible declares that grief and mourning come in many ways and for many occasions.

The revolutionary message of God's Word regarding mourning, however, is that the ransomed of the Lord (God's people) will return to Zion, and they will obtain gladness and joy while sorrow and mourning will flee away (Isaiah 35:10, 51:11). The New Testament echoes this sentiment in the Beatitudes (Sermon on the Mount) as Jesus taught, "Blessed are they who mourn, for they shall be comforted" (Matthew 5:4). There is a glorious promised deliverance from the condition of sorrow, grief, and mourning for God's own, and it shall not fail.

## Grief/Mourning and Death

The majority of Old Testament references of the terms for grief/mourning deal with the loss of loved ones. Examples of death abound.

Abraham went in to weep and mourn for Sarah (Genesis 23:2). The sons of Israel wept and mourned for thirty days at the death of Moses on the plains of Moab (Deuteronomy 34:8). King David led the people in a collective day of lament for the death of Abner as they buried him in Hebron (2 Samuel 3:31ff). Bathsheba mourned over Uriah the Hittite (2 Samuel 11:26). And in a lavish display of the wealth of Egypt, Joseph ordered the embalming (Egyptian custom) of his father Jacob, as the people wept nationally for seventy days. This was followed by one of the most elaborate funeral processions in Scripture as the family of Jacob moved out of Egypt and made their way to bury the patriarch in the land of Canaan. So elaborate was the spectacle that it left a lasting memory on those of other countries who, when they saw it, immediately recognized the "greatness of the mourning for the Egyptians" (Genesis 50:1–14).

One marked feature of Near Eastern (i.e. biblical) mourning was what is called its studied publicity and careful observance of the prescribed ceremonies. So often in the Scriptures, immediately following the account of some crisis, we read the familiar reaction: "And then he tore his clothing, wore sackcloth . . ." What follows is an accounting of the particular forms which were usually observed by an Orthodox Jew of his day.

1. Rending (tearing) of the clothes (Genesis 37:29, 34; Job 1:20).
2. Dressing in sackcloth (2 Samuel 3:31).
3. Ashes, dust, or earth sprinkled on the person (2 Samuel 13:19).
4. Black or sad-colored garments (2 Samuel 14:2).
5. Removal of ornaments or neglect of person (Deuteronomy 21:12).
6. Shaving the head and/or plucking out the beard (Job 1:20; Isaiah 50:6).
7. Laying bare some body parts (Isaiah 20:2).
8. Fasting or abstinence in meat and drink (2 Samuel 1:12).
9. Diminution in offerings to God (Deuteronomy 26:14).
10. Covering the head (2 Samuel 15:30).
11. Cutting the flesh (Jeremiah 16:6).
12. Employment of hired mourners (Amos 5:16; 2 Samuel 14:2).
13. Friends joining in for lamentation (Judges 11:40; Job 2:11).

14. Sitting or lying in silence (Job 2:13).
15. The cup of consolation (Jeremiah 16:7–8).
16. A designated period of time for mourning (Genesis 50:3; Numbers 20:29; Deuteronomy 34:8; Genesis 50:10; 1 Samuel 31:13).

In these practices Jews, Arabs, and Orientals, both ancient and modern, all tend to agree. Traditionally, men are mostly silent in grief while women scream, tear their hair, hands and face, and throw earth or sand on their heads. Both Mohammedans and Christians in Egypt hire wailing-women to wail at stated times. Some women shave their heads upon the death of a near relative, a custom prevalent also among Egyptian peasant tribes. In *The Arabian Nights* are frequent allusions to similar practices. Modern Egyptian women raise cries of lamentation called *wilwal*, uttering the most piercing shrieks, and calling upon the name of the deceased. The females of the neighborhood come to join with them in this conclamation, and usually bring two or more public wailing-women. Each brings a tambourine, and, while beating it, exclaims, "Alas for him!"

We conclude that from these examples of Near Eastern customs and practices, the Israelite "mourner" is readily identified in the society of his/her day.

## The Grief Process (working through loss)

There are points of likeness and contrast between oriental and occidental burial customs even today. We have seen that one nearly universal similarity is the conceptual idea that working through the loss of an individual is a process that involves personal involvement and adherence to certain prescribed customs. What follows is a biblical development of a pattern of typical Jewish funeral practices from death to the grave.

## Quickly

In the Near East the burial of the dead is done in such a way as to suggest haste to the Western mind. Burial among Israelites today seldom takes place later than ten hours after death, often earlier. It is suggested that the rapidity of decomposition, the excessive violence of grief, and a reluctance to allow the dead to remain long in the houses of the living explains what Westerners would see as the indecency of haste. In part, it explains the quickness with which the bodies of Nadab and Abihu were carried out of the camp (Leviticus 10:4), and those of Ananias and Sapphira were hastened off to burial (Acts 5:1–11).

What further explains their haste is that the Bible makes much of the idea of defilement from contact with a dead body, and the judgment that might come upon a house for harboring the body. The begging of the body of Jesus by Joseph of Arimathea for burial on the very day of the crucifixion (Matthew 27:39ff) was in strict accordance with the provision of the Mosaic Law, as well as in compliance with humanity. Jewish burial took place, if possible, within twenty-four hours after death, and frequently on the day of death. Today, the dead are often in their graves, according to custom, within two or three hours after death. As soon as the breath is gone, the eldest son, or nearest of kin, closes the eyes of the dead (Genesis 46:4). The death is announced, as of old, by a lamentation preceded by a shrill cry, and the weeping and wailing of professional mourners (Mark 5:38).

## Preparation

In Acts 5:6 we read of Ananias, "The young men . . . wrapped him round, and they carried him out and they buried him." What they probably did was unfastened the girdle, loosened the under-garment and wide cloak worn above it, and used them as a winding sheet to cover the corpse from head to foot. Little ceremony, much haste.

Usually, however, there would have been more ceremony and more time taken. It is still customary to wash the body (Acts 9:37), anoint it with aromatic oils (Mark 16:1), wrap hands and feet in gravebands of linen (John 11:44b), and cover the face with a napkin (John 11:44a). It was also common to place in the wrappings of the body aromatic spices and other preparations to retard decomposition (Luke 24:1; John 19:39–40).

That this was a very old custom is witnessed by such passages as 2 Chronicles 16:14, where it is said that King Asa was laid "in the bed which was filled with sweet odors and diverse kinds of spices prepared by the perfumers' art." Apparently there was, in later times, a confraternity of young men whose business it was to attend to these preparations on behalf of the dead (Acts 5:6 and 8:2). Perhaps they were the funeral directors of their day?

## On the Way to the Grave

Coffins were unknown in ancient Israel. When the time came, the corpse was carried to the grave on a bier, a movable stand on which a corpse is laid (2 Samuel 3:31). The bier sometimes had a pole at each corner by which it was carried on the shoulders to the tomb.

The procession of mourners was made up largely of relatives and friends of the deceased but was led by professional mourning women who made the air resound with their shrieks and lamentations (Ecclesiastes 12:5; Jeremiah 9:17). Among some Jews of today, it is said, the funeral procession moves swiftly because there are supposed to be innumerable evil spirits hovering about desirous to attack the soul, which is thought to be in the body until interment takes place, and the corpse is actually covered.

Some believe that the passages in Matthew 9:23 and Mark 5:38, "came into the official's house and saw the flute players," allude to the custom of a dirge song which was chanted by the participants.

## At the Grave

When the body was let down into the grave, only a heap of stones was piled over the shallow grave to preserve the dead from the dreaded invasion of hyenas, jackals, or thieves. Dirt followed.

It was customary for each family to have a family tomb: either a natural cave, prepared with stone shelves to receive the bodies, or one cut out of rock in the hillside, each tomb having many niches in which the bodies could be placed (Genesis 25:9–10). Many examples of such caves are given in the Bible: Joshua at Timnath-serah (Joshua 24:30); Samuel in the house at Ramah (1 Samuel 25:1); Joab (1 Kings 2:34); Manasseh in the garden of his house (2 Kings 21:18); Josiah in the same tomb as his father and grandfather (2 Kings 23:30); and Asa (2 Chronicles 16:14). According to custom, no Jew was to sell his burying place if it was at all possible for him to hold it.

When the tomb was a cave, or was dug out from rock, the entrance was often closed with a large, circular stone set up on its edge or rim and rolled in its groove to the front of the mouth of the tomb to close it securely. Often the stone was further secured by a strap or by sealing. In such cases it could easily be seen and discovered if the tomb had been disturbed (Matthew 27:66).

A lack of proper burial was regarded in ancient times as a great indignity or even a judgment of God. It gave men untold distress to think that they would not receive a suitable burial. For a corpse to remain unburied and become food for beasts of prey was the epitome of indignity or judgment: (1 Kings 13:22, 2 Kings 9:37, Jeremiah 7:33, Psalm 79:3, Revelation 11:9). Uncovered blood cried for vengeance; the belief was that the unburied dead would not only inflict trouble upon his own family, but also bring defilement and a curse upon the whole land. It was, therefore, an obligation resting upon all to bury even the dead found by the way. Even malefactors were to be allowed burial (Deuteronomy 21:22), and the exceptional denial of it to the sons of Rizpah gave occasion for the touching story of her self-denying care of the dead found in 2 Samuel 21:10.

## How Were the Graves Marked? / Places of Burial

Ordinary graves were marked by the heaping of crude stones. In some cases hewn stones and sometimes costly pillars were set up as memorials of the dead (Ezekiel 39:15; 2 Kings 23:17). Jacob set up a pillar over Rachel's grave (Genesis 35:20), and her tomb is marked by a monument to this day. Absalom's grave in the woods of Ephraim had a heap of stones raised over it (2 Samuel 18:17), but in this case, as in the case of Achan, it was not for honor but for dishonor. In New Testament times the place of burial was usually outside the cities and villages (Luke 7:12), and there was public provision made for the burial of strangers (Matthew 27:7). In the closing days of the monarchy, there was a public burying-ground at Jerusalem (Jeremiah 26:23), probably where it is to this day between the city wall and the Kidron Valley. Thousands of Jewish graves on the sloping sides of the Valley of Jehoshaphat, where the Jews have come from all lands to be buried, bear witness to the belief that associates the coming of Messiah with a blessed resurrection. Many Jews hold that Messiah, when He comes, will descend upon the Mount of Olives and will pass through these resting places of the dead as He enters the Holy City in glory.

On a less glorious note, the Bible speaks concerning an area southwest of Jerusalem known as the Valley of Hinnom (lamentation), a deep and narrow ravine with rocky sides separating Mount Zion to the north, from the sloping rocky plateau of the plain of

Rephaim to the south. It was originally a boundary line between the tribes of Judah and Benjamin (Joshua 15:8), and later became an area where Solomon erected high places for Molech and evil rites were revived from time to time under later idolatrous kings. Ahaz and Manasseh made their children to "pass through the fire" in this valley (2 Kings 16:3). To put an end to these abominations, the place was polluted by Josiah, who rendered it ceremonially unclean by spreading over it human bones and other corruptions (2 Kings 23:19; 2 Chronicles 34:4). That location appeared to have become the common cesspool of the city, into which its sewage flowed, to be carried off by the waters of the Kidron. From its ceremonial defilement and from the detested fire of Molech, if not from the supposed ever-burning funeral piles, the Jews later applied the name of this valley, Ge Hinnom, (Gehenna, land of Hinnom), to denote the place of eternal torment. It is in this sense it is used by Jesus in Mark 9:43: "It is better for you to enter life crippled, than having your two hands, to go into hell, into the unquenchable fire, where the worm does not die and the fire is not quenched."

As a final note, in an effort to better understand contemporary practices of the Jewish tradition, Congregation Shaarey Zedek (Rabbi Irwin Groner) has provided a guide/booklet explaining the procedures of mourning and the healing process. Governed by respect for the dead and concern for the mourner, the booklet is intended to help individuals better face the trials of death and honor the memory of loved ones. Their website is *http://www.shaareyzedek.org/gbereave.htm.*

# How Should We Then Mourn?

With the model of biblical Israel set before us, we turn our attention to the present. The common thread is that loss occurs. It happens to everyone at some time or another. With loss comes grief and mourning, and in that way, we are no different from those who have gone before us. Though cultural customs may change from place to place and from era to era, we all continue to work our way through loss as best we can.

## Disclaimer

There are volumes and volumes of books written and available concerning grief, bereavement, mourning, death and dying, loss, SIDS, suicide, unexpected death, sorrow, right to die, depression, mental anxiety, widow/widowers, children's deaths, loneliness, single parenting, emotions, shock, numbness, reality, handling the holidays and special days, adjusting, getting back into the flow, dating, the length of grief, and on and on it goes. Many individuals have distinguished themselves over the years as credible and trustworthy writers in this area. Their specialized books can be obtained through any library, bookstore or many funeral homes.

When writing a book of this nature, it is difficult to decide how much one should include pertaining to that which is so psychologically diverse and complex. I choose to allow the bulk of the vast complexity of the issue to be handled by the specialists in each arena. Hopefully I will leave you, the pastor, with a solid overview of what I believe are the most relevant and succinct considerations of which a clergy person would need to be aware.

## Defined

Dr. Glen W. Davidson writes in his book, *Understanding Mourning:*

STRONG
SHOULDERS
NEED TO
CRY TOO.

The idea of mourning is extremely old and has been preserved in two of humanity's most ancient languages. The root meaning in Sanskrit is "to remember" and in Greek is "to care." Mourning is an emotion that results from the universal experience of loss: the way in which mourners adapt from what was to what is. To grieve (to be burdened by sorrow) and to be bereaved (to be robbed of someone or something precious) are part of—but only part of—the mourning process. Mourning is a process of recovering orientation—becoming involved once again in human relationships.[2]

## The Normalcy of Grief

Grief is an emotional experience in deprivation. We lose something that we have cherished and do not want it taken from us. Death is the most extreme form of deprivation in our lives. It is not only that we lose what we have loved, but that we sense losing some important part of our own being as well. It is almost strange that we seem to be so ill prepared for this experience since much of life is this way. Any time we make a choice, we are giving up one alternative in order to take the other. A pastor will find that much of his/her time in grief counseling is spent in re-affirming an individual that what they are experiencing is quite normal. The patterns of emotions that an individual experiences (fears, anger, confusion, emptiness, anxieties) are common to all who have undergone deprivation. Our role often is to listen and encourage.

I remember some years ago reading an article on grief. The author said, "Jackie Kennedy had set back grief counsel ten years." For those who are old enough to remember, Mrs. Kennedy (perhaps on the advice of her political peers?) in the name of national bravado, took on a rather stoic approach to the untimely assassination of her husband. Because mourning is often misunderstood, individuals with this reaction are sometimes viewed by the community as recovering well because they do not "break down" or "fall apart" emotionally. Such was the public reaction to her demeanor. While the magazines and newspapers applauded her heroics, the psychological world wondered if her tearless show was due to good, misguided coaching, or perhaps a public admission of a less-than-admirable marriage? When individuals have sacrificial, intimate relationships in life, it is quite normal to display hurt, sorrow, and a tear or two. In fact, it is abnormal not to. The general equation is that the depth of grief we experience is commensurate to the intimacy of the relationship. We may show up for the funeral of the guy down the street, but we probably won't lose any sleep over his death. We didn't live with him, eat with him, sleep with him. Not so with loved ones. With loved ones, we cry. To express grief then is a normal reaction to the experience of deprivation.

## A Biblical Account

The account of David and Bathsheba in 2 Samuel, chapters 11 and 12, was an embarrassment for the king and an affront to his God. We cannot excuse in any way the willful actions of "the man after God's own heart;" however, the story does reveal an interesting observation of what could be called normal grief.

The prophet Nathan had delivered the hard message to David that the ill-conceived child was going to be taken by God as a judgment upon him and his sinful actions (verse 14). This was followed by the illness of the child (verse 15). David then did the only thing that he could do, which was to pray and fast before God and beg for mercy. His efforts did not stay the hand of God, and the child died (verse 18). Fearfully, the servants reasoned that to tell David about the death of the child would bring harm (verse 18). However, when David reasoned within himself that the death had occurred, he ended his fast, cleaned himself (shaved) and went to the house of God to worship Him. It seems from the passage that this confused his servants since they expected him to grieve after the death of the child, not before. This would seem to be the normal course of events.

David argued that as long as the child was alive, there was still hope for God's mercy. But since the child had died, there now was no way in which David could bring the child back to life. Then David demonstrated that his only hope after the death was that he would some day go to where the child was and see him again, but the child could not ever come back. I believe that since David had heard the pronouncement of the death of the child by the prophet (who would always be right, see Deuteronomy 18:14ff), though he held out for possible mercy, David was doing his grieving before the death of the child. Once the death occurred, and God had had His way, the proper thing was to move on in the grieving process and reinvest in life again, which is what David did.

## Tasks for Mourners

J. William Worden, Harvard professor, identifies four tasks for mourners.

1. **Accept the Reality of the Loss**
   The first task of mourning involves facing the stark fact that the loved one is dead. This sounds ridiculously obvious, but if it is true that we first move into denial, then we must counter it. Most of our lives we think we are in total control. To experience something which is irreversible is a shock. Young children, for example, do not have the concept of irreversibility. All they know is that Daddy and Mommy fix everything that goes bad. As adults, we are made painfully aware that this is not the case. When our imaginations are confronted by reality, we must change our orientation. At some point then, like it or not, we must begin the awful task of accepting the finality of death.

2. **Accept and Experience Grief**
   It is abnormal to seek pain. It is also abnormal to deny pain. We tend to avoid pain, but like a nagging alarm clock, it won't necessarily go away.

The griever will often make attempts to avoid people and places which remind the individual of the loved one. It is ironic that when we remove ourselves from familiar surroundings in an attempt to flee, usually disorientation becomes more profound, and problems multiply. There is no way to avoid working through painful experiences.

I read a book written by a widow in which she had a chapter entitled, "Take a Cruise." It seems that she had received constant well-meaning counsel from her friends that a cruise was all she needed to get herself straightened around. She concluded the chapter by saying that what they forgot to tell her is that she had to come home sometime, and all of her familiar memories would still be there waiting for her. Humans can no more run away from their problems than they can outrun their own shadows.

3.  **Begin to Adjust**

    We don't realize just how important another person is until that person is gone. The loved one played important roles in the mourner's life. Death takes away the cues that those people provided for orientation. Sights, smells, sounds, habits— these all were a large part of life orientation. They now are gone. Therefore, much of the grieving process involves identifying how the individual now gone played important roles in life and realizing, that in those areas, there would need to be change.

4.  **Reinvest in Other Relationships**

    Studies have shown that mourners who isolate themselves are likely to become severely disoriented and may even die prematurely. People who invest themselves only in themselves are likely to become chronically ill. For instance, counselors have known for a long time that adults who are untouched do not thrive, particularly those who are oriented to physical expressions of affection. Often we have not incorporated this insight into acceptable rituals of relating. Any grandmother can tell us about the value of hugging. Reinvesting emotional energies in other relationships, though threatening, is an adjustment that becomes one of these necessary tasks of grief work.[3]

# Healthy Grief

Dr. Glen Davidson identifies for us five factors which have been useful in identifying mourners who are likely to adapt in a healthy manner.

1. **A Nurturing, Supportive, Social Network**
   This is the most important factor, especially for short-term health. Loneliness increases the risk of illness and premature death. People cut off from society, without spouses, friends, or community ties, have a death rate twice as high as those of the same age who are socially involved. People become disoriented when deprived of human contact over long periods of time.
   Therefore, participation in mutual help groups, telephone or internet networks, and regular social activities like weekly worship seem crucial if a mourner is to maintain vitality. Everyone, it seems, needs a viable social network in order to keep his/her orientation.

2. **Adequate Nutritional Balance**
   Without social interaction, the loss of appetite and the use of junk foods are more likely. High-risk health habits such as smoking and heavy alcohol consumption are far more prevalent among the socially isolated. No matter how different people are in age, race, size, or activity, each person needs the basic nutrients. Use of a variety of foods from each of the food groups helps to assure desirable intake of nutrients.

3. **Adequate Fluid Intake**
   Mourners need to drink more fluids than they feel they need. Adequate fluids, the amounts varying depending on gender and body weight, are necessary to carry away the body's toxic waste and to maintain appropriate electrolyte balance. Alcohol or beverages with caffeine cause further dehydration, and thus should be avoided.

4. **Daily Exercise**
   Muscles should be kept in good tone. For the person with sedentary habits, reasonable daily exercise is doubly important. Regular exercise is also the most effective means of controlling depression. Inadequate oxygenation of the blood is often relieved by exercise.

5. **Daily Rest**

Rest needs to come at the same time in each twenty-four-hour cycle. It is important that regular rituals for rest are followed even if it is impossible to sleep. Many mourners make the mistake of working into the night because they are restless when they lie down. Then they begin to sleep later and later into the day. In no time, their rest cycle is radically changed—sleeping in the daytime and staying up at night. The internal clock then becomes unsynchronized with the rest of society and with the usual areas of orientation which provide the sense of place, time, and well-being. In short, a mourner should maintain the same rest patterns. If unable to sleep throughout the night, the mourner may find it necessary to rest for an hour at midday.

## Unhealthy Grief

A griever who persists in what psychologists call unhealthy or abnormal grief should seek professional help promptly. According to Dr. Davidson, here are five danger signs.

1. **Persistent Thoughts of Self-Destruction**

Some mourners wonder if readjusting to their loss is even worth it.
Though fleeting ideas of self-destruction are common, habitually focusing on this is a sign to seek professional help.

2. **Failure to Provide For The Five Basic Survival Needs**

It is often difficult to give proper attention to one's own needs. Though every mourner fails to meet some of these some of the time, an inability to maintain in these areas may signal a need of help from either friends or a professional.

3. **Long-term Depression**

The characteristics of grief should change over time. To still be in shock months after a death could be a sign that help is needed. If a mourner has chronic dysfunction, or has "no feelings," or does not express any grief following a loss, these too could be warnings.

4. **Substance Abuse**

Any time controlling substances are used on a long-term regular basis, the user should request professional monitoring. Suppression of disagreeable symptoms does not address the underlying cause of those symptoms.

5. **Mental Illness**

Characteristics of mourning can mask mental illness. This is usually seen in people with a family history of mental illness. People who have been depressive or manic-depressive should be alert to recurrence of their illness.

At close range it is difficult to separate the normal from the abnormal. We must ask ourselves, as counselors, whether an act that may seem abnormal is part of a whole pattern of unusual actions and reactions or merely an isolated occurrence. We want to see whether this new way of acting and reacting is becoming more firmly fixed or less so.

The abnormal usually shows up in extremes. Most people are "back to normal" in a few months. If people are not able to function effectively after this period of time, it is a fairly specific indication that they should have some special help in their readjustment.

## On Death and Dying

In 1969 Dr. Elizabeth Kubler-Ross, at that time medical director of the Family Service and Mental Health Center of South Cook County in Illinois, published the findings of her oncological studies in a book which would be hailed as one of the most profound works in this area of psychology and medicine. *On Death and Dying* has come to be known as the care-givers' bible of grief management and, for that reason alone, should be mandatory reading for all clergy.

Perhaps her greatest fear was stated in her disclaimer (Preface) that says, "It is not meant to be a textbook on how to manage dying patients, nor is it intended as a complete study of the psychology of the dying . . . but we will learn much about the functioning of the human mind, the unique aspects of our existence, and will emerge from this enriched and perhaps with fewer anxieties about our own finality."[4] It was as if she could foresee the potential abuse, for in the ensuing years her categorizing of the "Five Stages of Grief" (denial, anger, bargaining, depression, and acceptance) were nearly canonized as the textbook for managing dying patients by the care-giving community. Still, her observations have served as legitimate landmarks for the counseling profession whereby we identify the normal processes of the difficult grief work, whether it be with the dying or with the living who are left to grieve.

## What about Help?

With the advent of such groups as the Hospice Movement in America in the last thirty years, there has been a substantial raising of the bar of awareness regarding death, dying, and bereavement. And Hospice is not alone. There are numerous other organizations which have literature and information available to aid ministers in this critical area of care giving. Funeral homes are now typically either in-house equipped or keenly aware of resources to help us all in serving hurting people. It is incumbent upon ministers to move ahead in this area of service and to avail themselves of the multitude of aid ministries available.

# CHAPTER FOUR

# Opportunity

Show me the manner in which a nation cares for its dead, and I can measure with mathematical exactness, the tender mercies of its people, their loyalty to high ideals, and their regard for the laws of the land.

—William Gladstone

After sixty years the stern sentence of the burial service seems to have a meaning that one did not notice in former years. There begins to be something personal about it.

—Oliver Wendell Holmes

## The Minister's High Calling

As I observe the American scene, it is distressing to me to see the glaring imbalance in our values and priorities. As I spin the channels on the television, I see poorly educated, crazily clad young people on display as the music leaders of the culture. The philosophies of life they espouse in their songs are about drugs, immorality, and violence. They talk a language of which I know nothing. I cannot identify and do not want to. We reward them with lots of money. Some become millionaires before they are twenty-one.

We take promising athletes and sign them to multi-million dollar contracts, the bill being picked up by a combination of liquor companies, TV advertising revenue, and confused Americans who will pay great sums of money to worship the sports gods who come and go. We gamble and bet money on them and their teams and make the wrong people rich while the common man loses his paycheck. In a situation where one would think the athletes would pinch themselves to check reality, instead their wealth and fame more often than not breeds arrogance, which demands more of the same.

On the other side of the ledger, we often pay little attention to organizations, individuals, and benevolences who roll up their sleeves and get down where the people are. We barely applaud these servant types. We call a minister who will come into a crisis situation, help people find their way through life's most labyrinthine maze (death), and hardly recognize their efforts at all. We pay him a hundred bucks (more about that later).

If we look to our world for a proper balance, we will most often look in vain. Something is wrong here. Unless, of course, our own priorities are governed by God and His Word. In truth, these are the opportunities in life that have eternal value. Jesus said, "Whoever in the name of a disciple gives to one of these little ones even a cup of cold water to drink, truly I say to you he shall not lose his reward."

I wonder how much heaven will reveal the things which really counted and discount what the man on the street perceived as having value. A right perspective about these things should surely cause us to welcome eternal opportunities.

Dr. David Wesley Reid, in his article, *Generic Funerals*, summarizes this wonderful pastoral privilege:

> More than anything else, I believe it's the pastor's privilege and duty in working with grieving families to have his personal investment in their lives serve as a signpost, pointing to a God whose character is unquestioned, whose love is unbounded, and whose lordship over life is not limited to this earthly time and space.[1]

## Why Do People Get Religious?

> They sent therefore and gathered all the lords of the Philistines and said, "Send away the ark of the God of Israel, and let it return to its own place, that it may not kill us and our people." For there was a deadly confusion throughout the city; the hand of God was very heavy there. And the men who did not die were smitten with tumors and the cry of the city went up to heaven.
>
> —1 Samuel 5:11–12

In many years of active ministry, I have discovered an interesting truth among Americans: most of us have been influenced by the Christian faith in one way or another. It may have only been Mrs. Sellinger's Vacation Bible School, or Sunday school, or the neighbor lady, but something stuck. We have picked up on the idea that we are supposed to get religious when we go through special passages of life. Public school systems (often anti-Christian) still invite ministers to speak at their graduations because they sense that to ask for God's blessing in the lives of young people going out into the world cannot hurt.

Trouble also serves as a strong motive to get religious. In the example above from 1 Samuel 5, the Philistines (pagans) had been visibly witnessing a duel between Jehovah and their god, Dagon. Their daily frustration of defeat brought them to the conclusion that the ark of the Lord did not belong with them, and bad things had come upon them because of it. The account says that because of their condition, ". . . their cries went up to heaven." They prayed to a God whom they knew not.

Another example, Psalm 107, repeats the same theme four times to illustrate this similar pattern. In this psalm, the author tells us that distress, rebellion, and foolishness all served to bring God's people into a dark situation whereupon they "cried out unto the Lord in their trouble, and the Lord delivered them from their distress." Perhaps the old adage, "There are no atheists in the foxholes," is more true than we know. When distress overtakes us, it is good to seek God.

Moreover, weddings are religious too. With the number of failed marriages in the United States, we sense that we need some help. Perhaps it's wisdom, maybe it's just fear of the future; maybe it's a dutiful loyalty to the traditions of the family (after all, we want Aunt Jodie's blessing and wedding gift). Whatever the reason, the point is that people still get married in "the way of religion," though admittedly sometimes from a less than correct heart motive of true love for God. They sense they just need to do it that way (God's way). Under it all, people seem to say, "Perhaps God is here somewhere and could help us. We're open."

We sense a need of God's presence and His blessing. And I would say this is especially true regarding the death of an individual. The vast majority of people will tolerate God in the equation when they are in distress. There is an interesting obvious observation about death: It is absolutely the most sure fact of all of life. Playwright George Bernard Shaw said, "Death is the ultimate statistic: It claims one out of every one." There are many things in life which may or may not happen, but this is not so with death. We all die. And yet most of us go about our lives acting as if there is no possibility it will claim us. If we thought as we should, we would always reflect on our mortality since we never know when that time will come. Though perhaps considered morbid and nega-tive, the Puritans were on target when they espoused the philosophy that man should live as if today was his last day on earth.

Yet to live as the Puritans did is not the practice of twenty-first century Americans. Often ministers encounter situations where an individual has died, and the family, with whom they are dealing, is completely in the dark. They have avoided the certainty of death all of their lives. Absolutely unprepared for the event, they do not know what to do. Uneducated in the reality of death, they look to others (funeral directors and clergy) for guidance and direction. An encouraging observation is that many people will actually search for God at this time. It is at this point ministers of the gospel must see this situation as a positive opportunity to advance God's kingdom. If that is so, what then should be the attitude of the clergy?

## Seizing the Moment

When a minister is called to officiate at a memorial service of an individual who has not graced the door of the church, that minister can react in a number of ways. One consideration is to conclude that since the individual who died never knew God or sought after Him in his life, he would therefore want no part of a typical orthodox Christian service. That would seem logical. But remember that people often get religious in times of trouble. Again, their true motive may be less than pure; they may simply want the pain to go away, but they're willing to tolerate God in the equation. And they do not know where to begin. In an opportunity such as this, it is the role of the faithful minister to serve these people by giving them Christ and truth, for that is what they need. Should the policy be to only officiate at services of individuals within our local churches? What about friends or relatives of church members? Should we be open to serve anyone? If not, where is the cut-off point? How is that determined?

Once I was called to officiate at the service of a gentleman from Guam who had lived in the United States for twenty years. Nearly all of his family members were still living on the island and had come to the U.S. for his burial. His Guamanian relatives were devout Roman Catholics and, because of that, had attempted to contact a local priest to conduct the service of their brother. Because the deceased was not an active member of the local parish, the priest rejected their appeal, and they were left without an officiant. When called upon, I reminded both the funeral director and the family that I was a protestant minister and, because of that fact, there were some serious differences between how I would conduct the service and how a priest would do it. This did not concern them, however, because their religious "superstitions" led them to believe that unless their brother had some minister preside, his eternal chances might be in jeopardy. I told them I would be glad to help as long as they understood the clear difference, and they would not require me to "become a catholic priest." They held their own rosary before the service began (led by one of the ladies in the family), and then I did the memorial service. Since they were religious, they gave me a wide open door to preach the gospel of salvation by grace through faith. Sometimes opportunities present themselves in mysterious ways.

## The Imago Dei

> Then God said, "Let us make man in our image, in our likeness, and let them rule over the fish of the sea and the birds of the air, over the livestock, over all the earth, and over all the creatures that move along the ground." So God created man in His own image, in the image of God he created him, male and female He created them.
>
> —Genesis 1:26–27

The Latin term for "image of God" is *Imago Dei*. The term is of great significance and means many things. When I was a young boy, I didn't concern myself with such theological terms, nor did I even care to. Little did I know that years later, it would make sense to me in a rather profound way. Let me share two illustrations which have shed some light on this.

On Saturday nights, like many Americans, my family watched "Gunsmoke." Matt Dillon, Miss Kitty, Chester, and Doc. About once every four episodes, you could depend upon seeing a familiar scene: Two gunfighters striding out into the street in front of the saloon would walk a designated number of paces, turn around and stare at each other. The music would build as the two would often exchange some snarly remarks about being a two-timing, forked-tongued sidewinder. The tension mounted. One of them then drew first, and the other would respond. Guns a-blazin', the smoke would clear, and we'd sit there watching to see who got killed. Well, it probably didn't matter which one got killed because they didn't count anyway. Matt Dillon did count, but he never got killed. Nobody could outdraw him, and we knew that because he was, well, he was Matt

Dillon. What happened next, however, may have had more significance than I ever imagined. A couple of town folk would come out into the street and grab the dead guy by his boots ("ten toes up") and drag him out of the street. As they put him in a box made by the undertaker, one of the people would comment, "This rascal never did nothin' worth a hoot in his whole life. He was just no-good." And the other guy, never imagining his theological profundity, would say, "We're goin' up to Boot Hill and do this right 'cause everybody deserves a proper burial!"

Illustration number two: Through the years we have had the good occasion to have pet goldfish at our home. Why goldfish die is one of the great mysteries of life, but they do. One day there they are, floating upside down in the bowl. Kids have a difficult time with their first goldfish death, but it does get easier each time the inevitable happens. Initially we make a big deal of the death, but eventually we treat it as most people do: we flush them down the commode. We have even come to the conclusion that this practice is not all that degrading. They lived in water; we bury them in water. That makes sense. Now forgive me for sounding crass, but we'd never think of flushing Great Aunt Sally down the commode when she dies, would we? Why is that?

When God pronounced that He created man in His image, He was distinguishing the essential difference between the rest of creation and the apple of His eye—man. We are different. We have been different from the beginning. This fact makes many among us creationists and not evolutionists. Yes, kids lay their small pets in shoeboxes and talk about going to kitty heaven, but the truth is that the Bible clearly distinguishes this differential between mankind and the rest of creation. There is a special dignity, integrity, value, and worth which is attributed to mankind which is not afforded to any other area of God's creation.

Furthermore, it is key to recognize that the pronouncement given by God in Genesis 1:26–31 was made in conjunction with creation, and not redemption, which was to follow later. This tells us then that every life, because it comes from God Himself and bears His personal signature, is special, whether that life is redeemed unto His glory all of its days, or whether it is wasted in foolish selfishness. Indeed, we may stand at the graveside and shrug our shoulders in disgust reflecting on the sheer waste of a life, but as the guy on Gunsmoke said, "Everybody deserves a proper burial." It's all about the *Imago Dei.*

## Accentuate the Positive

Finally, brethren, whatever is true, whatever is honorable, whatever is right, whatever is pure, whatever is lovely, whatever is of good repute, if there is any excellence, and if anything is worthy of praise, let your mind dwell on these things.

—Philippians 4:8

On occasion I have found myself visiting the family of a rascal. Initially, the people are rather quiet when I ask them about the life of their loved one. This is often a tip-off that the individual has not lived a life to be remembered. The Westminster Confession of Faith tells us that "The chief end of man is to love God and to glorify Him forever." Usually their reluctance to tell the life story indicates that his was anything but that. At some point one of the family members will speak up and tell me that the individual was a certain way or had certain habits which would just as soon be forgotten, and certainly not mentioned at the service. I have adopted the policy of Paul's injunction in Philippians 4:8 at this point. Good scholarship demands understanding this passage as an exhortation of Christian virtues that we are to follow, and in so doing we will become examples to others. One commentator believes that this passage may be the best brief biography of Christ in the entire Bible. It truly is a great encouragement.

But I have wondered over the years if there may be another application from this passage. I believe that it may be the signpost to direct us in eulogizing the life of that guy from "Gunsmoke." The application then would be to focus on the good things of the life in question, and leave the rest alone.

Consider this: We naturally tend to remember the not-so-goods of life and probably don't need to be reminded of them. Focusing on the negative would not be a comfort to the bereaved in any way. Though it could be instructive as to the way not to live, this goes without saying to the listeners who knew this truth better than the officiant. Furthermore, the eternal decisions of life are complete and cannot be reversed. The implications are obvious to all. But more, in the name of the *Imago Dei*, we want to recognize the good that the individual has done in his or her life.

Dr. William Hendriksen in his commentary on Philippians supports this idea:

"To be sure, the believer is not at all blind to the fact that 'there remain in man, since the fall, the glimmerings of natural light, whereby he retains some knowledge of God, of natural things, and of the difference between good and evil, and shows some regard for virtue and for good outward behavior'" (Canons of Dort III and IV, article 4). In a sense even sinners do good (Luke 6:33), and even publicans love (Matthew 5:46). To deny this, in the interest of this or that theological presupposition, would be to fly in the face of the clear teaching of Scripture and the facts of everyday observation and experience.[2]

In short, all people have some good that they have done in their lifetimes. We dare not take these things as ushering in eternal life (as some preachers are prone to do at funerals), but we should be as positively honest as we can be. Remember the good, and allow the bad to die, if it will.

For this reason I have come to the belief that when a minister is summoned to officiate at a "religious" memorial service, he should, with biblical conviction, seek to honor that individual and be the mouthpiece before God regarding that life in the Image of God. The difficulty comes in the representation. I have found what people who attend funerals resist and resent is the exclusive presentation of God as judge without any recognition of the deceased as the *Imago Dei* (eulogy). We need to strike a balance.

## The On-going Tension

As ministers we are ruthlessly concerned about a proper representation of God in the context of death. The error of the universalists is that they overemphasize the love of God in such a way as to emasculate Him as the equitable and necessary fair judge of which the Bible speaks. Most of us have attended a memorial service where we began to believe that we might be at a wrong location, since the deceased of whom the presiding minister was speaking had become an angel—and we knew better. Even the theologically untrained individual senses that if there is both a heaven and hell, then surely there are certain individuals (whom we've known) who must occupy such locales. In the name of comfort to the living, the liberal minister often nearly empties hell. In doing so, he both protects the image of God (the deceased), while also protecting God's image as a harsh, non-benevolent, judgmental God. I suppose he means well.

The conservative, on the other hand, may tend to have his blind spot as well. Since death is such an urgent representation of God's judgment and affords the minister the one-time-only opportunity to advance the message of hope in the gospel (salvation from hell) to people who otherwise would never be an attentive audience, he often speaks exclusively to the issue of needed redemption and nearly leaves the deceased out of the picture. After all, life has ended for the individual in question, and there is nothing we can do for him/her now. Preach to the living. "Let the dead bury the dead." But in doing so, though he does defend God's image as a just judge, he likely does a disservice to the image of God (i.e. the deceased).

## The Formula

Working within this tension (speaking positive truth about an individual and yet not compromising the gospel), we need to reach a balance. Both the deceased and God must be represented well. Reducing the purpose of a memorial service into its most simplistic form, my belief is that it should accomplish at least two things:

A memorial service is *for the dead*—a memorial service is *for the living*—and the formula for success in accomplishing these two purposes is:

**Honestly give them their space (eulogy)—and they will give you yours (presentation of truth).**

## For the Dead

This is why we have funerals—not only to dispose of our dead, but to bear witness to their lives and times among us, to affirm the difference their living and dying makes among kin and community, and to provide a vehicle for the healthy expression of grief and faith and hope and wonder. The value of a funeral proceeds neither from how much we spend nor from how little.[3]

—Thomas Lynch

I think most people would like to be remembered, even though most of us will never make it into the history books. Was Andy Warhol right? Do we all really get fifteen minutes of fame? Perhaps not, but that does not mean that a life does not have a very significant meaning and purpose to it. Dads and moms sacrifice for their children. They become Boy Scout leaders, den mothers, Little League coaches, and Big Brothers. They work hard to provide for family with two, even three jobs sometimes. They serve on community committees; they attend fundraisers and write checks; and they serve in their churches. They take their kids camping, and one day those kids will have special stories to share with one another at reunions. They make great accomplishments throughout their careers. They become grandparents and mold small lives that will some day become great. Is this the "stuff" that makes it into history books? No. Is this the "stuff" that is the backbone of life and should be remembered? Absolutely!

I have often used the words of Proverbs 31:10–31 as a text for a service of an elderly woman who has lived a sacrificial life. We notice that the things that God highlights in this passage are great attributes such as virtue, goodness, honesty, enterprise, consideration for others, generosity, provision, strength, honor, wisdom, kindness, and especially a delight in shining the spotlight upon her husband. These are not necessarily the kinds of things which our current society holds high. They will not guarantee one's way into the history books, but they are the characteristics that God says are the golden threads of the life of a virtuous woman (a woman who is God's delight). When a woman has lived this way, it is altogether right and proper that it should be duly noted, and that she should be held high as a role model for others, especially younger women.

When I was a young boy, there was a television show on each week called, "The Naked City," a cops and robbers show situated in New York City in the fifties. In the epilogue of each episode, there was a concluding tag line that ended the show, "There are eight million stories in the Naked City. This has been one of them." Such is the value of eulogy. Every life is a story. Often that story is one which is downright fascinating, if we take the time to hear it. And every life, despite not having been lived to the glory of God, is still innately special and valuable under the banner of the *Imago Dei*. This is why we eulogize one another. It is to the honor of the dead.

## For the Living

There is a second reason why we have memorial services. We can wax eloquent regarding the life of old Uncle George, but if that is all we do, then we've missed something vital. We have the opportunity to address people who have been arrested by the sobriety of the message of one's own mortality and the spiritual side of life. In this regard, they/we become a people who have a desperate need of a message of hope on two levels.

First, for Uncle George we want to know that his destiny has been decided and that we can leave with a feeling of assurance and comfort. But admittedly, this is a message that may or may not be conveyed since our knowledge of his personal faith was limited.

And in the final analysis, it is ultimately between George and God. It is at this point that we may be tempted to fudge the truth. Our hearts want the best for Uncle George.

Secondly, we want and need a message of hope for ourselves. Every time we view a dead body, it is a reminder that we will pass this way just like our friend. We try to avoid this fact and put death at arm's length, but it is there just the same and will not go away. As ministers of God's good news, we know that the only message that can bring release from this bondage (Hebrews 2:15) is the biblical supernatural message of Jesus Christ—His life, atoning death and resurrection, and our necessary faith in Him for everlasting life. This must be shared with the living if they are to have any real hope for themselves. As predicted in God's Word, this message will be received in a number of different ways (Matthew 13:1–23). To some, this truth will be seen as foolishness (1 Corinthians 1:18) and will be resented and resisted to their own destruction. To others, the gospel is the liberating message which gives absolute confidence in the face of the most dastardly enemy, death. It is also at this point that we may be tempted to compromise the truth.

One comforting observation regarding this point: I have nearly always found that the above formula is a solid one, "Give them their space, and they will give you yours." If we do well in showing genuine consideration for the individual (*Imago Dei*) and represent that individual fairly (eulogy), the family will usually not only allow, but actually *expect* the minister to share the gospel with them, and they will be attentive to the message of God's truth. An imbalance on either side of this formula is perhaps an abuse.

## Is There a Service Not to Take?

By asking this question, we recognize that all ministers draw the line at some point. On occasion a funeral director who has met with the family will contact me and will say, "They want a chaplain, but they don't want one who is religious, and they don't want one who talks too long." Could there be a worse directive to a preacher? After all, it's all about religion (Christ), and we preachers tend to talk too long. When asking what the family means by that, usually they share that they are anti-Christian and have been turned off by organized religion in the past. My practice is to *not* officiate at a service where the only element of the service is the eulogy. I gently inform the people that I come as a Christian minister, no more, but no less, and that this includes a Bible representation of mortality. They are also assured that I will do my best to do justice to the life of their loved one and, that with their help, the service will be quite honest and fulfilling. Having made myself clear, the decision is then turned back to the family to determine whether we "have a marriage." If not, I either turn them back to the funeral director or suggest that they look to another chaplain of a little broader philosophical ilk. Happily, most funeral directors are savvy as to which ministers will work well in which services; hence, this issue should not arise often.

# Epilogue

In this chapter I have attempted to establish the innate value of the significance of the *Imago Dei*, being created in the image of God. Every life under God has special meaning and purpose before our Creator and before mankind. The personalization of that life through eulogy is our final attempt to capture that significance.

Pastor and grief management guru Doug Manning says the opposite of significance is trivialization. When ministers, though well meaning, use glib traditional religion in a non-personal way to memorialize, they have trivialized the life. It is an injustice before God and man to represent the finality of a life without the personalization which meaningful eulogy provides. I was reminded of the power of eulogy some years ago in my own Christian experience.

My wife and I had just finished listening to a series of taped sermons on the topic of hospitality and the Christian duty to be willing to open one's home to those around us. Since we lived and worshipped directly adjacent to Fort Lewis, Washington, (U.S. Army post), it was not uncommon to meet many transient soldiers who visited our church as they were stationed in the Northwest. For a few consecutive weeks, we noticed that two young G.I.'s had attended our church. As I casually spoke with them regarding their hard-core Army experience (The Ranger Battalion), they related to me that the one thing they desperately missed was a home cooked meal with all the fixin's. Under the conviction of those tapes, my wife and I covenanted that if the two returned the next Sunday, we would indeed invite them to our home for that which they so desired. They did, and we did. I remember that she not only prepared a roast, potatoes (mashed and yams), corn, beans, applesauce, and homemade bread; but she baked two pies as well. We fed them—the event was a thing of beauty.

A few days later, I picked up the daily newspaper and read about a tragic Army air crash. The article reported that during a night maneuver outside of Las Vegas, Nevada, one of the transports, due to a miscalculation, drove the plane straight into the night desert killing all who were aboard. One of the two boys we had hosted at our home just seventy hours earlier was on that plane. I collected my thoughts and emotions over the next day and then sat down to compose a letter. I told his single mother how she would have been proud of her son as he had been attending church regularly while away from home. My wife shared that his manners to our family, while in our home, were impeccable. We shared with her the blessing that we had received by having him for Sunday dinner and how genuinely thankful he was to us. We tried desperately to share our deepest heartfelt condolences for her loss. I licked the stamp and sent it off.

About two weeks later I received a cassette tape of the memorial service of her son, the Ranger. During the eulogy, the minister had read our letter. The accompanying letter from the mom told us of how thankful she was for us, both to take him in and to take the time to write the letter. She shared that her greatest comfort by far was to know that her son had been going to church, and that God had surrounded him with special people just before he went home to be with the Lord. The reading of the testimony of the final days of this young man's life was the highlight of that memorial service. To be used by God to be a part of the eulogy of this life was one of the greatest privileges of my lifetime. To be able to share something about a life and how it had been lived made all the difference in the world between sorrow and comfort. Such is the case with eulogy.

# CHAPTER FIVE

# The Visit

## Building Confidence and Trust

Confidence is a plant of slow growth in an aged bosom.
—William Pitt, 1708–1778

In life there is absolutely no substitute for relational trust. Confidence in another individual is a growing annuity and is gained and won over time. The depth of trust we feel from our comrades is granted in return for the investment of time—our lives. It is established through past successes involving reliable and predictable integrity and is earned by being transparent and approachable to people. It is through the door of confidence and trust that the minister will be allowed to walk with his message of hope and comfort. Though sometimes difficult to establish in a short-term relationship, it is necessary. Without this relational trust, the memorial service is a cold and hollow religious exercise. The first step toward initiating this trust comes by visiting the family of the deceased.

It can hardly be overstated that the visit with the family of the deceased is of utmost importance. We must remember that the individuals involved are most likely unfamiliar and uncomfortable in this foreign land and are actually looking to the minister for direction and guidance. The visit is *the most important element* contributing to the success of the memorial service; for it is in this visit that relationship begins. As a rule, I do not consider officiating at a memorial service unless I can be assured of this visit. The only exception is if the next of kin are from out of town and/or there is no possibility of a visit prior to the service. In that extreme situation, I make every effort to convince the family to come in at least one hour early on the day of the service so that we can spend time together. It is my professional opinion that a minister who flies in at the time of a service and casually meets the family for the first time is insulting the family, the deceased, and the funeral director in the dispensing of his duties. And it is a sure formula for disaster.

Once the minister has been notified of his desired presence as officiant, that minister must make arrangements to visit with the parties who are the decision makers of that service. Though most often it is a spouse and/or children of the deceased, this is not always the case. For instance, I once met with a nephew and niece who were making all the decisions because the spouse of the deceased was in ill health. Legally, the spouse was still the next of kin in every way, but had waived the decision-making to someone else. It is important to determine exactly what the legality of the situation is since the minister must see to it that he honors the wishes of those who are the legal representatives. Divorced individuals, though they may still be in close contact and may be the legal parent of surviving children, under the law have no rights to decision making. Usually, the rule of thumb is that the person who is honoring the funeral bill will be the person in the power seat. At any rate, this is an issue on which the clergy must be clear in order to avoid potential confusion and offense.

At this meeting the clergy person is actually beginning to wear an assortment of four hats. In order to minister to the family in the fullest sense, these different perspectives should come together at the time of the service. The minister becomes fact finder, coordinator, friend and counselor.

## Fact Finder

It is always wise to begin by taking good notes regarding time of service, names of family members, dates of significance, place of birth, age, and other important data that would have been gathered by the funeral home. I do not assume that the information which has been passed to me by the funeral director is correct. It usually is, but this should not be assumed. By following this procedure, I am assured that these facts will be on target, and that if there are any errors, they will be caught before the time of the service. An error on a name, or even the mispronunciation of a name, is seen as a personal affront and nearly unforgivable to the family. Even a newspaper obituary may have errors in it. The practice of double checking these facts can actually be a great check and balance with your funeral director that will serve to enhance your relationship with him/her.

Sometimes when meeting with a family, I will try to put myself into the role of the family members and ask myself how I would want the service to be conducted.

Or, another question to ask is, "How would I want someone to represent me?" As the officiant, my role is to be the representative of the deceased. I am the ambassador, the go-between for these people. It is important to me to have thoroughly prepared myself for that role so the service will be successful, for their sake as well as for mine. The facts are important.

## Coordinator

The family is usually looking to the minister for leading and direction in this foreign experience. In keeping with the two-part formula (eulogy—for the dead, and hope—for the living) and to instill confidence, the minister should establish the parameters of the service during the visit, and in a winsome way, let the family know that the usual format of a memorial service will involve those two main components. We explore the first of these two components (eulogy) while wearing the hat of coordinator.

## Funerals are for the Dead / Eulogy

> Nothing can help us face the unknown future with more courage and optimism than remembering the glory moments . . . and everyone has a few of them.
>
> —Eda LaShan

In the introduction to the movie, *Gandhi*, there is an immediate disclaimer that appears on the screen before anything else is told.

> No one can do justice to a life. You cannot adequately represent that life and all that it has entailed. You cannot tell all of the stories, the highs and the lows, the lives that have been impacted. But what you can do is (you can) find your way to the heart of that individual, and you can be true to the record that has been left behind—you can represent them well.
>
> —*Gandhi*, the movie

It would seem that the screenwriters, in their quest to represent the life of this giant of leadership, encountered the same dilemma that confronts an officiant of a memorial service. The question is, "How does one condense a lifetime of memories, often 70, 80, even 90+ years, into a block of time thirty minutes long, and do justice to it?" Well, the answer is, you can't. But as the screenwriters said, perhaps by eulogizing the life, what we can do is find the heart and soul of the person and then represent that person well.

According to Webster, eulogy is "a speech or a writing in praise of a person . . . especially a formal speech praising a person who has recently died." Therefore, the key to a successful eulogy is personalization. I have discovered three ways to personalize the service around the life of the deceased.

## Gather the Facts

I do this in two ways. Begin by asking very direct questions about the deceased. Check the date and place of birth. Ask questions regarding the deceased's parents. Inquire concerning where he/she grew up and how many siblings. Ask about years of marriage, where and how they met, if applicable. Inquire as to how the individual moved to the area. If it's an older man, ask about military service. We want to know especially about work and career. Ask about organizations to which the individual may have belonged, and his/her service within that organization: and hobbies, travel during retirement, special interests, etc. When they tell me that Dad always made regular trips to Las Vegas and lost lots of money gambling, I tell them that you can't tell the preacher about those kinds of things, because I can't repeat them. They usually laugh.

The Batesville Casket Company has for years served the funeral industry with a resource information group called Batesville Services (Batesville Management Group). This group published a helpful flyer for pastors that suggests "Five L's" to aid the minister in the preparation of the eulogy of an individual:

> Live—Think of five words that describe her most.
> Love—What relationships were important to him?
> Laugh—What type of things gave her pleasure?
> Learn—A member of clubs or organizations?
> Legacy—What stories can we pass on; how would she want to be remembered?

After gathering this data, I move to the second way in which I obtain facts. Moving away from the didactic, it is time to put down my pen, sit back in my chair, and address the adult children (or whomever) and simply say, "Go back a bunch of years and tell me about Aunt Mary. Tell me about your memories as a kid. Tell me about camping, Little League, Girl Scouts." In this way, I'm putting them on the spot so they will really open up and do two things.

First, I'm looking for the special memories of life which that individual has left behind which might be used at the memorial service. These are the things that probably mean the most to the family. These things, in their minds, are the summation of that individual. "He was a great dad. He never said a bad thing about anyone." "Mom was always there when we came home from school." "You could always get fresh baked cookies at Grandma's house 'cause she baked almost every day." "I don't think there was one person who disliked our dad."

Perhaps more importantly, I'm looking for these individuals to open up because it signals the beginnings of their move toward emotional catharsis. The grief professionals tell us that the way a person works through loss is not by avoiding it, but by opening up and "dumping," by working through the loss and meeting the reality of the death through things such as sharing these special thoughts. In this way, I am, without apology, encouraging this process in the grievers. It is healthy for them, whether they realize it or not. It also is the path to the next way in which I can personalize the service.

## Encourage Involvement in the Service.

Many years ago I began the practice of encouraging family members to participate in the service. I had found that even when a person had been a member of a church for many years, it was likely not the minister who knew that person best. So, in one sense, it is the family and friends who should be doing the eulogizing. Therefore, I always attempt to get those closest to the deceased involved. They, and they alone, can tell the stories about how "he lost the car keys in the snow bank up at the hunting lodge." I cannot.

I often ask the family how they feel about a time of sharing during the service. This means that during the eulogy, I will open the floor to all in attendance to share with us any memories, anecdotes, or stories about the deceased. This seems like tricky business, and you do have to assume the role of referee sometimes, but in the vast majority of occasions, this practice has been tremendously valuable. I assure these friends that sharing has great value to the people attending, as we all are able to re-live some special moments from the life. And that is true. However, my altruistic motive for doing this is that it is also very good for the sharer to do this, though that individual may not recognize it. It will help, as others participate.

I never know how the family will react to this appeal. Sometimes they let me know immediately that they are not a "talking bunch," and they just couldn't do it. Sometimes they are hiding the fact that the individual did not live his/her life well, and there is not much good to say. On the other hand, it is not uncommon that, as I am suggesting participation, some of the immediate family have already thought about this very thing and have written something out to be read; or someone has already decided to speak at the service. However, in most cases, it is still a tall order.

Many times the people will say something to the effect, "There's lots I could say, but I'm afraid I'd lose it." I tell them, "That's okay. Don't think of that as a disqualifier, since there's a sense in which we're all here to lose it. It's one of the values of a memorial service. We can legitimately lose it." At the very least, I always plant the seed for their participation. If they decline, so be it. If they don't decline, I now have the right people representing the deceased.

Poems have a special place in the eulogy, especially if they have been chosen by the family members. My first choice is to encourage someone from the family to read them. If not, then I assume that duty.

Another valuable activity is for family members to write down their thoughts about the deceased, and I will read them at the service. This allows the people to express their thoughts, though they may be too timid to speak

As you can see, all of these attempts to get individuals involved in the service will help immeasurably in personalizing it.

There is another way in which we can personalize the service.

## Music

Admittedly, not all ministers will be comfortable with this suggestion. Music is such a subjective art that it's impossible to imagine what styles of music appeal to certain individuals. Couple that with the fact that music conveys a message (philosophy), and there is the potential for a real "can of worms." I have a pastor friend who officiated at a memorial service which included a friend of the family (an Elvis impersonator) singing "How Great Thou Art" in full regalia.

If however, the minister believes that only gospel music should be played at a memorial service, the idea of incorporating secular music is an area into which one does not want to go. If however, Willy Nelson doing Georgia can be tolerated, go for it. My worst nightmare is that the family says that Dad's favorite song was Old Blue Eyes' version of I Did It My Way: "The record shows, I took the blows, but through it all, I did it my way." Years ago after listening carefully, I came to the conclusion that there may not be a more self-condemning humanistic song than that one. When people think that bravado is the best way through life, they live in accordance with Frank's sentiment. That's scary. My choice, of course, is that we'd play "I Did It The Lord's Way" at every service.

Interestingly, in the 80's and into the mid-90's, Bette Midler had three hits in a row, each of which became very popular and were often requested as memorial service songs for the un-churched. Little wonder, since each one hit a nerve. Did You Ever Know You Were My Hero speaks of a special platonic relationship with a friend: The Rose talks about a love relationship: and From a Distance tells us there is nothing to worry about even when things don't look good because, "God is watching us."

I think the point regarding music is this: music often says what is in our hearts regarding life. It also stands for special junctures in life and the memories that go with those times. Whether it's Dorsey's In the Mood, Vaughan Monroe's Ghost Riders in the Sky, Sarah McLaughlin's Angel, or Rock of Ages, people identify with the music of their day. How a minister deals with the incorporation of the family's choice of music, or any music, plays an important role in the personalization of the service.

It can be a Chinese puzzle.

# Friend

You are building bridges which will be the foundational basis of a relationship that may well extend into the future. I have had countless people approach me after a service and ask about our church and the time of our services so they could attend. But this did not happen until after the ties had been formed by working through this difficult time together as friends. I try to get to know all the family members and friends who are gathered for our meeting time by asking how they knew or were related to the deceased.

Personalization of the service is key to its success. If I can build bridges of friendship, I am on my way to serving the family well.

## Counselor

I have a theory that when it comes to what is called grief counseling, there is a distinct difference from what we generally think of when we talk of counsel. The dictionary defines a counselor as a person who gives advice; an adviser. When people break down and go to a counselor, usually they are admitting they have problems (often self-inflicted) which need to be rectified. They are searching for answers to those problems. Rubber-ball Rogerian counsel notwithstanding, at some point they need to identify habits which have led to their pain. It is the counselor who identifies (defines) patterns and suggests (advises) changes of mind and attitude which will give them deliverance.

It is at this point where I suggest that grief counsel is different. When people are experiencing the pain of grief, generally there is nothing wrong with their attitude or habits. What they are feeling is real and is a universal reaction to their particular circumstance. They don't need counsel. Like Job's friends, who ". . . sat down with him upon the ground seven days and seven nights, and none spoke a word unto him: for they saw that his grief was very great" (Job 2:13), what people need is our empathy. The apostle Paul says in Romans 12:15b that we are to weep with those who weep. The primary role, therefore, of the minister at this juncture is to be a sympathetic listener; to allow the griever to work out the internal hurt through emotional catharsis.

One way this is encouraged is by allowing the people to re-enact and re-live the events of the day or days leading up to the death of their loved one. We should not be afraid to ask them how their loved one died. Chances are they are aching to tell the story. The variety of emotions shared will be the guideposts that will indicate the emotional condition of that individual and how well or how poorly he or she is coping with loss.

Memories not only tell us the story of the life, but also occupy a large place in the grieving process. Nostalgia is a wonderful thing when kept in balance. Too much and we are clearly operating in the realm of fantasy. Too little and we miss the special magic of our minds to embellish the best of what has gone before. It is the role of the pastor/counselor to listen carefully as people share their memories of prior days. By doing this, we encourage the griever to begin to take the very first steps in a long process of what the psychologists call the grief work.

The role of counselor is one which begins with the visit, but should continue well after the memorial service has ended. It's just good counseling common sense to check with key persons of the family from time to time in an effort to monitor the progress in their journey. Being familiar with specific community social services such as WICS (Widowed Information Consultation Services), Grief Management Services, Hospice Follow-Up and others, is a real aid to the minister in guiding the bereaved into helpful available networks. Many churches have begun specialized ministry in this area as well. Any conscientious minister should acquaint himself with those available services in his/her community.

Though ministers might shy away from it, there may be legitimate situations where the survivors might be gently encouraged to consider making pre-need funeral arrangements for themselves in order to unburden their family from this duty upon their own death. My personal feeling is that if there were domestic problems in the family while making arrangements, it will likely happen again and should be avoided in the future if at all possible. Also, having money in hand from insurance policies makes it an opportune time to take care of it before the event. Though I confess that this may not be an area in which the minister feels comfortable, I have witnessed that there clearly are situations in which an ounce of prevention is worth a pound of cure. This demands a discretionary call by the minister.

## Summary

Visit the family. Build bridges of confidence and relationship. Find out all you can about the deceased. Encourage their participation. Include music. Become friends. Do these things well from a genuine caring heart—and you will find they will "give you your space" and allow you to share the glorious gospel of eternal life in Jesus Christ. Don't do these things, and they will likely resent you.

# CHAPTER SIX

# The Message

## PREACHING TO THE LIVING

### For The Living / Resurrection

> Christianity is a religion of miracle, and the miracle of Christ's resurrection is the living center and object of Christian faith."
>
> —Alan Richardson

In the previous chapter I suggested a simplistic definition of a memorial service: "Funerals are for the dead; funerals are for the living." For the dead, for we are eulogizing and remembering the life and contributions of the deceased individual. For the living, for we desire to leave behind a clear message of hope for those who grieve the loss and must move on in life. I also proposed a formula for balance and success: "Honestly give them their space, and they will give you (and expect) yours." That is, legitimately eulogize the deceased, and we will most often find the door of advancing God's message of hope ajar.

Up to now our attention has been on the first aspect, eulogy: gathering facts to personalize the service, visiting to encourage participation, meeting family members, and building relational bridges. Having looked at eulogy, we now turn our attention to the message—hope for the living.

## Funerals are for the Living / Hope

> I am the resurrection and the life; he who believes in me shall live even if he dies, and everyone who lives and believes in Me shall never die.
>
> —John 11:25–26

In the second aspect of the memorial service (for the living), we want to leave a strong message of hope for those who go on. During the visit the minister should leave the family with a clear explanation that as a Christian representative, the gospel message will be presented. The heart of the message of hope lies in the apostolic preaching of the Christian truth of Resurrection—the Easter message—Christ has triumphed over sin and death.

If the family is so antagonistic to Christianity that they deny this presentation, then they do not want a Christian minister representing them. I would carefully suggest to them that they would probably want to choose another individual to officiate at their service. I must stress again, however, that I have discovered that when the minister takes pains to work through the first consideration (eulogy), the family will nearly always welcome this liberating message of hope.

## Advancing the Gospel

Every Christian minister should genuinely desire to advance the good news (gospel) in the context of bad news (death). Most of us feel duty bound to do so since we are convinced that it is the only (exclusive) message of hope which can overcome the fears and pangs of death. While we desire to represent the deceased well by eulogizing their life, we do not want to compromise the message of God's Word. This is the tension into which the minister steps. I believe that there are two factors then, that a minister must consider when deciding how to present the gospel message: How much can/should I say?" and "How shall I present it?"

## How Much?

When we ask the question, "How much?" we are taking into consideration two principles.

First, I know that I will not be able to relate the full gospel account to the individuals in attendance. By full gospel, I do not mean it in the modern-day charismatic sense, but rather in the sense of fully representing the entire unfolding drama of redemption as revealed in God's Word. That presentation would entail the Trinitarian covenant made in eternity past (Ephesians 1:3–12), to the eternal state (Revelation 21–22), and everything in between. The people in attendance would not be able to comprehend or tolerate it.

Additionally, if we have the major elements of a service—scriptural reading, music, obituary reading, poetry, eulogy and participation by other individuals, we ask, "How much time is left to give a genuine presentation of the gospel?" One of my early mentors in the faith used to say to us young "preacher boys," that we had roughly one-half hour to communicate to listeners. He was convinced that after that, the attention span was spent, and (he would add) if we hadn't said it by then, we probably ought to sit down anyway. Experience has taught me that he was not too far off.

These two factors force us to take pains to condense our message into a gospel presentation that is tolerable both theologically and temporally. I have found the text of 1 Corinthians 15:1–4 to be instructive in this area.

> Now I make known to you brethren, the gospel which I preached to you . . . that Christ died for our sins according to the Scriptures, and that he was buried, and that He was raised on the third day according to the Scriptures.

This would seem to indicate that Paul's presentation of the gospel was a condensation of Jesus' atoning death, burial, and resurrection, all in absolute accordance with the Old Testament Messianic prophecies. If we present these elements, we have represented the gospel according to Paul.

## How?

Anytime a minister has an opportunity to speak the truth, he should attempt to ascertain who the listeners are. By who, I am referring to who the people are in regard to their beliefs in spiritual things. When it comes to the attendees at a funeral service, there are a couple of givens. One fact is that we can never know since there will always be a cross section of beliefs represented. The good news is that this cross section will nearly always fit a recurring pattern.

First, we know that the attention of these people is somewhat riveted since they are a captive audience. Most often they have come either out of a sense of love or duty. They may squirm, but generally will not leave, out of respect for the deceased and the family.

Second, some of those in attendance are people who would otherwise never place themselves under the preaching of the gospel. Pastor Mark Coppenger comments:

> We don't think of funerals as laughing matters, but it's hard to keep from smiling when you see some of the folks who attend them. People who never come to church, whose lives are as dissolute as any to be found, find themselves seated before a preacher. They're usually black-sheep family members or rough-edged fellow workers. Whether they exhibit the florid face of the lush, the hair and jewelry of the lounge lizard, the affected sophistication of the socialite, the smug impatience of the self-made man, or the eyes that match a drug-fried brain, they look lost. Some squirm in borrowed Sunday-go-to-meetin' suits. Others posture in expensive, dress-for intimidation outfits. And there you stand with Bible in hand. If you'll pardon the expression, 'What a setup.'[1]

Third, the philosophy of relativism (no absolutes) is sure to be espoused by a number of people in attendance. The truth as absolute (Jesus said, "No man can come unto the Father but by Me") will be resisted by those people as narrow and offensive.

Fourth, though many of these people are unchurched and spiritually dull, it can be assumed that God may cause some degree of spiritual awareness, especially in the area of recognition of mortality. I knew a Baptist pastor who always advocated having the casket left open before, during and after the service. He felt that any time an individual viewed a dead body, by implication it was a reminder of one's own mortality; the viewer would be forced to admit that he/she would go the way of all others. Though I have wrestled with this view, his point was well made. The Bible declares that the natural man (the man without God) goes about in denial of God's claims upon him, and life itself demonstrates how much most people live as if they are invincible.

If these four conditions are present in the people who attend a memorial service, the question that we need to ask is, "How, then, can I reach them?" We need to know as much as we can about our contemporaries. We should stay alert to how they think. We need to observe people and their culture. Then, we should suitably apply the message of the gospel as we have opportunity.

How can we effectively present the gospel to these kinds of people? I believe the answer lies in a historical passage in the book of Acts, when the apostle Paul, while waiting for his traveling companions, appraised the city of Athens, Greece. What he found was a situation like we might find at a modern day funeral/memorial service. It is found in Acts 17 and may be prescriptive for us today.

## Mars Hill, Areopagus (Acts 17:22–31)

During Paul's visit to Athens, his discussions with the philosophers of the day led him to appear before the court of Areopagus—an institution revered since the city's earliest times. This court met upon the hill called Areopagus (Mars Hill), and its purpose was to decide religious maters. It was there that certain members of the court expressed some curiosity about Paul's proclamation of their own god.

There are many parallels to Paul's discourse at the Areopagus and the situation of speaking to a mixed philosophical group of listeners (funeral attendees). His speech provides a prescriptive (not merely descriptive) model for communicating the gospel to a group that has no Bible background. According to E.M.Blaiklock:

A portion of Athens' inspiration, to be sure, had been incorporated in international Hellenism, had gone east with Alexander, and was remembered and admired in the complex of lands where, after his conquests, Greek had become a second language, the Greek spirit a mental stimulus, and cosmopolitan Greeks an element in the population. But over all these long years of historical development, the city lay dead as though exhausted by the outburst of her fifth-century . . . .The vibrant life which made the glory of the fifth century, lingered into the fourth with Plato, and flickered briefly as Demosthenes fought looming dictatorship with his tongue, was dead, and a proud people lived incongruously on the memory of it. The third century had seen the rise of the systems of the Epicureans and the Stoics, both philosophies of breakdown and despair. The old questing spirit sickened into curiosity, and the search for truth into cynicism. Such was the city to which Paul of Tarsus came.[2]

We are told that Paul was moved by the vast array of symbols, shrines, and items of pagan worship, so much so that he could not keep silent. William Ramsay, in his work, *St. Paul the Traveller and Roman Citizen* remarks regarding Paul's approach to the situation:

The mere Jew could never have assumed the Attic tone as Paul did. He was the student of a great university, visiting an older but yet a kindred university, surveying it with appreciative admiration, and mixing in its society as an equal . . . the extraordinary versatility of Paul's character, the unequalled freedom and ease with which he walked in every society, and addressed so many races within the Roman world . . . Luke places before us the man who became "all things to all men," and who therefore in Athens made himself like an Athenian and adopted the regular Socratic style of general free discussion in the agora; and he shows him to us in an atmosphere and a light which are thoroughly Attic in their clearness, delicacy, and charm.[3]

Paul, following the policy of adaptation (1 Corinthians 9:22), which was part of his method, adopted in Athens the Socratic practice of free discussion in the market place. It was easy to talk in Athens, and a man with a burden soon found occasion to put his convictions into speech.

The first listeners were the Epicureans, followers of Epicurus whose philosophy of materialism and despair which sprang naturally from its circumstances, parallels much of the philosophies of today. He taught that pleasure was the chief end of life. It was an available philosophic refuge for the hedonist and the sensualist who sought excuse for self-indulgence.

Also there were the Stoics, who taught that the highest expression of nature was reason. To be virtuous then, i.e. to live in harmony with reason, was the only good; not to be virtuous was evil. All other things—life, death, pleasure, pain—were indifferent. The Stoic, therefore, should be absolutely brave, absolutely continent, absolutely just, with an emphasis on the supremacy of rationality over the emotion in man, which included the right to suicide, and a stern, unbending endurance. Stoicism had a great attraction to the Roman mind. Its faults were a certain coldness and spiritual pride.

Having assessed his audience, Paul's homiletic in Acts 17 is impeccable. He begins with an arresting, yet not disrespectful, statement declaring his listeners to be a "religious people" (verse 22). Undeniably so from the surroundings (verse 16), this would open the door to their willingness for Paul to proceed. He then chooses a theme which would be familiar to his hearers: the altar to the Unknown God (verse 23). Since its very label declared their divine ignorance, this allowed Paul to be bold in declaring to them what they admitted they did not know. The essential doctrines of his discourse are God as Creator (verse 24); God's self-sufficiency (verse 25); the equality of all mankind before Him (verse 26, which was calculated to cut at the root of pride and bias); righteousness, repentance, and judgment (verse 30–31); all reinforced by a quote from a verse of a Stoic poet (verse 28; Aratus of Soli in Cilicia, Paul's native country).

The important capstone of Paul's discourse is in verse 31b, where he declares that the resurrection from the dead of Jesus (the "appointed man") by God, validated the authentication of the message. The truth regarding resurrection was the issue which stopped Paul's discourse, as they could not accept it (verses 18, 32). Many of the Athenians were not responsive to Paul's teaching, and so Paul left their midst.

A key observation that I note from Paul's message was that clearly it was the message of resurrection which affected the listeners in at least four ways. First, we are told that Paul's invitation to come from the synagogue and market place to the Areopagus was due to their religious curiosity in this doctrine (verse 18). Second, the same message caused some to become cynical rejects ("sneered", verse 32). Third, others, still seeking, left the door open for further debate (verse 32). And finally, some (Dionysius the Arreopagite and a woman named Damaris) joined up with Paul and believed.

We conclude from this instance that the proclamation of the doctrine of the resurrection has the power to separate people in their philosophical bents. At one and the same time, it is both good and bad news. It is bad news in that it verifies Jesus as the prophesied Messiah (Christ) of the Jewish writings and judge of all mankind. It is good news in that it is the down payment placed in history of that most glorious truth which applies to all believers in Him. Because of this, it became a central element in all apostolic testimony during the infancy of the church.

## Resurrection Appearances

How was it that this one singular truth had such an impact on the dynamic of the growing Christian church in the world? In 1 Corinthians 15:5ff, Paul outlines how Jesus ". . . appeared first to Peter, then to the twelve . . . after that to over 500 of the brethren, then to James, then to all of the apostles and last to Paul himself." He then goes on to demonstrate the absolute importance of the resurrection and its link with all other Christian teaching (verse 12–19), the order of the resurrection (verse 20–28), the moral implications of it (verse 29–34), and the identification of the bodies of the resurrected dead (verse 35–50).

We who have toiled in proclaiming the truth of resurrection all of our days have become blasé to the tremendous impact which the appearance of the resurrected Jesus had on those who experienced Him. Whether it was the heart-moving appearance to Mary Magdalene outside the tomb (John 20:11ff), the humbling experience of Thomas (John 20:26ff), a lesson in fishing on the Sea of Galilee (John 21:1ff), the commissioning of the eleven in the upper room (Luke 24: 36ff), the revealing appearance to the two on the road to Emmaus (Luke 24:13ff), the dramatic conversion of Paul on the road to Damascus (Acts 9:1–9), or the ascension into heaven from the Mount of Olives (Acts 1:1ff), the experience resulted in changing the lives of the people who partook thereof. In one accord they ran to announce to the world, "We have seen the Lord, and He is risen from the dead!"

# ACTS—TRANSITIONAL PREACHING

The instance on Mars Hill is only one of many occasions where the apostles took advantage of their situations to advance the teaching of resurrection.

## Acts 2:14–41; Peter

In the familiar message on the Day of Pentecost, Peter declared with boldness that it was the *resurrection* of Christ which was the truth to which David looked forward as the fulfillment of Psalm 16:8–11.

## Acts 7:56; Stephen

The vision that empowered the first Christian martyr to conquer was an extension of the glorious truth of *resurrection*. The lofty view of the ascended Jesus in heaven welcoming His servant with open arms becomes the earnest to all who would follow and die in faith.

## Acts 10:40–41; Peter

Likely referring to the question of Judas (not Iscariot) in John 14:22 regarding Jesus' revealing of Himself to a select group, Peter instructs that it is the resurrected Christ who has commissioned them to "preach to the people regarding judgment to come."

## Acts 13:14–34; Paul

At Pisidian-Antioch on the Sabbath, upon invitation by the synagogue officials, Paul instructs the Jews and God-fearers in his midst that the promise made to the fathers, has been fulfilled in the *resurrection of Jesus*. He contrasts the fundamental difference between the death of David and the on-going life of Jesus as the proof that both Psalm 2 and Psalm 16 looked forward to this resurrection of Jesus as Messiah.

## Acts 24:15, 21; Paul

In Paul's defense before Governor Felix, after declaring the certainty of a general resurrection (compare 24:15 with Daniel 12:2), he makes it clear that it is the doctrine of the hope of the *resurrection* for which he stands accused (Acts 23:6). This should not have been ground for any accusation since it was believed by the Pharisees of Paul's day.

## Acts 26:23; Paul

In his defense before King Agrippa, Paul shares his conversion experience on the road to Damascus: an encounter with the resurrected Christ, who validated the Old Testament Scriptures (the prophets and Moses) in being the fulfillment of the One who would "proclaim light both to the Jewish people and the Gentiles."

All these passages make it crystal clear that both the personal experience of seeing the resurrected Christ, along with the obvious truth of fulfillment of Old Testament prophecy, together constrain the apostles to highlight the teaching of resurrection in their proclamations. It was the one greatest passion born of conviction which dominated the preaching of the early church. In truth, this realized empowering truth of the New Testament was not novel, for it had been deposited among God's people long before the days of the resurrected Christ.

## Job

> And as for me, I know that my redeemer lives, and at the last He will take His stand on the earth. Even after my skin is destroyed (KJV "worms destroy this body"), yet from my flesh, I shall see God.
>
> —Job 19:25–26

Many scholars believe that the book of Job is the earliest writing contained in the Bible. If so, it is here that we are first introduced to the doctrine of bodily resurrection. This is evidence that from the very beginning of the old economy, the immortality of the soul and a future state of unending existence were revealed and believed.

The story of Job's testings and his resulting dire condition is well known. His sufferings are set before us as a mortal measuring stick, and as such, there are many lessons which can be learned from his experience. One observation is that the pain and despair which the patriarch experienced seemed to heighten the awareness of his mortality. In chapter 19, sensing that his days may be numbered, he cries out in pity that his experience would be recorded for posterity. Under a strong sense of divine desertion, these laments and moanings give testimony to Job's sorrowful earthly perspective. Interestingly, through it all he clings tenaciously to his belief in the glory of his Redeemer and his own interest in Him.

John Calvin states:

Besides, when Job says that he will see his Redeemer from his flesh, he intends that he will be restored in a new state, his skin having been so eaten. For he says that even his bones will be consumed and that nothing will remain whole; and then he adds, "From my flesh I shall see God." And how will he see Him from his flesh? That is to say, "I shall be restored as I was previously, and I shall yet see my God." And so he confesses that God will be powerful enough to raise him up, though He has entirely consumed him and plunged him in the depths. This is the condition for which we ought to hope in God: when He will have cast us into the sepulcher, we may know that He extends His hand to withdraw us from it.[4]

According to Matthew Henry:

When we think of the approaching death of our bodies, and their destruction and dissolution in the grave, like Job, let not that discourage our hope of their resurrection, for the same power that made man's body at first, out of common dust, can raise it out of its own dust.[5]

Job comforts himself with the believing hope of happiness in the other world, though he had so little comfort in this one. It was a solemn confession of his faith in something supernatural and carried him through his trial, no matter what his temporal condition. It was founded in resurrection truth.

# Abraham/Isaac

> By faith Abraham, when he was tested, offered up Isaac; and he who had received the promises was offering up his only begotten son; it was he to whom it was said, "In Isaac your descendants shall be called." He considered that God is able to raise men even from the dead; from which he also received him back as a type.
>
> —Hebrews 11:17–19 (Genesis 22:1–10)

In Jewish tradition Abraham was said to have been tested by God on ten different occasions. Genesis 22 contains the story of Abraham's greatest test of faith: the offering of his son Isaac as a sacrifice. The classic faith chapter of Hebrews 11 includes this test as a defining moment of one of the true heroes of the faith. In this passage what the author of Hebrews emphasizes is Abraham's resolute faith in the promises of God, though it was Isaac who had to be sacrificed. This must have seemed absurd to Abraham, since the fulfillment of the promise (Abrahamic progeny) depended upon the survival of Isaac. Yet at a time when Abraham must have been bewildered by God's command, he continued to believe and refused to act in any way other than the way the Lord had told him. We ask, "Why was that?"

Dr. F.F. Bruce comments:

Our author's statement that Abraham believed in God's ability to raise the dead is not a gratuitous reading into the narrative of something that is not there. The plain meaning of the text is that Abraham expected to come back with Isaac. But how could he come back with Isaac, if Isaac was to be offered up as a burnt-offering? Only if Isaac was to be raised from the dead after being sacrificed. Abraham reckoned, "that God was bound to restore Isaac's life if his life had to be taken." He received him back from the dead, says our author, "in a figure" meaning, probably, in a manner that prefigured the resurrection of Christ.[6]

So, while the passage fundamentally speaks of the unique faith of Father Abraham, we must remember that the object of his faith was, like Job's, the sure promise of God which was founded in the supernatural truth of resurrection.

# THE TEACHING OF JESUS

And Jesus answered them, saying, "The hour has come for the Son of Man to be glorified. Truly, truly, I say to you, unless a grain of wheat falls into the earth and dies, it abides by itself alone; but if it dies, it bears much fruit."

—John 12:23–24

In John 12:24ff, Jesus took a natural event in everyday living to teach the harvest principle. The illustration was clear, especially at the moment it was spoken, not more than a few days before the harvest feast of Passover. Some appreciation of this principle, manifested in the recurring sequence of seed time and harvest, even underlies the fertility cults of the dying and rising gods, familiar in the ancient Near East. But more than that, this agricultural principle is likely chosen because it transcends time and is familiar to all of us in any age.

Dr. John Mitchell, in his commentary on the Gospel of John, states:

I came across a jar of seeds the other day, seeds I used to plant when I had a little garden plot. In all these years in that jar they haven't sprouted once. They abide alone. But if you take them and put them in the ground, they die. There is no fruitage until there is death.[7]

When the Greeks came to seek Jesus, it was the signal that the hour of His glorification had come (John 12:20). His immediate reaction (unexpected) was to reveal a principle to Philip and Andrew (and to you and me): the mighty foundational truth that Christ's death was to be the source of spiritual life to the world. His death, like a grain of seed corn, was to be the root of blessings and mercies to countless millions of immortal souls. Jesus said, "If I be lifted up from the earth, I will draw all men unto Myself."

The universal principle that is obvious in farming is that unless the seed is planted in the ground, there will be no crop. The grain dies as grain, but what emerges is not grain but a plant. If the seed is not sown, it remains alone, producing no fruit. So also if Jesus does not die, He will remain alone, without spiritual fruit. His death, however, will result in a rich spiritual harvest. The principle of the gospel was once more exhibited—that Christ's death (not his life or His miracles) was to bring forth fruit to the praise of God and to provide redemption for a lost world. It illustrated what William Barclay calls "the amazing paradox," that new life emerges from death, a truth which is at the heart of the message of Christian hope.

# The Teaching of Paul

So also is the resurrection of the dead. It is sown a perishable body, it is raised an imperishable body, it is sown in dishonor, it is raised in glory; it is sown in weakness, it is raised in power; it is sown a natural body, it is raised a spiritual body.

—1 Corinthians 15:42–44

The apostle Paul takes the same concept which Jesus had taught in John 12 and enlarges upon it in its application to the Christian. By using the metaphor of sowing (Greek, *speiro*), the idea of burying is put in a different light, and the possibility of life from death is indicated.

The context indicates that Paul is dealing with a problem in the Corinthian church, as he has in much of First Corinthians. He is answering a two-fold objection against the doctrine of the resurrection of the dead, concerning first, how the dead are raised up and second, with what body do they come (verse 35)?

Matthew Henry is helpful here:

To the objection, the apostle replies by telling them that this was to be brought about by divine power, that very power which they had all observed to do something very like it, year after year, in the death and revival of the corn; and therefore it was an argument of great weakness and stupidity to doubt whether the resurrection of the dead might not be affected by the same power (vs. 36). It must first corrupt, before it will quicken and spring up. It not only sprouts after it is dead, but it must die that it may live. And why should any be so foolish as to imagine that the man once dead cannot be made to live again, by the same power which every year brings the dead grain to life? It is a foolish thing to question the divine power to raise the dead, when we see it every day quickening and reviving things that are dead. Burying the dead is like sowing them; it is like committing the seed to the earth, that it may spring out of it again.[8]

One of the finest illustrations of this harvest principle is the following excerpt from a sermon entitled, "God's Ways Are Unreasonable—Psalm 126," by missionary professor, Del Tarr.

Those who sow in tears will reap with songs of joy. He who goes out weeping, carrying seed to sow, will return with songs of joy, carrying sheaves with him.

—Psalm 126:5–6

"I grew up in a preacher's home in the little towns of Minnesota and South Dakota. I spent most of my time with the deacons' kids on John Deere tractors, International Harvesters, Cases, Minneapolis-Molines. I learned how to drill oats, plant corn, and cultivate. And never once did I see a deacon behave like Psalm 126 says. What was there to weep about at sowing time?

"I was always perplexed by this Scripture, until I went to the Sahel, the vast stretch of savanna more than four thousand miles wide just under the Sahara Desert, with a climate much like the Bible lands. In the Sahel, all the moisture comes in a four-month period: May through August. After that, not a drop of rain falls for eight months. The ground cracks from dryness, and so do your hands and feet. The winds off the Sahara pick up the dust and throw it thousands of feet into the air. It then comes slowly drifting across West Africa as fine grit. It gets inside your watch and stops it. It gets inside your refrigerator (if you have one).

"The year's food, of course, must all be grown in four months. People grow sorghum or milo in fields not larger than a sanctuary. Their only tools are the strength of their backs and a short-handled hoe. No Massey-Fergusons here; the average annual income is between eighty-five and one hundred dollars per person.

"October and November, these are beautiful months. The granaries are full—harvest has come. People sing and dance. They eat two meals a day—one about ten in the morning, after they've been to the field awhile, and the other just after sundown. The sorghum is ground between two stones to make flour and then a mush with the consistency of yesterday's cream of wheat. The sticky mush is eaten hot; they roll it into a bit of sauce, and then pop it into their mouths. The meal lies heavy in their stomachs so they can sleep.

"December comes, and the granaries start to recede. Many families omit the morning meal. By January, not one family in fifty is still eating two meals a day.

"By February, the evening meal diminishes. People feel the clutch of hunger once again. The meal shrinks even more during March, and children succumb to sickness. You don't stay well on half a meal a day.

"April is the month that haunts the memory. The African dusk is quiet, you see, no jet engines, no traffic noises break the stillness. The dust filters down through the air, and sounds carry for long distances. April is the month you hear the babies crying in the twilight, from the village over here, from the village over there. Their mothers' milk is now stopped.

"Parents go at this time to the bush country, where they scrape bark from certain trees. They dig up roots as well, collect leaves, and grind it all together to make a thin gruel. They may pawn a chair, a cooking pot, or bicycle tires in order to buy a little more grain from those wealthy enough to have some remaining, but most often the days are passed with only an evening cup of gruel.

"Then, inevitably, it happens. A six—or seven-year-old boy comes running to his father one day with sudden excitement. "Daddy! Daddy! We've got grain!" he shouts.

"Son, you know we haven't had grain for weeks."

"Yes, we have!" the boy insists. "Out in the hut where we keep the goats—there's a leather sack hanging up on the wall—I reached up and put my hand down in there—Daddy, there's grain in there! Give it to mommy so she can make flour, and tonight our tummies can sleep!"

"'Son, we can't do that,' he softly explains. 'That's next year's seed grain. It's the only thing between us and starvation. We're waiting for the rains, and then we must use it.'

"The rains finally arrive in May, and when they do, the young boy watches as his father pulls the sack from the wall, and does the most unreasonable thing imaginable. Instead of feeding his desperately weakened family, he goes to the field and—I've seen it—with tears streaming down his face, he takes the precious seed and throws it away. He scatters it in the dirt! Why? Because he believes in the harvest.

"The seed is his; he owns it. He can do anything with it he wants. The act of sowing it hurts so much that he cries. But as the African pastors say when they preach on Psalm 126, "Brothers and sisters, this is God's law of the harvest. Don't expect to rejoice later on unless you have been willing to sow in tears."[9]

# Summary

It is right and natural to grieve when we lose someone we love. To not grieve speaks of the lack of intimacy within a relationship. Even Jesus Himself wept at the tomb of Lazarus. In First Thessalonians, Paul tells us that Christian grief is distinctly different from other grief, because other grief lacks the encouraging hope of the resurrection. Contrary to that, the Bible teaches that, "If we believe that Jesus died and rose again [resurrection], even so God will bring with Him those who have died in Christ." In verse 55 of First Corinthians 15, Paul paraphrases the Old Testament prophet Hosea (13:14): "Where, O death, is your victory? Where, O death, is your sting?" His form of rhetoric demands the answer that Christ has won the final victory over death, and has overcome the grave.

Although the death of Christ is what He explicitly came to accomplish, the resurrection is no less important historically. Evangelist Reuben A. Torrey called the resurrection "the Gibraltar of Christian evidences, the Waterloo of infidelity." The resurrection is the historical base upon which all other Christian doctrines are built and before which all honest doubt must falter.

James M. Boice states:

The "empty tomb" verified the person of Jesus Christ as the Son of God, transformed the character of the disciples and changed the day of regular Christian worship. Because of the resurrection, "Death is swallowed up in victory," and what a victory it is. It is the entrance of the soul and spirit into the presence of God, to be followed in time by a physical resurrection. Assurance of these things is ours because of the resurrection. Jesus' own resurrection provides powerful assurance of the Christian's resurrection.[10]

And for our purposes, it is the only message of ultimate hope that an individual can take with him from a memorial service. We may not be certain regarding the destiny of the deceased, but we certainly can speak to the living. And so, whether it be for loved ones who have died, or for us, the living who must go on and pass this way as well, the message of hope is the same: resurrection truth!

In closing, consider the contemporary poetry of John Updike:

Make no mistake: if He rose at all it was as his body; if the cells' dissolution did not reverse, the molecules reknit, the amino acids rekindle, the Church will fall.

It was not as the flowers, each soft Spring recurrent; it was not as His Spirit in the mouths and fuddled eyes of the eleven apostles; it was as His flesh: ours.

The same hinged thumbs and toes; the same valved heart that—pierced—dies, withered, paused, and then regathered out of His Father's might new strength to enclose.

Let us not mock God with metaphor, analogy, sidestepping transcendence; making of the event a parable, a sign painted in the faked credulity of earlier ages: let us walk through the door.

The stone is rolled back, not paper-mache', not a stone in a story, but the vast rock of materiality that in the slow grinding of time will eclipse for each of us the wide light of day.

And if we will have an angel at the tomb, make it a real angel, weighty with Max Planck's quanta, vivid with hair, opaque in the dawn light, robed in real linen spun on a definite loom.

Let us not seek to make it less monstrous, for our own convenience, our own sense of beauty, lest, awakened in one unthinkable hour we are embarrassed by the miracle, and crushed by remonstrance.[11]

A real resurrection gives birth to conviction and comfort. He has risen, yes risen indeed. He has overcome death!

# CHAPTER SEVEN

# Memorial Texts

All Scripture is inspired by God and profitable for teaching, for reproof, for correction, for training in righteousness.

—II Timothy 3:16

Over the years I have accumulated a number of "little black service books." Among other things, a service book is an anthology for use in funeral services. Usually it is a compilation of contributions by various authors on the subjects of weddings, funerals, the sacraments or ordinances, dedications and church governmental functions such as convocations and the like. I have found them to be of some (though minimal) use, especially when there is no time for preparation. I also have located certain works of poetry in these books which have been especially helpful. To my understanding, the reason they are usually small is so they will fit into a jacket pocket or an automobile glove box, and be retrieved at a moment's notice. They are often signed by a funeral home or funeral director and presented as useful gifts to the clergy of the community.

Pastor J.R. Hobbs, in the preface to his *Pastor's Manual* comments: "The suggestions in this little book relating to how to perform the various tasks of a pastor are the outgrowth of a varied experience. The author does not claim that this work is perfect, but believes that it may prove helpful and suggestive to all pastors, especially the young brethren just entering upon pastoral work."[1]

I agree with Brother Hobbs. Anything that will contribute to the success and better performance of the duties of a pastor is to be appreciated.

However, one area that I have found to be nearly offensive and quite unhelpful is the Sample Funerals section of these books. The titles read, "For the Funeral Service of a Young Man," "Funeral Service of an Aged Man," "Funeral Service of a Woman in Mid-Life." I fight cynicism at this point, but someday I expect to see one titled, "For the Funeral Service of a Middle-Aged Left-Handed Male Born on the Second Tuesday of October between 9:00 A.M. and noon." My experience has taught me that attempting to plug into a pre-prepared generic "typed" funeral service is asking for trouble. I can hardly think of a way to make a memorial service less personal. When asked, I tell pastors that if they are not able or willing to go and meet the family and learn about the deceased so they can construct the service around that person's own unique life, don't do the service! It is that important.

Other than mentioning the main elements of a memorial service (prayer, music, obituary reading, Scriptural reading, eulogy, poetry and/or personal involvement), I would never attempt to suggest by way of a sample how a minister should construct the actual mechanics of the service. That, to me, seems like an insult.

What I do submit to you is a collection of Scriptural verses or sections of Scripture which have passed the test of time as being either confirmations for the dead, comforting remarks for the living, or launching pads for eulogy. These texts will prove helpful to all who explore them.

## The Inevitability of Death

Job said, "We brought nothing into this world, and it is certain we can carry nothing out." What is equally certain is that all die.

Psalm 90:3–6, 10
Hebrews 9:27
Ecclesiastes 9:5
Job 14:14
Psalm 23:4
Psalm 90
Psalm 116:15

## Consolation For Those Who Grieve

It is consoling to know that God is faithful and will, according to His promises, provide for us in every strait.

Lamentations 3:31–33
Psalm 103:13–14
Isaiah 51:1–3
Isaiah 55:6–7
Isaiah 61:1–3
John 14:16–19
II Corinthians 1:3–4
Psalm 27:5
Psalm 40:1–3
Psalm 73:24–26
Isaiah 40:28–31
Isaiah 43:2
Amos 5:8
Philippians 4:7
I Thessalonians 4:13
Luke 8:52
James 4:8,10
Revelation 22:17

## Hope for the Righteous Who Die in Faith

Paul reminds us that godliness (righteousness) not only carries the "promise of the life that now is," but also "of that which is to come" (1 Timothy 4:8). The good hope in death is that when we quit the body, we have the promise of full enjoyment of all the privileges afforded the righteous as well as the blessing of the Savior's presence.

Numbers 23:10
Proverbs 4:1–13, 20–27
Ezekiel 18:22

John 14:1–9
I Corinthians 2:9
II Corinthians 4:16–18
II Corinthians 5:1–9
Matthew 25:34–40
Matthew 19:28–29
Luke 12:35–44
Luke 18:18–30
John 5:25–29
John 6:37–40
John 11:24–26
John 14:1–9
Romans 8:31–39
I Corinthians 15:35–50
Colossians 3:1–4
I Thessalonians 4:14–18
I Thessalonians 5:1–11
II Timothy 4:6–8
Revelation 7:14–17
Revelation 14:13
Revelation 21:1–7

# Children

Who so happy as I am, even now the Shepherd's Lamb? And when my short life is ended, by His angel host attended, He shall fold me to His breast, there within His arms to rest.

—Hymn writer, Henrietta L. Von Hayn

Matthew 19:14
Mark 10:14
II Samuel 12:23
Luke 8:52

# The Abolishing of Death

And when my task on earth is done when by Thy grace, the victory's won even death's cold wave I will not flee since God through Jordan leadeth me.

—Poet, Joseph Gilmore

Hosea 13:14
Isaiah 25:8
I Corinthians 15:26,54
Ezekiel 37:12–13
I Corinthians 6:14
Psalm 16:9; Job 19:26
Psalm 17:15
Psalm 73:23–24
John 5:28
II Timothy 1:10

# Transformation

Soon shall close thy earthly mission swift shall pass thy pilgrim days; hope soon change to glad fruition, faith to sight, and prayer to praise.

—Hymnist, Henry Lyte

I Thessalonians 4:15,17
Philippians 3:20,21
I Corinthians 15:51,52
I John 3:2
I Corinthians 13:12
II Corinthians 5:1
Philippians 3:20–21
I Corinthians 15:49

## Together with the Saints

When Jesus appears, the dead raised and the living changed meet and rise together as the completed Church to greet the Savior.

Hebrews 12:23
I Corinthians 15:23
Genesis 25:8
II Samuel 12:23

## The Promise of Heaven

Paul said that to depart and be with Christ was far better than anything earth could offer. In heaven our unfinished service, incomplete consecration, partially appreciated divine gifts, and undeveloped capacities will all reach perfection. Here is a brief classification of that which awaits the Christian when he or she dies.

WHAT LEMMINGS BELIEVE

II Corinthians 5:1, 8 - An eternal building
Luke 23:39–43, 16:22 - Paradise
I Peter 1:3,4; Ephesians 1:18; John 14:2 - An inheritance incorruptible
Luke 12:22; Matthew 13:43, 25:34 - The Kingdom
II Peter 1:10,11; Revelation 22:14, 21:27 - The entrance in
Colossians 3:1; Romans 8:18; I Corinthians 2:9–10 - Heavenly things
Romans 8:2,17–18, 30; Psalm 16:11; I Corinthians 2:9 - Pleasures
II Corinthians 5:6–8 - Presence with the Lord
Revelation 21:4, 22, 27: 22:5–7 - No night, defilement, tears, death, sorrow, pain
Hebrews 4:9 - Eternal rest

# An Elegy For King Saul

Elegy: A mournful, melancholy poem, especially a lament for the dead.

And David lamented with this lamentation over Saul and over Jonathan his son: and he bade them to teach the children of Judah the song of the bow: behold, it is written in the book of Jashar: Thy glory, O Israel, is slain upon Thy high places! How are the mighty fallen! Tell it not in Gath, Publish it not in the streets of Ashkelon; Lest the daughters of the Philistines rejoice, lest the daughters of the uncircumcised triumph. Ye mountains of Gilboa, let there be no dew nor rain upon you, neither fields of offerings: For there the shield of the mighty was vilely cast away, the shield of Saul, not anointed with oil. From the blood of the slain, from the fat of the mighty, the bow of Jonathan turned not back, and the sword of Saul returned not empty. Saul and Jonathan were lovely and pleasant in their lives, and in their death they were not divided: They were swifter than eagles, they were stronger than lions. Ye daughters of Israel, weep over Saul, who clothed you in scarlet delicately, who put ornaments of gold upon your apparel. How are the mighty fallen in the midst of the battle! Jonathan is slain upon thy high places. I am distressed for thee, my brother Jonathan: Very pleasant hast thou been unto me: Thy love to me was wonderful, passing the love of women. How are the mighty fallen, and the weapons of war perished.

—II Samuel 1:17–27

Following the death of King Saul and his son Jonathan, David took hold of his clothes, and rent them, mourned, wept, and fasted. Though the way was now opened for David to aspire to the throne of Israel, he denied himself joy at Saul's demise, but rather with those about him, vented his grief. Regarding David's attitude toward the king despite Saul's continual attacks upon him, biblical writer Arthur W. Pink comments:

There are many who secretly wish for the death of those who have injured them, or who keep them from honors and estates, and who inwardly rejoice even when they pretend to mourn outwardly. The grace of God subdues this base disposition. David mourned for Saul out of goodwill, without constraint: out of compassion, without malice; because of the melancholy circumstances attending his death and the terrible consequences attending his death which must follow. "Rejoice not when thine enemy falleth; and let not thine heart be glad when he stumbleth" (Proverbs 24:17).[2]

In the 2 Samuel account, we see David as the master of the pen (Psalms), as well as the sword. In this elegy of both Saul and Jonathan, David leaves us with a poem of tribute of lasting value to the lives of these two great men. Not only are poems moving and affecting, but as Matthew Henry comments, "Some gain information by poems who would not otherwise read history." From Joshua's reference to the Book of Jashar (Joshua 10:13), it is believed that it was likely a book of (non-inspired) state poems, which would explain his commandment in verse 18 for the teaching of it to the children of Israel.

David's elegy is concerned with the curse upon the land of Israel. He sees the death of these two men as defeat at the hands of the ungodly (verse 20), which is a sorrowful condition. This theme is repeated three times within the poem (verses 19, 25, 27) which highlights a key concept and is a poetic device in which misery and sorrow were seen as useless and unproductive. We identify at this point for this certainly is not far from our own experience of inability and unproductiveness while in the context of grief. Perhaps the most relevant application which we can take from this passage is the attitude of generosity that David brings to his tribute (eulogy) toward a man who had been an adversary for many of his days. I highlight six observations:

1.  David celebrated Saul's valor and military renown (verse 22). It had been earned legitimately and should have been recognized.
2.  David concealed the faults of Saul. Much like the passage of Philippians 4:8, David restrains himself to "thinking on these things." Matthew Henry states, "We ought to deny ourselves of making personal reflections upon those who have been injurious of us. Let the corrupt part of the memory be buried with the corrupt part of the man."
3.  There is nothing said of Saul's piety because David will not utter lies. This is often quite different from today's eulogies that are so contrived.
4.  David recognizes the qualities and devotion of both Saul and Jonathan during their lifetimes (verse 23).
5.  David calls upon Israel (others) to remember and grieve (verse 24). Remember, for Saul had truly enriched the country with spoils which had benefited one and all. Grieve, for it is the normal thing to do at a time of loss.

6. (Regarding Jonathan) David laments for what Jonathan had already been to him ("pleasant and wonderful"), highlighting especially the genuine affection which the two had shared. Keeping in mind that David would soon take Jonathan's rightful crown, the non-selfish love of Jonathan is described as that which surpassed the love of women. As A.W. Pink comments, "Nothing is more delightful in this world than a true friend, nothing more distressful than the loss of that one."

This elegy of David is both a noble tribute of respect unto King Saul and a plea of tender affection for Jonathan. As such, it is a model eulogy for those of us who are in ministry.

## Proverbs 31

The end, it is said, of the book of the Proverbs, is to set out a system of practical instruction, generally applicable. The truth, as it is in Jesus, is practical truth. There is not a temper, a look, a word, a movement, the most important action of the day, or the smallest relative duty, in which we do not either deface or adorn the image of our Lord and the profession of His name.
—Preface: *Proverbs*, Charles Bridges

Matthew Henry called Proverbs 31 (the virtuous woman) a "looking glass for ladies," which they are encouraged to open and dress themselves by; and if they do so, their adorning will be found to praise, and honor, and glory, at the appearance of the Lord. The author, King Lemuel (?) was endowed, like many of God's people (Psalm 116:16; I Timothy 2:9–10; 1 Peter 3:1–6; II Timothy 1:5, 3:15), with the invaluable blessing of a godly mother; who, like Deborah of old (Judges 5:1), was honored of God to be the author of a chapter in the sacred volume.

The enquiry to "*find* a virtuous woman" implies the great value of the gift when found. No treasure is comparable to her. We note that the search is for virtues, not accomplishments, for internal worth, not outward recommendation. For this reason the proverb becomes a fitting passage to be used at the memorial service of any woman who lived for the deeper things of life. Her different qualities are given:

A wife; characterized by fidelity and oneness of heart—verse 11

The interests of her husband—12, 23
Personal habits are filled with energy—13–15
Leadership, self-denial—15
Enterprise—16, 24
Strength—17,25
Diligence—18,27
Benevolence—20
Proper adorning; femininity—21–22
Honorable—25
Joyful—25
Law of love in her heart—26
Active—27
Prioritizes; a correct perspective on beauty—30
Lives in the fear of god—30

Proverbs 31 concludes that there is no greater earthly happiness than her children's reverence and her husband's blessing. She, crowned with years, her grown children surrounding her, remembering her blessed example to them all.

The portrait, divinely etched, begins with the touch of a virtuous woman and ends with a woman who fears the Lord. All who see her and remember her at her passing recognize the grace of God and God's favor as the highest honor. There is no higher tribute to be paid a woman.

## The Assurance of Victory—I Corinthians 15:50–57

> But when this corruptible shall have put on incorruption, and this mortal shall have put on immortality, then shall be brought to pass the saying that is written, Death is swallowed up in victory . . . but thanks be to God who gives us the victory through our Lord Jesus Christ.
>
> —I Corinthians 15:54, 57

In this chapter the apostle Paul addresses what is likely the greatest doctrine of Christianity—the resurrection of the dead. In the early part of the chapter, he establishes the certainty of the Savior's resurrection (verses 1–11). From this truth, he then refutes those who said there was no resurrection from the dead (verses 12–19). Again, he confirms the Corinthians (and you and me) in the belief of this truth by some other considerations (verses 20–34), and then answers an objection against this truth (verses 35–49). From verse 50, Paul leaves the reader with the finality of his argument regarding the great change that will be to those still living at the sound of the last trumpet and the complete conquest the just shall then obtain over death and the grave. It is a powerful and liberating message to the faithful, for it speaks of our ultimate participation in the kingdom of God, that will break with this earth which is under God's curse. When Christ will offer the kingdom to the Father, those who are not alive in Christ will not and cannot be citizens of that kingdom. The transformation from corruption to incorruption is made quickly (unlike the process of the sprouting of a seed in his previous explanation), and the dead are changed. In the end, death is abolished, immortality is ushered in, victory ensues, and conquers. Paul quotes from the Old Testament prophet Hosea (13:14) to show that death, now defeated, can no longer conquer. Verse 57 tells us that since this is so, glory is due to God because of the great work He has done. Death and sin are no more and victory is complete.

Matthew Henry comments:

What can be more joyous in itself than the saints' triumph over death, when they shall rise again? Shall not their souls magnify the Lord? Such conquest and triumph shall tune the tongues of the saints to thankfulness and praise for the victory, and for the means whereby it is obtained, not by our power, but by the power of God; not given because we are worthy, but because Jesus Christ is so, and has by dying, obtained this victory. With what acclamations will saints rising from the dead applaud Him! Underlying this truth is the certitude that because Christ rose from the dead, there is a resurrection also for us. It is a powerful and liberating message at the time of death.[3]

## The Perfect (?) Death and Funeral

Then he charged them and said to them, "I am about to be gathered to my people; bury me with my fathers in the cave that is in the field of Ephron the Hittite, in the cave that is in the field of Machpelah, which is before Mamre, in the land of Canaan, which Abraham bought along with the field from Ephron the Hittite for a burial site."
—Genesis 49:29–30

In Genesis 47:29–31, we read that Jacob (Israel), at the age of 147 years, realized that the time of his death was drawing near. He called Joseph, his son, to his side and made him promise that after his death, he would take his body out of Egypt and bury him in the family burial place. This was the cave at Machpelah, in the field of Mamre in Canaan, which had been deeded to Abraham some years earlier from Ephron the Hittite, for the sum of 400 shekels of silver (Genesis 23:3–20). This passage not only speaks strongly to the issue of the value of special traditions, but also is a model regarding the special provision and cares this father had for his family to the very end.

Facing up to the obvious fact of mortality, Jacob first assured his son, Joseph, of God's faithfulness to bring Jacob back to the land of their fathers. Then he summoned all his sons together and commanded them to assemble so that he could prophecy to them regarding the future for each. Having finished his polemic, he then charged all the sons, as he had Joseph, regarding his instructions to be transported to the historical burial place at Machpelah. We read that "When Jacob finished charging his sons, he drew his feet into the bed and breathed his last, and was gathered to his people." It is a touching scene.

What follows in Chapter 50 is the account of the love and loyalty of his sons to follow their father's wishes. We are told that Joseph immediately displayed his affection and normal grief, "He fell on his father's face and wept over him and kissed him." After embalming his father (forty-day Egyptian practice) and honoring the required seventy days of mourning, Joseph requests permission of the Pharaoh to remove Jacob's body in accordance with his promise to his father. What follows is perhaps the most spectacular funeral procession in history. The entourage of Pharaoh's servants, the elders of the land, the households of Joseph, Joseph's brothers, and Jacob (no children, flocks or herds of animals), chariots and horsemen proceeded through the land until arriving at the threshing floor of Atad, whereupon they paused for a seven-day observation of mourning. The spectacle of their mourning was so great that the place became known as (a pun) Abel-Mizraim, or the "meadow of Egypt", by the Canaanites in the area. The sons then proceeded to the cave of Machpelah where Jacob was buried with father Abraham, Sarah, Isaac, Rebekah, and wife Leah.

An aside is that in Genesis 50, we read that Joseph did the same as his father, and made his doubtful brothers vow the same promise to him prior to his own death (verse 24). The passage underscores the power of tradition to compel family members to honor the requests of respected parents at the time of their death. In this way the children of Jacob displayed their great love for and veneration of their father for his provision on their behalf through all of their days.

## John Chapter 14—Prodromos—Comfort For The Disciples

In My Father's house are many mansions (dwelling places); if it were not so I would have told you; for I go to prepare a place for you. And if I go and prepare a place for you, I will come again, and receive you unto Myself; that where I am, there you may be also . . . He that has seen me, has seen the Father.

—John 14:2–3, 9

For many years I sat under the tutelage of a Baptist minister named Everett Bramblet. Having been a pastor for nearly fifty years and having started four or five mission churches, he knew people and the reality of their problems. He also knew God's Word and His promises. During the time I was a member of that church, there were seven young men at the church who were enrolled in a nearby seminary. One of the most memorable truths that he shared with our group was the day that he told us about crisis situations. His counsel was that whenever we found ourselves ministering to people in crisis, make sure we didn't stray too far from John 14. The passage contains one of the most powerful heavenly promises in all of Scripture—*Prodromos*.

Jesus' words, "Let not your hearts be troubled," were spoken to a small group of confused men. The "heart," of course, refers to the whole of the inner man: thoughts, feelings, and will, as well as the emotions. Jesus knew that in a very short time, life for the disciples was going to fall in. Their world was going to collapse in chaos around them. At such a time there was only one thing to do—stubbornly hold on to trust in God, "I believe that I shall see the goodness of the Lord in the land of the living" (Psalm 27:13).

William Barclay comments regarding the *honesty* of Jesus:

Jesus told men bluntly that the Christian must bid farewell to comfort, accept persecution and hatred, and carry a cross. But He also told of the glory that was theirs if they followed Him. One of the great words that is used to describe Jesus is prodromos. Used as a noun, it means those who were sent before to take observations, acting as scouts, especially in military matters. In the Roman army, the prodromoi were the reconnaissance troops. They went ahead of the main body of the army to blaze the trail and to ensure that it was safe for the rest of the troops to follow. In Hebrews 6:20 it is used of Christ who has gone in advance of His followers who are to be where He is, when He comes to receive them to Himself. That is what Jesus has done. He blazed the way to heaven and to God that we might follow in His steps.[4]

Jesus states this truth as an absolute certainty that what He says about His Father's house is so and should never be doubted. It was, after all, His mission. To come, to live a perfect life, to die a perfect death, to rise from the dead, to ascend to heaven, and to send the Spirit (Comforter). This is all theologically matter-of-fact. If we were to comprehend just these facts, that should be enough to deliver us through any trial, even death itself.

But the power of the passage finds its fulfillment in the ninth verse. The concept of heavenly provision by Jesus is tied in with a clear declaration of deity. Heavenly promises are lofty thoughts to our minds, and carry with them tender sentiment.

However, if you or I were to say such things to one another they would be empty words since we lack the supernatural power to back them up. Not only did Jesus make such powerful claims, but He drove them home by reminding us that not only could He make such claims, He can deliver, since He is nothing less than God come in the flesh (incarnate). He declares, "He that has seen me has seen the Father."

Down through the centuries these first few verses of John 14 have been a tremendous comfort, strength, and hope to God's people under all circumstances, especially death.

My Baptist pastor was right. In times of crisis, don't stray too far from John 14.

## 1 Corinthians 2:9

But as it is written, eye hath not seen nor ear heard, neither have entered into the heart of man, the things that God has prepared for those who love Him.

—1 Corinthians 2:9

I include this Pauline passage because it is an often-used text at memorial services. The tendency among preachers is to isolate the text and highlight the lofty notion of the unimaginability of the heavenly rewards that will be dispensed to the saints in glory. This is an exceedingly comforting concept and perhaps declares that the salvation which God provides (including heavenly rewards) far surpasses the ability of the mortal mind to comprehend. However, the use of the text in this way does not do justice to the contextual use by Paul in addressing the issue of "the wisdom of this world" (verse 6–16) and the absolute necessity of divine spiritual revelation in order to understand it. Interestingly, the text used as a promise beyond the grave, though perhaps textually dishonest, is always readily accepted by listeners since it is both pleasant to our minds and truthful.

## Psalm 6—Praying Our Grief

I am weary with my sighing; every night I make my bed swim, I dissolve my couch with my tears. My eye has wasted away with grief . . . for the LORD has heard the voice of my weeping. The LORD has heard my supplication. The LORD receives my prayer.

—Psalm 6:6–9

Though this psalm is principally about David's adversarial conflicts, it conveys the inspiring message that to know spiritual wisdom is to know how to behave under severe and deep trials. Some hearers melt away, some harden their hearts and withdraw from God, but to the tender hearted, it is a time to draw near to God for refuge. The psalm teaches us that whatever our afflictions may be, Eternal rest - let us betake ourselves to God in prayer. Grief is a process which takes time. During that time, faith in God will dispel any sadness.

. . . every tear becomes a sparkling gem in his crown: when to sighs and groans shall succeed the songs of heaven, set to angelic harps, and faith shall be resolved into the vision of the Almighty.

—A.G. Horne

# Difficult Services

**Dif'-fi-cult** adjective; hard to understand, hard to deal with, get along with or please, arduous, trying.[1]

When we use the philosophical term "hedonism," we tend to think of the lifestyle of a person such as Hugh Hefner. A hedonist, by our contemporary definition, lives life to the fullest, eating well, playing well, "getting all the gusto," desiring only pleasure from life. The reality is that this definition is only half true. In fact, philosophy defines ethical hedonism as the view which affirms that pleasure is intrinsically desirable and that displeasure (or pain) is intrinsically undesirable. In other words, not only does the true hedonist seek the greatest good, (pleasure) he also avoids that which will bring displeasure. And if that is so, then perhaps it is so that life has a tendency to make each one of us a bit of a hedonist, especially as we age. Life, we find, takes the starch out of our sails.

True enough, we desire to be people who, as the axiom goes, "when life gives lemons—make lemonade." But by and large, difficulties (true hedonism) are something to be avoided. Our problem, of course, is that difficulties cannot be avoided. And as ministers, when we walk into the room, "all of the waves must calm." We are expected to make good come out of the bad.

Handling services of little old ladies who lived for the Lord, died in their 90s, sang in the church choir, and just peacefully passed on in their sleep at their daughter's home are easy. Those people lived as they should, took care of themselves, did not outlive their children, and died as they should. But now we enter the deep water of the other side of life. Now we consider the difficult services.

Examples of difficult memorial services abound. As I have analyzed these situations over the years, I have found that one of the conditions which make difficult services so difficult, is that they have their own peculiar set of difficulties.

Consider the following:

SIDS (Sudden Infant Death Syndrome)
- trauma of the unexpected
- philosophical wrestlings of theodicy (God?), emotions of anger, confusion
- unnaturalness of outliving one's child
- tremendous implied guilt feelings
- domestic problems (marriage) as a by-product

STILL BIRTH, MISCARRIAGE
- no identification with child
- no meaning to the life of the child
- father's inability to identify with wife's grief
- futility of having carried and labored to "come up empty"
- immediate disposition of fetus, no memorialization (extended grief)

DEATH OF A YOUTH
- unnatural to outlive one's offspring
- robbed of maturing into productivity, lost potential
- theodicy—God? (sometimes misplaced blame, anger toward the medical community)
- impossible to replace
- guilt of parents when death is either intentional (suicide) or irresponsible

TRAUMA/VIOLENCE/UNUSUAL DEATH
- sudden and unexpected
- blame society, government, laws
- implied guilt, no closure with the individual
- theodicy
- revenge, justice

AIDS
- moral/immoral issue, lifestyle
- frustrations of incurable disease (What is medical science doing?)

SUICIDE
- morality issue (mortal/unforgivable sin before God?)
- vast multitude of emotions (guilt, anger, regret, shame, neglect)
- haunting memories, images (guilt letters, discovering the body)

DEATH AND HOLIDAYS
- birthdays, anniversaries are reminders for evermore
- Christmas is especially difficult

And, from my personal files, I could add to this list these instances:

The sudden death of a husband who took sole responsibility in the family. I had a woman in her sixties say to me in her frustration that, "The S.O.B. died on me." As I probed, I found that they actually had enjoyed a rather good marriage, but he handled every duty all their lives. Not only could this woman not pay a bill or balance the checkbook, but she had never gone to the grocery store alone. She didn't know how or where to start. Therefore, his untimely death was seen as a personal affront to her. How rude! In reality of course, hers was a misdirected anger which was rooted in his never having either encouraged or allowed her to become the woman who would have to care for herself someday. The service was difficult.

Often the death of an individual will bring domestic and family problems to the surface. Usually, people have worked hard for many years practicing destructive habits and patterns that at the time of death become visible to all. This situation is not just with spouses, but also with children, adult and young alike. I recall officiating at the service of a gentleman in his mid-forties who had died somewhat suddenly, and all three of his previous wives came to the funeral "dressed to the nines" in black. They behaved themselves at the chapel, but when we got to the rural cemetery they "lit up." Each one in turn, put on a display at the grave. One of them had to be restrained as she threatened to jump in the grave. No fooling. The humorous thing was that as the funeral director and I stood and watched, we came to the somber conclusion that since the guy had been a rascal in life, we were not certain whether these gals loved him—or hated him. He must have been a charmer. Difficult.

In a family with which I was very close, the father died leaving a large number of adult children (ten) and their mother. The family was split over the disposition of the father's antique gun collection; some thought the proceeds should go to the mother exclusively, others wanted a share for themselves. Following the funeral service, the family met at the home and had a verbal brawl which split the family for years to come.

I officiated at a service of a young man (late 20's) who, in the throes of a drug problem, took his own mother hostage in her home. He was holed up there for some time until, negotiations breaking down, a SWAT team was finally called. After much deliberation he came out of the house and, with a towel draped over his right arm, made a run for his truck in the driveway. The officers not only shot the tires out of the truck, but took him down with about 70 rounds of ammunition. That's what SWAT teams do when lives are at stake and a situation seems hopeless. Tragically, it was revealed as he went down that he had no weapon under the towel as suspected. It seems that he had come to the end of himself in his problems, and either lacking the courage to take his own life or, for his dear mother's sake, elected to exercise his death wish and have the police do the deed for him. They complied. There wasn't much to say at his service. Extremely difficult.

In one of the most icy services at which I have officiated, the police escorted the spouse of a deceased young lady into our chapel. He was dressed in orange prison coveralls, shackled and handcuffed, sat in the first row and glared at me. He was being held on suspicion of murdering his wife, and yet won his appeal to the judicial system which allowed him to attend her funeral service. Not pleasant.

## What is the Problem?

I can think of at least three reasons why these services are so difficult.

1.  In nearly all of the above-described situations, the issue of good and evil (theodicy) is alive and well. I have found that no matter what the outwardly professed philosophical beliefs and habits, most people are wrestling with God in these circumstances. They may confess to not knowing whether God exists, but in their heart of hearts they are wondering if planet earth makes much sense. If the individuals involved have no personal faith, the situation seems even more despairing. It is one thing to have to confess that "we know not why things happen, but we know that there is a God who does know and is in control." It is quite another thing to have no belief and relegate occasions such as these as nonsensical fate. Despair reigns supreme. That is why chapter two is in this book.
2.  The tension of the moment is so high that the individuals are unable to behave rationally. The intensity level is at a fever pitch. Our ability to focus on anything other than the emotional pain is nearly gone. We hear well enough but do not retain much of what is said. We do not think very well when in crisis. These are all factors that should guide the clergy in his actions with the bereaved.
3.  The subjective side of our being becomes dominant. Our emotions are everywhere. Our lives are captured by denial, guilt, anger, regret, jealousy, revenge, shame, disappointment, numbness, a feeling of bondage, separation from God, and countless more.

# What Can We Do?

The most fundamental principle is to realize that the ability of the bereaved to focus and thereby hear is limited, and much of what we say or do will probably not be retained. Here are six considerations I have found helpful.

1. Expect a high level of *emotion and tension*. Tears and emotional outbursts are not uncommon. I have officiated at services where there were estranged individuals in attendance who harbored dangerous feelings toward the others, and the minister needs to be aware of these potential personal confrontations. I have ended some of these potentially volatile services with an uncomfortable feeling, and yet had to confess that the service probably didn't go that badly. In these situations, it is normal to experience this tension.

2. Above all, *be brief*. By this I do not mean to exclude portions of the service, but rather make certain that words are succinct and to the point. There is nothing much worse than the droning on of a preacher at a highly charged emotional memorial service.

3. When dealing with people individually, and in officiating at the service, *avoid the natural tendency to run too easily to your comfort zone*. This is why people make the glaring mistake of overusing all-too-familiar phrases and clichés. To say to the mother of a child who has suddenly and mysteriously died, "God must have a special need for your little one in heaven," is not only theologically incorrect, but gives no comfort to the bereaved. When we move into the "uncomfort zone," it is better to be silent and express our concerns in other ways than to utter *regrettable* words. Paul says to "weep with those who weep" (Romans 12:15). Hugs go a long way.

4. If there is any *participation in the service by others*, seek this input outside of the immediate family and closest relatives. In an exceptional case I have had next of kin say something at a service of this type, but generally it is asking too much to expect these individuals to contribute, outside of the information obtained at the time of the visit. There are times, however, when perhaps a grandparent, working colleague, close friend or neighbor will add the personal touch.

5. *Focus on one point in the message.* It can be drawn from Scripture or a poem or the life itself. I have found that to consider the truth of brevity and urgency of life is usually tolerated and is of course a great reminder for all of us. Be sure that the presentation is done in a loving and winsome way that will draw the listeners to consider their own lives in light of the circumstances before them. Since the attention is automatically drawn toward our mortality, it is perfectly legitimate to apply God's ointment (gospel) to the exposed area.

6. *Use the Bible.* God has promised to honor His Word unlike any other vehicle. Perhaps we must conclude that in one sense the most difficult service of all is just handling the dynamic that exists when an individual has died, and it is known to all attendees that the individual's life was scandalous and completely without faith in any way. The following anecdote illustrates this dilemma.

The story is told of the known "rascal" who died suddenly. The man's memorial service was being handled by the deceased's brother. The brother approached the minister who had been named as the officiant and informed him that no matter what else the minister said, he must declare his brother to be a saint. This was a tall order, since everyone knew the man as anything but. The man assured the minister that if he followed his request, he would be paid handsomely, and if not, he would not be paid at all. When it came time for the eulogy, the minister declared that the deceased was indeed a troublemaking rascal who was known by all as an evil, low-life individual, but when compared to his brother, he truly was a saint.

This light-hearted story defines the tension. To those who believe, the implications of a situation like this one are obvious, though no one will want to verbalize it. We hope for the death bed or death moment conversion experience but we recall the words of Bishop J.C. Ryle who said, "The Bible records one death bed experience, and only one (the thief on the cross). One, so that none may despair, but one so that none shall presume." We leave it to almighty God. To those who have not faith, it will not matter to them for they will neither believe nor care. In such cases, we cannot compromise the truth though many a minister has preached individuals into heaven despite obvious life evidence to the contrary. We can then only eulogize in the areas in which the individual excelled, while preaching ultimate accountability before God to the living.

I have officiated at numerous services over the years. Generally, I am not emotionally charged while serving as their chaplain. First, I am a professional extending a service that must be done with precision and integrity. Second, I have not been attached to the deceased, as were the family members, so the degree of bereavement that I experience will not be near theirs. Sometimes, however, I officiate at a service of an individual with whom I identify, and the emotional pain touches my heart deeply. I am a father, so the loss of children generally tugs at my heart and soul. I see myself sitting in the front row as if the preacher were speaking to me. I cry once in a while.

Some services are more stress-filled and challenging than others. As ministers, we cannot give people what they truly want, i.e. the life of their loved one returned. What we can give them is our assistance through the most difficult time of their lives. We can take them by the hand and walk them down the path where no one wants to walk. And lovingly and truthfully, we can share with them the hope, comfort, and promise of assurance which is contained in the gospel of Jesus Christ and His resurrection.

# CHAPTER NINE

# Clergy and Funeral Directors

## WORKING TOGETHER... TO SERVE TOGETHER

### Clergy/Funeral Director Relations

Do not lay up for yourselves treasures upon earth, where moth and rust destroy, and where thieves break in and steal. But lay up for yourselves treasures in heaven, where neither moth nor rust destroys, and where thieves do not break in or steal.

—Matthew 6:19–20

In Matthew's account of the Sermon on the Mount, Jesus teaches His disciples (and you and me) concerning true wealth. The clear teaching is that we must distinguish between the treasures which this world offers which are tarnishable and destructible, and those that extend into eternity and are everlasting.

Some time ago while preparing a message on this text, it occurred to me that if the distinction lies in "everlasting-ness," then we would have to conclude that all investments made in this life would ultimately come to naught since we take nothing with us into the next life—with one exception: relationship. Relationship, whether vertical with God or horizontal with our fellow man, has eternal consequences. We are currently nurturing a relationship with God and His Son which will extend forever. When we say that we will meet our loved ones in heaven, we are confessing this extended relationship process. Therefore, I conclude, Jesus is encouraging us to invest in relationship in this life as investments forever. I have found that life also bears this truth out. The longer I live, the more I am convinced that lasting fulfillment lies in relationships.

In every area of life, knowingly or not, we are constantly forming relationships. To care for our bodies, dentists drill our teeth, chiropractors crack our spines, podiatrists rub our feet, radiologists read our bone structure, and endocrinologists meter the stuff inside which none of us understands. Add to that our spiritual guides, and on it goes. It seems that this cadre of relational community is not only advantageous but also necessary, for by it we maintain the whole man by bits and pieces. The sum of the parts *is* equal to the whole. All the disciplines come together to serve the whole man.

So it is in death. The combination of the funeral director/clergy is our society's way of best ministering to those who are going through the death and dying process. When the two disciplines come together, we become mutual servants of God and man. We interact to serve our fellow man—we invest in professional relationship with one another.

Interaction

> Two are better than one because they have a good return for their labor. For if either of them falls, the one will lift up his companion . . .
>
> —Ecclesiastes 4:9–10

## Coming Together—to Work as One

When a death occurs, many disciplines become involved. Allow me to exaggerate my point. The medical community is nearly always involved in attending to the deceased in one form or another prior to the demise. Many die in rest homes where numerous *nurses* and *caregivers* tend to us. With on-going illness which leads to death, our *primary family physicians* and other *secondary M.D.'s* typically care for us. In sudden death, usually *emergency or trauma units* are involved. Often *EMT's, firefighters* and *police* have necessarily stepped in. With terminal illness the *social caregivers* (hospice) are called in to help with the actual dying process. If the death is due to suicide, often the *psycho-socio* divisions of medicine are involved. A *man in the morgue* ties a tag on our toe. The *government* actually gets involved, since there is official paperwork (death certificates) to be filed. The individual branches of the *military* will make an appearance at the cemetery if the deceased so merited their attention. *Florists* are called to supply flowers of remembrance. *Musicians* play a part in the memorial service. A *casket salesman* sold the casket or cremation container to our funeral director. *Cemetery men* dig a hole in the ground in which to put us. The *burial vault man* drives his truck to the cemetery to deliver the large concrete container in which they will place the casket. The *ladies group* of the church prepares a potluck following the service for a time of fellowship. *Neighbors, friends* and, of course, *family* combine in their individual ways to walk through the steps of moving through the death of you or me. And so it goes with any number of combinations of all these people. Little wonder Grandpa in his sarcasm used to say, "Don't make a big fuss, just dig a hole in the back yard and throw me in."

Of all the disciplines which are involved in the death experience, none, in my estimation, are as necessary as the two who take center stage in this process. The *funeral directors* and *clergy* of a community are the team that is most closely aligned in this process and by definition must work in perfect harmony for the good of community. They are co-professionals in this effort. And though their roles and perspectives differ immensely, there is a gelling that must take place if we are to serve our fellow man well.

I have witnessed a wide variety of attitudes among funeral directors and clergy. In some cases the two are good friends and truly complement one another in their service. I play golf regularly with one of my colleagues. But in some situations these two professions have seen one another as something less than a good union. There actually can be animosity, depending upon how they perceive one another. I have known funeral directors who see the clergy as tending to be too pushy and involved even to the point of dictating the family's decisions. I have known clergy who resent funeral directors. They see them as the capitalistic exploiters of people in their weakest moment.

It is my observation that the effectiveness of this relationship, then, depends upon how well the cooperative effort works for both the benefit of the family and for the benefit of the two participating professional services. This is the common ground that we seek. And though most professionals work well together for the good of their people, it should not be considered a given. As Scripture says, "For lack of knowledge, the people perish." Knowing historical funeral industry changes and having an understanding of business peculiarities will help the conscientious clergy person to fit hand in glove without compromising his/her personal and theological convictions. In the same way, knowledge of the specialized concerns of the clergy in assisting hurting families will help the conscientious funeral director to better appreciate the enormity of the task of the servant of God in the context of crisis management.

# The Defining Components

I grew up in a small town suburb of Pittsburgh, Pennsylvania. In my day, Pittsburgh was recognized as the steel capital of the United States. Up and down the rivers which feed the Golden Triangle, steel mills had been built in the small towns along the Allegheny and Monongahela Rivers. Immigrants who had moved to America found prosperity in the steel industry. They worked the mills as did their children, as did their children's children, generation after generation. Kids grew up, got married, bought a house near their parents in the same town, and brought up their children to do the same. Families and friends tended to settle together in their own ethnic groups, and the people would live there, work there, raise their kids there and die there.

Today, towns can be identified as predominantly Italian, or Irish Catholic, or Polish, or Jewish. To some degree this dictates how the funeral industry is run. In the town next to ours (Jeannette), which is largely Italian, Graciano's Funeral Home does much of the business. In Squirrel Hill the business is split between Ralph Schugar and Burton Hirsch, both Jewish. And so it goes.

At the time I was growing up, in my town there were five funeral homes that served a population base (including the surrounding townships) of around 30,000 people. This represented around 450 deaths per year. Ethnicity, religious ties, social status, all were determining factors of how the total number of deaths was divided up. One old-line firm in our town was owned by a man named Leo Bacha (Polish), and so he buried all the Catholics. Coshey's Funeral Home had been around longer than the rest, so they tended to trade with the old guard. Barnhart's were Lutherans and, for some reason, also buried all the black community. Kepple's were country club folks, so they probably had most of the upper crust. The fifth business, Pantalone's, was new at that time, an Italian cutting his way into the Catholic trade. Five funeral homes serving 30,000 people—450 deaths.

Still today, the preachers and funeral directors know each other well. They deal with one another often and regularly. They associate with one another in many ways. They see each other at the Kosciuscko Club Dance. They know each other on a first name basis.

Contrast that small-town, ethnic scenario with the situation where I live in 2001. Tacoma, Washington, and the surrounding area has a population base of around 250,000 people. It is nearly ten times the size of where I grew up. Tacoma, like much of the West, is a melting pot of humanity. The Norsks may be somewhat predominant, but largely it is a hodge-podge of people who have settled here. I don't think I had ever met either a

Mexican or a Native American until I moved to the northwest. There are eight funeral homes and three memorial societies which serve the area that represent around 2700 deaths per year. By east coast standards, this would support around 30+ funeral homes. The average numbers of funerals per establishment are larger. The area is much less ethnic, more spread out, and less personal. There is no Kosciuscko Club. The traditions of the east coast hardly exist. Viewing of bodies, or wakes, are considered foreign.

The point is that funeral service is different because of differing traditions, ethnicity, and denominational beliefs. Clergy and funeral directors have a different working relationship in Tacoma than in Pittsburgh.

# Paradigm Shifts

I am just old enough to remember the 50's and 60's in rural Pennsylvania. It was common to embalm the body at the funeral home and transport it back to the home where it would be viewed for three days in the living room. What seems even more macabre to the modern mind is that prior to that time, the embalming was often done at the home too. Before the 50's, this practice was somewhat routine; today it would be considered barbaric. Like this one example, there have been many significant changes in the funeral industry in the past fifty years that have moved it from its old traditions and have either directly or indirectly affected the funeral director/clergy relationship. It is a wise minister who pays heed to the changing trends in funeral service, for by knowing this, he/she will understand the what and the why that the public demands of both professions.

Following are some important considerations and trends that have changed the face of the American funeral industry in the past fifty years.

1. **America has become a mobile society.**

So far away . . . doesn't anybody stay in one place anymore?

—Carole King

We connect by flight in hours to destinations that took days to reach in the past. Education gives us wonderful work opportunities, but we must go where that work is located. In short, we do not stay put like generations past. Because of this, funeral homes are more often dealing with first-generation families. Quite often these individuals are un-churched and do not have the old traditional ties with their community. There is no personal connection with old Parson Brown who buried Dad, Mom, and Grandma. In fact, there is no Parson Brown in their lives. An independent chaplain is called in to be the officiant.

In the old days, everyone knew George, the undertaker. The family knew George's dad (George Sr.) before that. Between the two of them in the last forty years, they've buried six people from the family. When we had a crisis, we called asking for George, not the other licensed employee, and certainly not the answering service—only George. But consider what it is like nowadays, particularly in urban areas. We go to the funeral home where we are met by a young man in jazzy flowered braces and matching tie who overwhelms us with prices from an itemized sheet of endless details regarding services performed. Having wearied us, he hands us off to another man who begins talking about cemetery property. After that, we talk with the man who sells us the grave marker. We don't know any of them. We can't really remember their names two days later. And as in many disciplines of life (medicine, banking, for example), we conclude that we've lost touch with the personal professional ties which were once so vital to our lives. In our mobility and growth, we have de-personalized.

## 2. The Changing Face of the Funeral Home

The traditional concept of a funeral home is in flux. Consider that in the last thirty years, there has been a growth of large corporate chains invading the smaller sector and acquiring firms to be centralized and operated under the banner of the large chain. With the inception of the two mega-powers, Service Corporation International (Dallas, Texas) and The Lowen Group (Canada), locally owned and operated firms have been transformed from mom/pop hometown businesses into standardized cookie-cutter machines which are controlled by out-of-state "suits." There are significant plusses and minuses to this approach. The concept is to retain the down-home feel by keeping the old guard around, while being controlled by the large mega-chain operators from a distance. It has not always met with success. By 2001, the Lowen Group found themselves in serious financial trouble as their stock value plummeted. So much so that some of their initial acquisitions had been put back on the market or returned to their previous owners. On the up side, standardization on a large scale tends to help the individual firm minimize its costs, thus passing it on to the consumer. On the negative side, many are convinced that this trend, like in so many other areas of American commerce, is the depersonalization of us all. As the metamorphosis of the funeral industry continues, the jury is still out. Nonetheless, corporate acquisition promises to continue to be a major factor in the landscape.

Consider also that the growth of the "one-location" combination funeral home/cemetery concept has moved us away from our traditions. Though there is no disputing the convenience of these operations, there has been a sacrifice in areas such as the somewhat majestic and regal magnetic flags, headlights-on, processions through the town to the cemetery. Police escorts are becoming a thing of the past. Limousines for immediate family are passé. The emphasis is on simplicity, "All your service needs, in one easy location."

Another factor that changed the funeral industry occurred in the late 60's when the U.S. Federal Trade Commission required the funeral industry to begin mandatory fee disclosure via itemization. The thinking was that funeral directors had a license to steal, especially since they could unfairly conceal prices. This had an eye-opening effect upon the general public. Prior to this time the typical consumer in America was not likely to shop-and-compare in the area of funeral service. The final fee that they paid was rolled into one total price which included all services and goods rendered. However, with itemization, not only was the consumer now able to see the actual breakdown of costs, but it made the industry much more competitive because everyone now knew everyone else's price rates. Such things as disclosure over the phone (required by law) made the consumer aware that perhaps shopping for a funeral could, in fact should, be no different from buying a car. And since the consumer became aware and conscientious, decisions such as the choice of funeral firm became based not solely on traditional loyalties, but more and more upon competitive pricing.

Competition—capitalism at its best. The result was something that the mid-American funeral director never dreamed of. Aggressive advertising and marketing became standard. Busses cruised down the streets with placards on the back advertising low cost cremation plans. The selling of pre-need funeral arrangements (death insurance) became a standard service offered by any competitive establishment. Having funeral directors or associates who were licensed in insurance sales became necessary for all progressive firms. Competitive free enterprise now existed in a new way in the industry. The American public had begun to shop and compare.

Furthermore, though most funeral homes have always maintained an area in their facilities to be used as a chapel, the use of that area was dictated by the strength of a family's ties with a local church. If a family had a strong link with a church, more often than not the service would be held at the church. If not, the funeral chapel would be used. As the number of churched/unchurched individuals in an area either waxes or wanes, so does the percentage of those who use the funeral chapel. In areas such as the northwestern United States, for instance, where the number of church-going persons is quite low, the funeral chapel has all but replaced the use of churches as the locale for the funeral service. In all these ways, then, it is clear that the face of the funeral home has greatly changed.

## 3.   The Changing Face of the Cemetery

One of the powers cemeteries hold is the inducement to private meditation. They move us to reflect upon the meaning of our own lives as well as on the lives of those who have gone before us.

—David Robinson, Beautiful Death

**THE FAMILY CIRCUS**          **By Bil Keane**

"It's a cemetery. That's where dead people live."

© Bill Keane, Inc. Reprinted with Special Permission of King Features Syndicate.

There was a time in this country when most of the cemetery/graveyards were owned and operated and located by a church. It is a most fascinating revelation to study the old churchyard cemeteries of the northeastern United States. The pithy inscriptions upon the old gravestones tell long-forgotten tales. It is safe to say that Europe is even richer in its heritage.

The trend among cemeteries today in the United States is taking a different direction. Many of our most productive cemeteries are either privately owned or corporate/board driven to make money without apology. Appealing to the common man, there are financial plans available for Mom and Dad at every level. Single interment, columbarium niches, mausoleum crypts, the urn garden (for ashes only), The urn wall (facing the pond), The promised land (infants), and DILC's (double interment lawn crypts, where two people can be stacked on top of one another), to name a few. With an emphasis on maintenance costs (lawn mowing), many have gone to flat ground markers only, which can be purchased on a payment plan from the office. Oh, and don't schedule your burial on the weekend because there's an overtime charge. Yes, the cemetery business is big business.

The government has cut back for veterans also. It used to be that any veteran could get $150.00 or more and a cemetery marker, but with President Reagan came more stringent guidelines. A free burial space is available for any veteran, but law requires that it be only at the nearest National Cemetery. Suffice it to say, cemeteries, as other aspects of the dying industry, are continually changing.

## 4. Cremation

In 1975 the cremation rate (choice of cremation as means of final disposition) in the State of Washington was around eight to ten percent. Twenty-five years later, that rate is at nearly sixty percent. Some believe that in America this shift is not so much one of philosophy (cremation vs. earth burial) as it is just simple economics. The cost of a minimum full-service funeral plan, including cemetery property will often range from $4,000—$10,000 (depending upon geographical location, etc.). As with most everything else these days, it is expensive to die.

In contrast to this, an immediate disposition cremation plan can still be purchased for about $1,000. It's pretty simple economics, but comes with its sacrifices too. Immediate disposition is, of course just that. I call it "down and dirty, out the door." There is no embalming (refrigeration instead) since there is no viewing of the body. If there is no viewing, then there is generally no service as well (optional for an extra charge). With no service and no memorialization, there is no need for a clergy person.

From a theological perspective, the question is, "which (cremation vs. earth burial) is more biblical, and therefore either smiled or frowned upon by God." For some ministers it is of great concern, others hardly recognize it. I have a standing response to people who appeal to me as a pastor and ask, "Which is better, cremation or burial?" I say that I've not found either one very attractive. There is literature which either endorses or condemns cremation, and both from a perceived biblical and theological perspective.

As an aside, conjecture exists among professional grief counselors regarding the shift toward cremation. For years the argument for the standard form of American funeralization was that the process of three days or so of rigorous involvement, including a healthy viewing of the deceased, provided a legitimate and necessary time of closure for all those involved. Since immediate disposition (cremation) does away with most if not all of the traditions, we wonder if we are not short-circuiting the process, and thereby creating a generation of people who have never really worked through the grieving process in certain situations. Time will tell. For now we conclude that the rather rapid rise in numbers of cremations in America has surely changed the large picture.

## 5. The Changing Role of the Funeral Director

What a scandal it would be if an undertaker gave way to cheerfulness and whistled at his work!

—Ed Howe

Once upon a time we had a community servant/merchant called an undertaker. His job was to care for the disposition of the dead. In days of yore, he often doubled as a furniture or cabinet craftsman. This was because he was the man who built the boxes into which dead people were placed. He was regarded to be a good man. In an area of public service in which most of us would not be terribly comfortable, his role was appreciated.

In the new millennium the American undertaker has become like a precious diamond, multi-faceted. No longer confined by the boundaries of at need (a term designating the time at which the actual death occurs), he is now a licensed insurance agent who sells pre-need funeral plans (death insurance). It is not uncommon for a funeral home to now require its entire staff to have completed the state licensing requirements for selling these products. The success of the pre-need program of a funeral home is also key for securing long-term commitment from families and individuals who otherwise will make their "at-need" decisions according to the marketing of the day playing upon the emotion of the moment. The necessity of pre-need commitment is marketed via the appeal to make rational, objective, non-emotional decisions before the need arises. And that, we would agree, would seem to be wise.

In addition, the funeral director of today is trained to be a follow-up grief counselor (post need), helping the living as they find their way through the varied stages of grief and into healthy recovery of life. It could be that the church has dropped the ball in this area of service, but perhaps the funeral director has built such a solid bridge of confidence and trust that the public sees him/her as their friend and counselor. Nonetheless, this mantle often has been passed to the funeral profession. Many progressive funeral homes employ a trained specialist to conduct regular follow-up meetings with their families to monitor their individual progress in the grief work. Some firms establish libraries in their facilities where people can find resources for their difficult journey. It is an extra step whereby the funeral professionals are able to say, "We care."

To sum it up, the role of the undertaker has truly become multi-plex. These five shifts then, have redefined the funeral industry in the past half-century. To some degree they dictate the direction of the future. There are other funeral traditions and issues within our American culture which impact the clergy and his/her role which we need to examine as well.

# THE ISSUES

The funeral process in America is driven by our time-tested choices which originate in tradition as well as cultural and religious beliefs. Like many areas of life, our practices are continually on trial and changing. We shift with the times. These matters define the clergy/funeral director relationship in our day, for often the minister is consulted by family members for counsel in these important funeralization decisions. To discover these areas of concern, we need only to ask the correct questions.

In the remainder of this chapter, I examine the issues of which a minister should be critically aware—which are particularly germane to a healthy on-going relationship between the clergy and funeral directors.

## What does a Funeral Director want or expect of the Clergy?

Often, the funeral director is asked to suggest an officiant for the memorial service and supervise the choice from the wide variety of personalities and theological representations in the community. Consequently, the success or failure of the minister is inextricably associated with the reputation of the funeral home. If the funeral director makes a good choice, his/her business is promoted in the minds of the community, and of course, vice versa. Generally, most funeral directors will make some effort to match the deceased individual's belief system and personality with a corresponding clergy representative.

For instance, a right-wing, conservative "Bible-thumping" Baptist would not typically be chosen to officiate at the service of an old-line, liberal Episcopalian. Funeral directors will always try to make a match. However, beyond the obvious theological and denominational distinctives that influence the decision, there are a number of other considerations which affect the funeral director's choice.

Funeral directors want clergy people who are *available*. There has been a notable change in this respect in the last twenty years. I recall that the funeral director, while making the arrangements, used to call the officiant immediately to *ask* if the proposed date and time of the service would work with his schedule. If not, the funeral director would change the time to accommodate the officiant's schedule. Though this practice continues, it is not done with as much frequency as in the past. Instead, often the funeral director now calls to *tell* the officiant the date and time of the service, and he/she is expected to adjust his/her schedule to fit the service time. This is especially true when dealing with a large funeral home which schedules numerous services daily. Therefore, funeral directors who know that the clergy person is available will most likely continue to call that person on a repeat basis. Often the relationship grows over time, thus becoming a win/win situation for everyone involved.

Funeral directors have learned that a clergy person who will make a personal telephone call and *visit the next of kin* are especially valuable. The visit with the family of the deceased becomes all-important in a number of ways. First, it is the primary process of personalizing the service. During the visit the clergy learns the special value of the individual's life. The facts shared by the family are the information that emerges as the "meat" of the eulogy. The inclusion of this information in the service becomes incredibly comforting to the family as well as rewarding to the funeral director.

Second, the visit provides an opportunity to ascertain that all the information that has been shared with the funeral home is correct. On numerous occasions I have discovered errors in facts and dates which had been related incorrectly to the funeral director. Mistakes in a released obituary or at the time of the service are items which are seen as nearly unforgivable in the eyes of the family members. People also change their minds between the time they made the original arrangements with the funeral home and when the minister visits them regarding such things as choice of music, having a reception, the order of service, and who will take part in the service. This then becomes a good opportunity to give them the chance to arrive at what they really want by working through it with them. In addition, some funeral directors will not take upon themselves the responsibility of relaying information received from the family to the clergy person. They want the clergy person to take that responsibility, thus lessening the possibility of inaccuracies.

Funeral directors are especially fond of ministers who are *conscious of time*. Most of the funeral directors with whom I have contact believe that a legitimate memorial service can and should be conducted in about one half hour. Beyond that, it is reasoned, the attention span of most individuals wanes. In addition, the balance between eulogy and gospel is something to be considered. If the majority of time is given to the eulogy, we have dishonored God and His truth. If the majority of time is given to gospel, we have probably dishonored the life of the deceased and his or her service to others. There is a balance.

Many funeral directors are not comfortable with ministers making a gospel appeal (altar call, decision for the Lord) during a memorial service. First, it makes the service inordinately longer than their perceived acceptable length, and secondly, the urgency of the gospel message coupled with the stark reminder of our mortality is a tension that most individuals (funeral directors included) would rather not face. Any element which adds tension to the service is something most funeral directors would rather avoid. This is an area of particular sensitivity since conscientious ministers will not compromise the truth of the gospel. Tact is of the essence.

Punctuality, of course, is also a part of the formula. To be late is unforgivable; to be on time is expected; to be early (accommodate changes, talk with family) is preferred. I have a funeral director friend who likes to choose clergy who are located in the same geographical area as the family of the deceased and who will continue to call on that family after the service. Conscientious funeral directors who are aware of the on-going needs of the bereaved appreciate ministers who will continue the steps necessary to help individuals through the grief process.

## What do the Clergy want or expect of a Funeral Director?

There are times when the shoe is indeed on the other foot. Occasionally, a minister is asked by the family to help in the selection of a local mortuary. As a young man I worked at a local funeral home in a small town in western Pennsylvania. The rumor mill made it clear that the Catholic priests of our town would, while consoling the families of individuals who were dying, freely volunteer that should the worst occur, those families should not forget that there was one of "their own" funeral directors in town. The clear implication was that the Catholic families were expected to trade with people of like faith. Truth be known, I think the Protestant funeral directors were probably jealous of the loyalties that were not afforded them by their own clergy. I never doubted the veracity of this rumor. And while I won't pass judgment upon the ethic of possibly exploiting a death situation, it is nonetheless true that clergy at times have the opportunity to be in the power seat regarding a family's choice of a funeral home/funeral director.

Knowing that I have been intimately involved with the funeral home selection process, people on occasion come to me to ask my opinion of the firms in our area and, in particular, which one they should choose. It can be a heavy responsibility.

So, in response to the query, "What does the clergy want or expect of a funeral director?" I believe the answer comes down to two primary considerations.

*Clergy desire that a funeral director be genuinely concerned for the people and their desires.* Clergy, as the rest of the public, recognize the acute tension between the business aspect of a funeral home and the service side. Funeral directors have the unglorified duty of the disposition of dead human remains, a job most of us would dread. It is a business that has bills to pay and salaries to meet. At the same time, the funeral profession is one of service, for it meets the consumer in his most critical hour of life and gently guides him through a maze of decisions at a time when his thinking is often influenced by the subjectivity of the experience. Should funeral directors get rich by exploiting the emotional decisions of those under stress, selling outlandish products that are beyond the means of the individuals involved? All would heartily say, absolutely not! Happily, in most situations, this exploitation is not the case. However, since the clergy are so thoroughly consumed in the genuine service of people in crisis, they in turn expect service to be the emphasis of other community leaders. When this responsibility of service is abused in any way, it is frowned upon by clergy. Ministers want funeral professionals to be sensitive to the peoples' desires and expectations.

Lack of this sensitivity can surface in a number of ways. I can illustrate this point best by sharing an illustration from my own experience. I was contacted by a large funeral home to officiate at the service of an individual who had died in middle age (50's), was successful in business, quite pro-active in his community, and had an opinionated family. When I met with the family, they informed me that having already thought through the funeral process, they knew that there were at least four people who wanted to speak at the service and that they wanted me to open it up to "sharing" from people in the audience. In addition there would be two special songs to be sung by another individual from the family. This meant that even if I assumed the role of a talk-show host and kept my part to merely shuffling individuals in and out, the service would probably be at least thirty-five to forty minutes or longer in length. This was entirely the family's choice. When I arrived at the funeral home on that Saturday, I was met by a funeral director (different from the one who had originally called me) who immediately informed me that since they had thirteen services scheduled for that day, I would absolutely need to make sure that the service went no longer than twenty minutes because he had flowers coming into the same chapel for the next service immediately following. I told him that that was not possible since the family had requested something quite involved. He told me that it was my responsibility to see to it that that would not happen. In a winsome and loving way, I told him to get lost and that in the "bigness" of their mechanized funeral plant, he had lost his perspective of what funeral service was all about—serving people. We went ahead and did what we had planned. He was furious (I didn't stick around to see how the rest of his day went), and shortly thereafter I found myself on the ministerial blackballed list of that firm. I concluded that if that was their attitude, it was likely better to be blackballed.

Preachers expect funeral directors to be genuinely sympathetic to the original calling of serving people in the funeralization process. Sensitive that people are hurting, and meeting their needs and desires is what is required. No more—no less.

The second area in which clergy expect consideration from the funeral profession is in *allowing them simply to be clergy.* Their role is distinctively different from that of the funeral director. Clergy are expected to share words of comfort (God-talk) in this time of need. Any restraints upon that is an offense to a conscientious minister.

## Show Me the Money

> For the Scripture saith, "Thou shalt not muzzle the ox that treadeth out the corn," and, "The laborer is worthy of his reward."
>
> —1 Timothy 5:18

A touchy area of discussion is always the idea of *honorarium.* There are mixed feelings within the church regarding remuneration for this pastoral service. Some see the dole as a necessary and legitimate response to a professional calling. Others see the role of officiant within the scope of the job description of a minister; thus, it is a duty covered by one's standard salary.

There is an interesting account in Acts chapter 8 regarding a local sorcerer named Simon Magus. This man had "bewitched" the people of his area and offered money to Peter and John if they would impart to him the power of giving the Holy Ghost to others. His appeal was met with a scornful and judgmental rebuke from Peter. Thus is the unenviable history of Simon the Sorcerer, as it is recorded in the New Testament. Later centuries have shown the estimation of the heinousness of his sin by employing his name to indicate the crime of buying or selling a spiritual office for a price in money. My dictionary reads: "*simony*—the making of money out of sacred things; sin of buying or selling positions, promotions, etc. in the church."

An interesting aside to this account is that according to Hippolytus, the earliest authority on the subject, Simon was buried alive at his own request, in the confident assurance that he would rise on the third day. It is speculated that perhaps under conviction for his actions, he made a turn-around? According to other sources, he attempted to fly, in proof of his supernatural power; in answer to the prayers of Peter, he fell and sustained a fracture of his thigh and anklebones; overcome with vexation, he committed suicide. We conclude that only time and eternity will tell.

The question of legitimate honorarium versus simony ultimately must be decided between the individual and God. If it is not proper to accept money for services extended to people within the church, is a minister justified in taking money for services rendered outside of their flock? Is not the time invested worth something? In one sense, we might ask, "With the question of time, expenses and other commitments to the local church, can a minister really afford not to get paid? If so, how much is legitimate? If there is a legitimate range, by what standard do we judge that?" These are all questions which will help make the decision. To my surprise, I was once paid by three different individuals for the same memorial service. The original honorarium was included on the funeral bill and paid by the next of kin. The two sons (a banker and a lawyer) had flown in from out of town and each one wrote me a check of his own freewill. The reason I accepted both was that first, I made it known to them that I had already been compensated on the original funeral bill. Secondly, they had each made it clear to me that they wanted to share the money with me in thanks for my service to their family. Did I "simonize" the people? I think I gave the money to my wife to assuage my conscience and comforted myself knowing that a triple honorarium doesn't happen often.

The question of the *amount of the clergy honorarium* is one which is debated. People are usually in the dark here and have no point of reference, so they're looking to the funeral director to lead them. I have discussed this with funeral directors, asking them how it is they arrive at the figure. The funeral directors with whom I work suggest a number "in the range of" (minimum to maximum) a certain dollar figure. This sets parameters while still allowing for a decision by the family. The funeral directors, in turn, ask me what I believe is a fair fee. I always remind them that if a minister visits the family (two hours) and then conducts the service (two hours), they have invested about four hours with that family. I can't imagine ever wanting to attach an hourly fee to my service, but I am without apology reminding my funeral directors that in order for a clergy person to do it well, our service and sacrifice should be recognized by all involved. When they press for an actual figure, I usually say, "The Roto-Rooter guy won't come out to your house for less than a hundred dollars." That may sound a bit hard, but in this way I'm conveying to them that if we fail to recognize and evaluate a minister's time and efforts on the same playing level as most other professions, we have missed the target. In 1980, clergy honorarium in the northwest was around $75.00. In 2000, it was $150.00.

In situations where legitimate charity is called for (families on public assistance, young unemployed couples, single parents), a minister should always be prepared to provide one's service—gratis. In my estimation, to miss this is to miss the essential aspect of Christian service.

To those who believe that a minister should *not* receive financial compensation, a Pennsylvania pastor's wife writes: "I once heard an individual say that they resented my husband taking an honorarium for 'saying a few words' at the funeral of a parishioner he has known for 20 years. If only it were a matter of 'saying a few words.' He spends many hours with sick and dying members of our congregation. He gets out of bed at any hour of the night to go to their bedsides. He prays with them, holds their hands and offers words of comfort. He is often the liaison between doctors and family. His presence calms heated situations when people are grieving and not at their best. When someone dies, my husband meets with the family, talks with the funeral director, arranges music, organizes a luncheon, prepares a service, prints a funeral bulletin and handles many other details, which can often take two or three days. This frees the family to grieve. Families may give a monetary gift to the pastor out of gratitude for his dedication to their loved one and appreciation for his time."

Here, here! (My comment)

There is another crucial point that I have discovered regarding the issue of honorarium. Generally, clergy and funeral directors agree that it should *not* be the responsibility of the clergy to procure the honorarium from the family. This is distinctively one of the duties of the funeral home and allows the minister to steer clear of the issue of money with the family. I have, however, seen an interesting twist at times. When the family is making arrangements with the funeral director, they are working through an itemized bill of their financial responsibilities. The clergy honorarium is one of those. At the time of the arrangement, this figure has no tangible value. In fact, it is possibly resented, since some individuals feel that clergy should just volunteer their services. That is, after all, what they do—help people. However, after the visit, almost always a relationship is begun. After the service is conducted, only then do they see and feel the tangible value of the role of the minister, and their attitude regarding the honorarium is completely changed. They are usually quite thankful and realize that the fee charged by the funeral home was more than fair and justified. In fact, they conclude that without this important ministerial aspect, the service would have been incomplete.

## Viewing the Body . . .
### Visiting the Deceased

A funeral among men . . . is a wedding feast among the angels.

—Khalil Gibran

Over the years individuals have asked me what a Christian should believe concerning some of the traditional practices of a funeral. It is good for a minister to thoroughly think through these issues, though we need to be careful to discern what are our views and what are God's.

One of these is the idea of viewing the body. Some think this practice is rather morose and unnecessary; others seem to need to do it. Our country is geographically divided on the practice of viewing. The old-line traditions of the ethnic east coast are generally still in effect. While in the western United States, where cremation and immediate disposition are more prevalent, the idea of viewing the body plays a more minor role. For years, grief counselors told us that the intrinsic value of viewing the body is that it forces us to move from the area of denial into the stark realization that the individual is dead. To move toward reality is good for our emotional health. Many of us have either said or heard the statement, "She's not really there. After all, it's just a shell. Her soul has gone on to be with God." I believe that this is an indication that the reality of death (viewing) causes us to immediately search for some other avenue of assurance for our loved one (and ourself). And right or wrong, it reflects a theological conviction which is intended to be understood as comforting.

*"You've got to admit—he looks good."*

We know that to some extent viewing has a positive benefit from studying the effects on the survivors of individuals who have died and disappeared. Drownings at sea, avalanches, POW/MIA's and the thousands who perished in the barbarous attack on the World Trade Center—are all situations where the person was here today and literally gone tomorrow. We observe that the next of kin of these people are never really given the chance to experience closure. They relate instances such as the eerie experience of imagining hearing the door open and seeing the individual walk in at dinnertime. From this we conclude that to be able to see and touch the deceased makes us own up to reality.

Three weeks following the World Trade Center event, New York Mayor Rudolph Guiliani announced that the city would be freely distributing, to all who were involved, wooden urns which contained dust from the wreckage of the site. It was suggested by the grief therapists that, in this way, the families would be better able to move toward acceptance while retaining a visible reminder of the body which would never be recovered and/or seen again. Without some sensory experience, our very being fights against this closure.

Commenting on the Alan Ball (Oscar winning writer of *American Beauty*) funeral home sitcom, *Six Feet Under*, essayist Thomas Lynch says, ". . . the Fisher & Sons Mortuary . . . where the living look the dead in the face. Not because we need answers, but because, in the face of mortality, we need to stand and look, watch and wonder, listen and remember. He (Ball) presses us to examine the difference between the fashions and the fundamentals (viewing the body) in the business of death."

On the other hand, in many situations viewing may not be necessary at all. For example, if a person has died of a terminal illness and was being visited moment by moment in the dying process, the survivors may feel that to remember the individual as he/she was in the fullness of life is actually a better choice. Hence, no viewing is necessary. Accident victims and disfigurement may also be situations where no viewing is a better choice for survivors. However, if denial is an issue, it may be warranted.

The debate goes on. There may be no hard-and-fast rules which govern this decision. The clergy should be aware that this is an area in which people may solicit ministerial advice. I have concluded that to steer people away from non-rational denial and toward objective admission is always prudent. If eventual healing is to take place, it must begin with the first step of admission of the death.

Another tradition which is questioned by some is the practice of having a wake. The dictionary defines a wake as a watch or vigil by the body of a dead person before the burial. Originally, the wake was instituted to make sure a person was really dead. History records that too many comatose people were buried alive. That sad fact created the lying in state practice among the high born; and later, this led to medical death declarations and death certificates. Over time and as medicine progressed, the practice became more of a social and cultural issue. The time spent at either the home of the deceased, or later at a funeral home, was seen as honoring both the family and, of course, the deceased individual for a life appreciated. We would pay our last respects.

In biblical times it was considered proper to pay one's respects even amongst enemies. There is a fascinating example of paying one's respects recorded in 2 Samuel 10. In an effort to show kindness to the son of the deceased Ammonite king, David sent a diplomatic entourage of his servants to console the king. King David's kind intentions being misunderstood, the princes consulted with Hanun (the king) and persuaded him that David's true intentions were not to console but to spy out the country that he might overthrow it. The Ammonites then humiliated the entourage by shaving one-half of their beards and cutting their garments into mini-skirts. David reacted by encouraging his men and, in time, defeated the Ammonites for their odious treatment of his men. We would only hope that our best intentions to console others at the time of a death would never parallel this strange story from the life of King David.

# What About Caskets / Vaults?

Coffin: a container small enough for bums, large enough for presidents.

—Anonymous

Coffin: Greek—kophinos, "a basket." Obviously, if earth burial is selected, a casket is a necessary purchase. If a casket is used, it must be placed into one of two types of receiving units in the grave.

From time to time pastors are brought into the decision-making process and asked their counsel regarding this selection. It is important since the choice of the casket can make a great difference in both the total cost of the arrangement and also what is known as peace of mind for those involved. They are manufactured in many sizes, colors, and shapes; they come in metals of differing gauges and composition, and are available in soft and hardwoods. A standard point of distinction is the designation of sealing and non-sealing, depending upon the existence of an air and watertight gasket between the lid and body of the unit. Some metal caskets are sealers, all woods are considered to be non-sealers. Prices range from low for a minimum burial container to very high for bronze, copper, and stainless steel metals and exotic hardwoods.

Caskets are marketed under the heading of protection, meaning their ability to with-stand years of corrosion and disintegration because of the earth's natural processes. The casket (along with the embalming process and burial vault) will preserve the body from decay. Copper, bronze, and stainless steel will withstand the elements longer than stan-dard steel. They are also considerably more expensive.

Additionally, the casket is lowered into the grave and placed into a receiving unit which prevents the grave from caving in. There are choices here as well. The unit is either a burial vault (sealing) or a grave liner (non-sealing). These units are constructed from either concrete and asphalt or steel and other metals. Again, the price is determined by the ability of the unit to preserve and protect.

Some Christian ministers have a difficult time with this concept for at least three reasons: First, the Bible clearly teaches that the resurrected body will be glorified, and we will receive new bodies, not these that were destined for decay; hence no need for emphasis on protection. Second, when one considers it, protective sealing caskets are something of a "Johnny-come-lately" in the scheme of things. Every person on planet earth, who lived and died prior to the 20th century, was never afforded the luxury of this protection. This means that only a very small percentage of people in all of history could have been protected. Everyone else who was buried in the ground prior to this time is essentially gone; bones, at best. A minister asks, "Why did God wait until now to allow us this somewhat exclusive privilege, if it is so superior?" For years, most casket manufacturing companies have extended twenty-five and fifty-year warranties on their products. Other than the standard business practice of backing one's product, I've never fully understood that. Have people ever held them to their warranty? Last, a conscientious minister will usually know the financial capabilities of his/her family to some extent. To counsel a family or individual to move into heavy debt in the name of protection should be a concern for the clergy.

The potential for extravagance in this area does not minimize the genuine attention we as a people should extend to one another as we exercise dignity in caring for the dead. Most European countries use hand crafted wooden coffins which quite tastefully lessens the gap between a poor man's box and excess. Perhaps we could learn from them.

My observation has been that Americans tend to die as they lived. The casket that a family chooses more often than not will reflect the standard of the lifestyle of either the deceased or the decision maker. Refrigerators, ranges, televisions, caskets (marketing and salesmanship aside): people generally choose something in the price range of what they're used to. If they drove Cadillacs in life, they choose Cadillac caskets as well. If they drove Chevies, they go to the cemetery in Chevies. Maybe in the end, the concept of resurrection may not have all that much to do with it, and neither does protection. Dignity, integrity, and common sense—all should be within the limits of one's budget.

In the year 2000, the State of Tennessee was challenged in what some believe could have been revolutionary precedental litigation. A black minister, tired of what he perceived as high priced casket sales, challenged the industry by opening a casket store in his community. His efforts to alter the funeral home monopoly on casket sales was met with resistance, his adversaries claiming the business to be unlawful. Those favoring the monopoly argued what they felt were two compelling justifications. First, they said that potential environmental hazards from the minister's caskets were risky (?); and second, it was proposed that only licensed funeral directors should be allowed to sell caskets since the sale is tied up with grief, and only funeral directors are trained in grief counseling (??). It was shown, however, that the minister was selling units identical to the ones sold at funeral homes. Moreover, Tennessee licensure of funeral directors required no formal training in grief counseling. The court did not feel that the justifications to exclusivity were sufficient and ruled for the minister. The state of Tennessee appealed the decision.

Is the day coming when we will purchase our casket from the casket man and transport it for use to the funeral home of our choice? Time will tell.

## Pallbearers

Now as He approached the gate of the city, behold, a dead man was being carried out . . .
—Luke 7:12

When we hear the term pallbearer, most of us think of the six men who carry the casket to its final destination. We have an illustration of this in the passage above from the gospel of Luke. The term is interesting since literally understood it means those who *bear the pall*, the cloth which covers the casket or bier. In more liturgical churches (high church), the use of the pall still exists; however, among non-liturgical denominations (low church) it does not. Aside from any meaning contained within the tapestry and design of the pall, its chief significance is that this covering reminds society that all are equal when we go to the grave. The draping of the cloth over the casket of rich and poor alike eliminates any possible ostentation or display of status conveyed by the ornamentation of the burial unit. In this way the church can dignify the life and death of prince and pauper alike. Obviously, some funeral directors would rather see the pall stay dead.

Regarding the role of the pallbearer as we know it (carrying or escorting the casket), there has been a shift in the last twenty-five years. I remember in the sixties when off-duty police were used as pallbearers of individuals who had no family. In those days they would usually receive a five-dollar honorarium for their service.

With the decrease of committal services (graveside), less emphasis on the funeral procession, and the increase of funeral home/cemetery combinations, today there is simply less need for pallbearers. Often the cemetery provides (and prefers) their grounds keepers as pallbearers who place the casket on the burial device prior to the arrival of the rest of the attendants.

It is interesting to note that my dictionary (published 1990) reads: Pallbearer . . . one of the **men** who walk with the coffin at a funeral. However, a sign of the times is reflected by this letter which appeared in the *Dear Abby* column of my local newspaper.

> **Dear Abby:** We are a family of six girls. In September, my sister Ethel was diagnosed with cancer. During my last visit, she was planning her funeral. When the subject of pallbearers came up, I told her I intended to act as a pallbearer. Her face lit up. "What if all of you could do that?" she asked. Ethel died at home and all her sisters and brothers-in-law wheeled her coffin into the church for her service. As my mother said, "You were all there to help her when she needed it; why shouldn't you help her now?"
> It's a memory I'll always treasure. It was the last time all six of us could do something together.
>
> —Ethel's Sister

> **Dear Sister:** Thank you for such a heart-warming letter. Read on.

> **Dear Abby:** I insisted on helping to carry out my mother's casket. I felt that since mother had carried me for nine months into my life, I could certainly bear her weight and carry her for the last time. It gave me an enormous feeling of peace and helped tremendously in my grieving process.
>
> —Jane in Ohio

**Dear Jane:** I'm sure it was both comforting and empowering during such a painful time. Read on.

**Dear Abby:** What's the big deal about female pallbearers? By the time I was thirteen, I had been asked to do it four times. I'm now 81, and I'll never forget those experiences. All of us were proud to help.

—Honored in Santa Ana,
California

**Dear Honored:** Your letter should put to rest the idea that women pallbearers are a recent phenomenon.

**Dear Abby:** The letter about the female pallbearers brought back the memory of a story my grandma told me about a woman who was planning her funeral back in the 40's. She insisted she wanted women to carry her casket when she died. Her reason: Since men didn't take her out while she was living, she didn't want them carrying her out when she was dead.[1]

—Betty in Florida

# Graveside/Committal

A grave, wherever found, preaches a short and pithy sermon to the soul.

—Nathaniel Hawthorne

Happy is the grave the rain falls on.

—Irish Proverb

Graveyards are a way of keeping the dead handy but removed, dear but a little distant, gone but not forgotten.

—Thomas Lynch

One of the most bizarre graveside service I can recall was the time that we listened to all seven and one-half minutes of Lynnard Skynnard's "Free Bird," and then released a couple hundred helium filled balloons into the sky. The song (his favorite) was in memory of the deceased. The balloons were a mild theological statement regarding release into the heavens and something greater than this life. I'd be lying to say I was totally comfortable with the whole thing, but I didn't feel it was the time or place to begin a theological polemic concerning the implications of our actions. And everyone should appreciate the Van Zandt brothers. I think the process worked for them.

In pondering our traditions, the issue of the necessity and value of graveside committal services should be considered. The transporting of the body (via hearse) with the "bearing of the pall," being seated at the grave, tossing a handful of dirt into the grave itself—these are all options that seem to have their own individual benefits. For example, the Latvian communities of the northwest bring back actual dirt from their country and have it available for all families to use. At the close of the graveside service, they first throw in some Latvian dirt and then pick up the shovels and fill in the grave. No cemetery workers are employed. This is a very important ritual to them.

Especially memorable is the involvement of military, when available, at the committal service. Taps, gun salute, and the folding and presentation of the American flag are all elements that leave quite an impression on all in attendance. Military posts have details that are devoted to just this service and when executed correctly, it is an inspiring occasion. In my estimation, there may be nothing better than "Amazing Grace" on bagpipes. It is guaranteed to stir the heart.

The issue of cooperation with fraternal groups (Masons, Elks, etc.) during a graveside service is met with mixed emotion by clergy. Theologically, some ministers are uncomfortable with these presentations, for while they accommodate a biblical perspective (God-talk), they are also shot through with organizational language which is lofty and heavenly but cannot be backed by Scripture. In addition, they are usually "universalistic" (everybody makes it to heaven) and often grossly misrepresent God and His nature. In a situation where cooperation must be accommodated, there are ways that a minister can distinguish himself from the fraternal group. One way to do this is for the minister to conduct only the chapel service and give the committal service to that group and their chaplain. This will draw a clear line of difference between the two.

As a rule, it is good to adopt the procedure that when officiating at both a chapel and a graveside committal service, devote the chapel time to eulogy and the graveside time to the biblical concept of the hope and assurance that is contained in the message of the resurrection. In one sense, in the first part (chapel), we are addressing the dead; in the second (graveside) we are really speaking about the dead to the living.

Very seldom is there a need or occasion for viewing at the gravesite. The exceptional case might be when a family member or friend has arrived late and was not able to visit at the funeral home. This is always the decision of the next of kin and family. The difficulty comes as we consider the aspect of closure. Usually the casket is shut after the family has made their final goodbyes. To re-open it always creates a tension of moving backward in the process and is quite disturbing to some.

## Headstones/Gravestones

A cemetery is a history of people, a perpetual record of yesterday, and a sanctuary of peace and quiet—today.

It is the little "dash" between the date of birth and the date of death which tells the story of the life. All that happens between the time we are born and the time we die, is wrapped up in that little dash which appears on the tombstone.

## Old Greek Epitaph

Pythonax and his sister here lie at rest
Within the grave's embrace,
While yet their lovely youth is unfulfilled;
Wherefore their father, Megaritos, willed
That in this place a consecrated stone should rise,
To mark his undying thanks that they have lived.

In Seattle the sod on the grave of rock 'n' roll guitar legend Jimi Hendrix has to be replaced a couple of times a year because it gets so worn out from people walking on it. It may not be the Lincoln Memorial or Gettysburg, but the idea is the same. We erect monuments of permanence to people so that we will remember their lives. Headstones (or gravestones if you prefer) serve at least three purposes.

Number one, they mark the *location* of the interment of the individual. That may sound obvious at first, until you consider that if we did not require this, we would have a great deal of legal confusion. Records have to be kept because once in a while we need to go back and identify people. It's nice to have a grave marker to tell you where to dig.

One of our local "less than honorable" cemeteries was caught red-handed in an incident due to a gravestone. It seems a family years previously had interred their father in a certain section of the cemetery which had been improperly platted. Due to incorrect identification, the number of actual grave lots in their section was one short. The lot below Dad, which they were told they also owned, did not exist. When it came time to bury his daughter, the shifty cemetery, upon discovering their mistake, attempted to deceive the family by moving them to another location near Dad, trusting that they'd not remember where his grave was located. What they did not count on was that a family member recalled that the father's grave was marked with a stone, located it, and asked why their graveside service was so far away from where their father was buried. Shame-faced, they attempted to explain away the error in the name of poor planning by the previous cemetery people years prior to their administration. Was there a lawsuit there? Gravestones can be important.

Second, we tell a *story of remembrance* on the stone. We use rocks such as marble and granite and bronze metal, (things that will last), because we want to be able to share this story for many generations to come. A fascinating Old Testament study is to appreciate the practice of Israel in erecting "stones of remembrance" in places where significant acts of God took place (Joshua 4). We carve inscriptions and graphics into the stone which encapsulates a memory of who the person truly was. Jimi Hendrix, of course, has a graphic of a Fender guitar on his headstone. We even recognize God in the life of the individual. We especially do this for infants, since their shortened lives are easily forgotten and seen as insignificant, and we don't want that. In the old cemeteries of a city, the size of the monuments becomes a factor because it speaks of prosperity and power in the community from days past. All these things say—remember.

Thomas Lynch in his book, *The Undertaking*, comments:

"Where death means nothing, life is meaningless. It's a grave arithmetic. The cairns and stone piles, the life stories drawn on cave walls, the monuments in graveyards, one and all, are the traces left of the species before us—a space that they've staked out in granite and bronze. And whether a pyramid or Taj Mahal, a great vault in Highgate or a name on

The Wall, we let them stand. We visit them. We trace the shapes of their names and dates with our fingers. We say the little epitaphs out loud: "Together Forever" "Gone But Not Forgotten." We try to reassemble their lives from the stingy details, and the exercise teaches us something about how to live. Is it kindness or wisdom, honor, or self-interest?" We remember because we want to be remembered.[2]

The third purpose which headstones serve is to be a special *point of focus*. People drive their cars to cemeteries, walk to a grave location, trim the grass around the stone, place flowered vases, share a special story with the deceased, and cry. Without this location, acts of remembrance such as this are hard to do. I once officiated at a service of a retired Navy man who had requested to be cremated and have his ashes scattered in the Puget Sound. His wife felt obligated to honor his wishes and did. Their adult children labored long with the mother to do something other than that, but did not prevail. Six months later, the woman began to come to the cemetery on a regular basis just sitting at the urn wall and crying. Six months after that, she purchased a niche on the urn wall and had her husband's name and data inscribed on the faceplate. There was nothing behind it. His ashes were in Puget Sound. She continued to come for years and to sit with her husband. Or at least, appeared to. Apparently, in this case, the kids were right. A place of focus seems to be important. In the Old Testament, God thought it was important. Should we spend money in this aspect of the memorial process? I think so.

An interesting aside to this topic is a group known as the Association for Gravestone Studies in Greenfield, Massachusetts. Through its publications, conferences, workshops, and exhibits, AGS promotes the study of gravestones from historical and artistic perspectives, expands public awareness of the significance of historic gravemarkers, and encourages individuals and groups to record and preserve gravestones. AGS publications describe methodologies and techniques for recording cemetery data, restoring cemeteries and gravestones, photographing and rubbing gravestones, utilizing graveyards as a teaching resource, and preparing legislation to protect gravestones from vandalism, theft, and demolition. There is an annual conference held which features lectures, slide presentations, exhibits and classes. They can be found on the Internet at *http:// www.gravestonestudies.org/*

# Pre-Planning

In the past 20 years, the concept of pre-need funeral planning and sales has become paramount to the funeral industry. For funeral homes it is pre-planning which locks people up for the future. Loyalty to the wind, families can no longer be counted upon to stay with one certain funeral home through the years. After an individual dies, follow-up with the next of kin is a must if that family is to be retained for the future. Since clergy are consulted as to what people should do regarding these future-plan decisions, it is good that pastors consider the pros and cons of pre-need arrangements.

The author of the Proverbs looks to the example of the ant to encourage us to think about the future, "Ants are creatures of little strength, yet they store up their food in the summer" (Proverbs 30:25). Surely from this example we learn that it is generally a wise and prudent action to consider our days ahead. On the other hand, Jesus in the gospels tells us that since we can't really do much anyway ("Who of you by worrying can add a single hour to his life?" Matthew 6:27), we should rather remember that God knows perfectly all of our needs. Somewhere between these two concepts lies balanced wisdom. Here, then, is my assessment of pre-need funeral planning.

1.  It breathes *objectivity* into the decision-making process. It is difficult to deal with the issues of death and funeral arrangements at any time. We are quite uncomfortable. It is doubly difficult to make these decisions when our emotions are uncontrolled, and we are physically drained. I'm certain that the average individual is more scrutinizing regarding price and other key decisions when the need is not at hand. Making these decisions ahead of time also eliminates the tyranny of the urgent.

2.  It can *eliminate "family" problems* in the decision-making process.
    Often, if an individual had a number of offspring, it means that there may be many people involved in the arrangements. If there are differing opinions as to how things should go, having made pre-arrangements may prove to be the tonic for potential domestic problems.

3.  Pre-arranging assures the deceased that *his/her own decisions will be honored.* There may be some decisions which are imperative to an individual, and in this way the family is obliged to see that they are carried out.

4.  If pre-planning includes pre-funding, *the expenses of the funeral are cared for* by way of an insurance policy. This, of course, will financially un-burden the rest of the family members from this responsibility. Also, with most pre-need plans, there is an interest figure which grows along with the policy which is intended to cover the increased cost of dying over the years.

5.  Pre-planning, in many cases, can actually be *an effectual bereavement exercise.* If an individual is terminal, securing one's own service can be a step in the direction of owning up to mortality, getting one's house in order, which is healthy. It does not need to be morbid.

For these reasons, as a pastor I feel comfortable suggesting to individuals that pre-planning their funeral is generally a good idea. More information regarding pre-planning can always be obtained from a local funeral home.

## Cremation vs. Earth Burial?

Fire is punitive.
We bury the treasure—
we burn the trash.

—Thomas Lynch

No issue has impacted the American funeral industry in the past 40 years like that of cremation. Until the 1950's the United States held the line against cremation, unlike Europe, Canada, and the East. Today nationally the number of cremations is over 50 percent, with highs of 70 to 80 percent in some areas of the country. It would seem that cremation is here to stay. Many funeral directors and theologians believe that the explanation for this increase is due to two reasons which are linked: a pragmatic financial choice (economics), coupled with a sliding departure from the biblical concept of bodily resurrection and its significance (theology/philosophy).

## Corporate/Economics

In any given area, facts are recorded which reveal the number of deaths per capita, per year. Though these numbers can fluctuate depending upon the rapidity of growth and declension, it can generally be said that it is most always a slow change. Even if an area is blitzed by new industry and housing to support it, the majority of the families who move into that area are somewhat youthful and do not impact the death numbers immediately. It happens over a long period of time. This means that in a period of twenty or thirty years, the maximum number of deaths in a given area is apt to stay close to the same figure for many years. That total number of deaths in the area is divided up between the total number of funeral homes. The funeral homes are all vying for their share of the market.

Consider also that years ago, when the percentage of funerals involving earth burial was much higher, the gross sales numbers were also higher, since it always involved the sale of a casket, which was the key component in the price of the funeral. Profits were tied up with high-end casket sales. Employee funeral directors were trained to sell well. Coppers, bronzes, stainless steels, and solid hardwoods—these were the units that funeral directors wanted to sell. So a great deal of their marketing was directed toward the sale of these caskets. Casket manufacturers made much of the idea of protection by highlighting the differing gauges of steel which went into the product, thus assuring the preservation of the body.

But, with the intrusion of cremation as the disposition of choice, that has all changed. Now we must make a distinction at this point. Cremation can be chosen as merely the *means of disposition*. When we say that, we mean that cremation can be the choice of the way in which the body will finally be disposed. It does not mean that viewing an embalmed body, celebrating a wake, having a service with the body present in a casket, etc., cannot accompany this. It just refers to the final end. The funeral industry uses the term *immediate disposition* to designate the choice of cremation as the means of disposition, but in the context of the immediate, i.e. no embalming, no viewing, no casket sale, no service. This is the type of service which is often marketed en masse by memorial societies on billboards. A large number of this country's population have made it their choice, and it is here to stay.

If a funeral home over the years sees its percentage of traditional earth burial services change to a significant number of immediate dispositions, the gross revenue of that firm will radically change as well. In addition, since the decision of immediate disposition does not involve a great deal of interaction with the funeral director and staff, it follows that no significant relationship is built. Because of this, there is no reason to expect personal loyalties to come into play in their choice of funeral homes selected, either at this time or for the future. The decision is one made simply by considering the economics of the issue; hence, the need for aggressive marketing and pre-need sales. For the funeral home, it is purely dollars and cents. Both the casket manufacturers and the funeral industry have adjusted along the way by countering with such things as craftily manufactured cremation urns, but the public has spoken and has had its way. Cremation, due to the escalating cost of dying, is not going away. And one reason why people choose cremation is to save money.

## Theological/Philosophical

Many clergy persons would admit that their understanding of the issue of cremation as a theological consideration has snuck in the back door. Most pastors at one time or another have been confronted by conscientious Christians as to the biblicity of this as a choice. Many have no answer. I do not recall ever discussing it during my time in seminary. There is theological literature available defending both sides of the issue, though I presume that the majority of clergy might be neutral (or worse, unknowing) on this issue.

With the cost of dying escalating, the issue becomes even more difficult. I liken it to the situation of a pastor who finds himself counseling a wife with children who have suffered ongoing abuse for years, only to be told by the pastor that they must stay because the Bible condemns divorce. How can we encourage geriatric people who are on a fixed-income budget to go ahead and run up a ten thousand dollar bill for a funeral, when for one thousand dollars they can do it through the vehicle of cremation? We are in a hard place.

Defining the dilemma, here are some of the pragmatic and theological arguments *for* cremation.

1.  A pro cremation position is a theologically liberal attack against those who hold the Bible as being *prescriptive* in this area. "Times have changed, and we should not be expected to behave as in Bible times. We have come of age."
2.  The *lack of space* (cemeteries have filled up) in our country requires us to utilize cremation as a rational and sensible option to this growing problem.
3.  Cremation is also a more *hygienic* means of disposition of the remains.

4.  To support earth burial as the biblical model is to miss the *geographical* truth that the Middle East (Bible land) is primarily rocky, thereby requiring entombment, not earth burial as we know it. Jesus was laid in a tomb. If anything, the Bible would then endorse above ground entombment and the use of mausoleums. Above ground entombment in the United States is used mostly in the South (Louisiana, Alabama, northwest Florida) where the swampy soil will not tolerate in-ground burial. And though the explanations for the southern United States and Israel are entirely opposite, the fact that geography dictates these decisions is the same.

Even if there is validity to the biblical argument against cremation, the question still needs to be asked, "Does the average American Christian who chooses cremation even concern himself with the issues of things such as the Image of God or the philosophical connection with pagan beliefs?" If it is not a religious issue (amoral), but financial, then *should we see it as willful sin*?

The philosophical arguments *against* cremation include:

1.  It is argued that cremation is part and parcel with *Eastern and pagan religions.* In religions such as Buddhism, it is a significant transference and release of the soul in a cyclical pattern which returns back at some point as re-incarnate. This then is not neutral, but in fact, anti-Christian and should have no part in Christian philosophy. In other philosophies, the idea of cremation is connected with annihilationism which attempts to avoid accountability and judgment.
2.  The biblical examples of burning are always associated with *bad situations and bad people.* Without question, whether speaking of God's anger burning, or burning incense before Baal, or burning the altars erected to do sacrifice to the false gods, the testimony is glaringly obvious that this is God's way of final purging and judgment against evil to bring about purification (Deuteronomy 32:22, Jeremiah 21:10, Malachi 4:1, Amos 2:1ff, Matthew 13:30, Luke 3:17, John 15:6, Hebrews 6:8, "the refiner's fire").
3.  To cite examples of people who have died in tragic accidental fires, plane wrecks, etc. is to beg the question. God's providence overrules all in this area.
    The problem with cremation is that it is a *willful choice* made by the individual, and, because of the prohibition, is an area which we must not enter.

4. Cremation is a willful act of desecration against God's special creation (Image of God), and as such, is a deliberate violation against the significance of bodily resurrection as it is revealed in God's Word.

There are noticeable *examples from Scripture* endorsing earth burial, not cremation: Sarah (Genesis 23), Abraham (Genesis 25), Jacob (Genesis 49), Miriam (Numbers 20), Abner, (2 Samuel 3), Josiah (2 Chronicles 34), John the Baptist (Matthew 14), Stephen (Acts 8), Annanias and Sapphira (Acts 5), Jesus (Luke 23).

## Scattering Ashes

One evening in his opening monologue, comedian Jay Leno reported that a certain lady had decided that she wanted her husband to be with her at all times even after his demise. She chose to use his cremated remains as the "filling" for her implantation augmentation devices. In that way she could be assured of having him with her wherever she went. When I heard this, I knew it would make my book. You've got to be kidding! But such is the case of the sublime to the ridiculous when it comes to the decision of what to do with the ashes?

A minister's perspective on this somewhat common practice will no doubt be dictated by one's view of cremation itself. Generally, if cremation is seen as an acceptable means of disposition, then scattering of the remains is also usually accepted and even encouraged. Though the scattering of cremated remains seems to me to be influenced by both Eastern and pantheistic thinking (and filled with implied allusion), it is seen as comforting to some surviving relatives and seems to be here to stay. My experience has been that scattering often appeals to people who either loved to work or play outdoors. Mountains, bodies of water, or golf courses are prime locations for this deed. I cite the following example:

When our youngest son—an avid skier, was killed in an auto accident on his way to ski three years ago, we were stunned. One of his friends asked if he could have some of his ashes to spread at a favorite ski run they had enjoyed together. That led to our decision to divide his ashes and place them in vials. After the memorial service, we invited anyone who wished to do so to take some to spread at a special place they had shared with our son and to let us know where and why they chose their special place. The responses delighted us.

His ashes are spread from Canada to New Mexico; the stories his friends wrote and shared with us are beautiful. We spread some of the ashes in Ohio where his youth was spent, and we took some to Scotland to scatter on his grandmother's grave.

I had a similar experience with the service of one of my favorite golfing buddies. His home was located on a bluff overlooking the Puget Sound, and his wife decided to scatter half of his ashes in the Sound and keep half to be buried at a later date.

I suppose the theological (especially eschatological) implications of this practice could occupy our ivory tower think-tanks for days. Regardless, one fact to always keep in mind is the obvious: scattering ashes is a once-for-all event. If asked for counsel by a family member regarding this practice, a minister should always direct the decision around this fact: when possible, make certain their decision is the agreed upon will of all those who will be affected by it. It cannot be reversed!

# The Dreaded "Plug"

There is one final issue that merits our consideration, though it does not actually involve clergy/funeral director relationship per se. Surely, one of the most difficult decisions an individual can face is the tension involved in the moral issue of choosing when or when not to continue life support for a loved one. A church friend of mine shares this true story:

My adult sister was chronically suffering from a nearly hopeless heart condition. Her quality of life was so diminished that she very consciously opted for surgery which was rated at somewhere between fifty and twenty percent survival rate. Truth be known, she probably did not expect to survive the surgery, but it was okay with her. The surgery went poorly, as the doctor said her condition was found to be even worse than expected.

The day following the surgery, she was put on dual life-support to keep her alive and breathing. Two days later, still on support, we had concluded that enough was enough. The only person who expressed any measure of hope was the surgeon, who kept advocating continuation. Even the nurses would call us aside and ask us how we felt about the situation. It was clear that they, having been through this numerous times, were sending us strong body language signals.

The tension was this: the natural inclination is to not give up hope and to want to continue to fight, even beyond reason. But I could not deny the thoughts that this surgeon was extending this condition just for the purpose of running up the bill for the sake of the hospital and his practice. Only after a nurse had actively persuaded us to do the only conscionable thing, did he begin to back down and admit defeat. By then, the hospital bill was probably 30 percent higher than it might have been. Looking back, I know that just one legitimate nudge by the surgeon would have encouraged us to make the decision sooner, especially since we knew how "ready my sister was to go." I would hate to think that hospitals encourage their doctors to do this at the sake of the psyches of patients and families, but I know the condition of the medical/insurance thing in America these days. Making money and paying bills is the bottom line for hospitals and doctors.

This story represents a very real tension that exists in America. Considering that it also becomes the gateway of the future to euthanasia, it truly is a hornet's nest. The living will is the instrument which can put these decisions to rest in advance regarding this sticky-wicket, but it requires forethought on the part of all involved. Also, the urgency of the moment, which comes with emergencies, does not allow for these decisions after the fact.

Often, a minister is either indirectly involved or is directly asked his/her counsel regarding these, life's most difficult decisions. Funeral directors, too, hear these stories being rehearsed to them in the context of funeral arrangements. They are real situations that demand the utmost attention of the minister if he/she is to serve well.

## Interfaith Funerals

A friend of mine was involved in the funeral of her brother. The man's two living brothers made the decision to inscribe, "Goin' To Kansas City" on his gravestone. The deceased loved the 60's blues hit, and the brothers felt it would be a fair representation. Two of his sisters (my friend included), strong orthodox Christians, felt that there were only two possible after-life destinations, and neither one was Kansas City. There was a multitude of mixed feelings among the family members, and the two sisters decided they were not about to contribute money for that flippant inscription. The brothers paid for the grave marker themselves.

The incident brings to light the potential conflicts that can arise when funeral decisions involve people with differing faiths and life philosophies. This story appeared on the religious page of my local newspaper:

Marzuq Jaami got so upset that he walked out of his sister's funeral. The Muslim man said he could no longer listen to the Christian pastor's sermon. "Everything was about his way of seeing Jesus," he said. "I have never been so worn down, my spirit broken." Jaami said he was offended that the pastor saw the opportunity to ask people to accept Jesus as their Savior. By the time it was over, the Dallas resident said, a ritual designed to bring comfort only added to his grief.

The number of interfaith families is growing, and many find that the funerals which bring them together also can pull them apart. The rate of intermarriages and conversions has skyrocketed in recent decades, creating families with members of different faiths including Christians, Jews, Buddhists, Muslims and many others. Though statistics on interfaith marriages are difficult to come by, a 1990 Jewish population survey found that fifty-two percent of Jews married people of other religions, but those numbers have been disputed. Still, it demonstrates a growing issue which concerns families, funeral directors, and religious leaders. The question is, "How will an American Christian pastor handle funeral services knowing that some of the family members are of other faiths?" Will a Catholic widow feel left out when her Jewish in-laws sit shiva, the seven-day mourning period? Can an interfaith couple find a cemetery that allows them to be buried together—and will both spouses be comfortable with that decision?

Interfaith situations like these raise the question about the purpose of the funeral service. Is it for the deceased or is it for the family? Since most of us (the premise of this book) feel it is for both, it becomes a tough balancing act. Funeral directors say that the growing number of interfaith families has made funerals a bit more difficult to plan. A typical planning meeting that used to take an hour and a half now runs closer to three hours, said Kelly Smith, spokesman for the National Funeral Directors Association in Brookfield, Wisconsin.

Some religious leaders say they make adjustments at funeral services to try to be sensitive to people of other faiths. Others, believing that it would compromise their theological integrity, will not budge. Sometimes there is no happy medium. A Unitarian minister conducting a funeral service for an atheist woman read the Twenty-third Psalm from the Old Testament. When her born-again grown children asked for something from the New Testament, the minister declined, citing that the funeral was for their atheist mother. They were not pleased.

One thing is certain—it is a bit of a conundrum. With the escalating numbers of interfaith marriages, it is a sure bet that the Christian clergy will continue to have to work through this issue more and more in the days to come. The issue may or may not be an area of tension and struggle to ministers and families and in the final analysis, the funeral director will give the obvious hard-counsel. Simply put, if the theological implications which cause a tension are too difficult to settle, then the person who is honoring the funeral bill is in charge. They make the decisions and the officiant must honor that individual's requests. If the minister cannot live within that tension, he/she should consider removing oneself from the relationship, and allow the family and/or funeral director to locate a clergy member or officiant who can satisfy the family's desires.

# MEMORIAL EFFORTS

## Video

In chapter five I discussed the value of music at a memorial service. Another spin on the use of music is the concept of a memorial video. I officiated at a service years ago where the next of kin had gathered a large selection of photos and had taken them to a local video person who arranged them and put meaningful background music to it. Today, many funeral homes are set up to accommodate these videos (i.e. big screen in their chapel), and most offer this service through a local merchant. The key to the success of this form of memorialization is operating within the tension of the urgent. This can be a heart-wrenching exercise to the next of kin at the actual time of death. Therefore, someone must take it upon himself to expedite this effort soon after the death, since generally there is a limited amount of time available. I have found that these videos represent well the high points of the life of the deceased and are generally effective and quite moving.

## Photo Collage

Another exercise which can be done quite easily by a group of family members or friends is to dig up the old photo albums and scrapbooks and assemble some of the significant memorabilia of the deceased individual's life into a collage to be displayed at the funeral home or church. Unlike the video, a photo collage can be put together rather quickly and is totally under the control of the family, eliminating the tyranny of the urgent. If cost is an issue, many funeral homes have easel stands for just this purpose and will help a family to facilitate this nice memento.

I have found that everyone genuinely appreciates this gesture since many of the people in attendance at a memorial service only knew the deceased in one short period of his/her life. To see pictures of a friend or colleague from youth and days gone by is always a special treat.

Another interesting by-product of this effort is that it begins the facilitation of the grieving process for those who are assembling the collage. Though it may hurt to do so, most would agree that it is a healthy experience of the grief work.

## Dates/Cards

> Anyone can be a friend when things are rosy; the time when friendship is needed most is when they're not.
>
> —Anonymous

When the death of a loved one occurs, it changes life forever. A vacuum is created. Any dependence within that relationship is gone. Eventually, whether we like it or not, the corner is turned and life goes on in a new way. Someone has said, "We never really get over it, but we do learn to live with it." And while we may learn to adapt, the memories still linger, especially at certain times. The date of death, birthdays, and anniversaries are all times which will spark the emotions of an individual regarding the loss of a loved one. This is quite normal.

Our modern times are often hectic, and it's all too easy to forget another's quiet grief in the hustle of our own lives. But by marking reminders throughout one's calendar, we can keep in mind our friends' and church members' needs for the months ahead. "A joy shared is multiplied; grief shared is grief divided."

Sending a thinking-of-you card at the appropriate time is a wonderful way to minister to people when they are hurting. Listen to these words from a griever:

Although flowers, lunch and service are important ways of showing you care, a card can be read in the middle of the night when sleep won't come or read again on a lonely morning. Words on a page can be wrapped around you like a warm hug, reminders that you care.

It is comforting to the griever to know that others are going through the difficult "first times" with them. Cards should carry a simple, encouraging tone. Notes need not be elaborate. Just say, "Thinking of you at this time," or share a happy memory of the deceased that is associated with the occasion. If a parent was lost, a note before Mother's Day or Father's Day can help them get past this holiday. In the loss of a child, send a card just before the date of the birthday. The first anniversary of a loved one's death should be commemorated. Invite a widow or widower to go to dinner with you on a wedding anniversary. Though the griever may decline, it's still good to let him/her know that you remember. The important thing is to send the clear message that "You're not alone."

## Funeral Etiquette

Things change. I remember when it was expected that people would dress up for a funeral service. Nowadays anything goes. Not only do young people honor their trends (leather, rings everywhere, multi-colored hair), but adults have adjusted too. Attire at a memorial service is much more casual now than in days gone by. Even jeans are accepted.

A writer to *Dear Abby*, reacting to her shock at the "lack of respect shown" (gaudy clothing), found this list in *Emily Post* regarding proper funeral etiquette. Dated perhaps, but you be the judge.

1. Don't be late.
2. Wear dark clothes.
3. Don't wear more black than the widow.
4. Wear minimal jewelry (wedding band, tasteful earrings, tie tack).
5. Humor is acceptable as long as it's tasteful and low-key.
6. If it is acceptable to the family, exes may attend or serve as pallbearers.

7.  Family members only are allowed to sit in the family section (no exes).
8.  The time for hugs and acknowledgments is when the family is receiving guests at the funeral home or at the cemetery—NOT as people pass by the coffin to pay their last respects to the deceased.
9.  Don't bring babies or unruly toddlers.
10. Don't get up and leave during the service.

I would add one more which I have experienced and is particularly relevant to our day. TURN OFF cell phones and pagers. It is a bad thing for phones to ring in the middle of a service. It is a very bad thing when it is the minister's pager or phone which goes off.

## The Future

Like any discipline, funeral practices are subject to changing trends. What the future holds, only time will tell. The year 2002 marked some events which represent the extremes within funeral service from which we can learn.

Early in the year, crematory owner/operator Ray Brent Marsh found himself at the center of a ghastly discovery in the pine woods of northern Georgia. It seemed Mr. Marsh, a youth football coach

*"I hate how informal everything has become."*

The New Yorker Collection © 1992
W.B. Park from cartoonbank.com.

and respected businessman in his community, was abusing the trust of his clientele at his local crematory. Instead of cremating bodies as contracted, he was leaving bodies wherever it was convenient. Hundreds of decaying or mummified bodies were found stacked in pits, caskets and above-ground vaults on the Marsh family property behind their business, the Tri-State Crematory. The newspaper reported that, "The towns-people were struggling to understand how he could have done such a thing and lived such an outwardly normal, respectable life." Pearl Goodloe, a longtime neighborhood friend, said that maybe Marsh was just desensitized to death after so many years around the crematorium, which was run for years by his parents. Mr. Marsh's father, Ray, was also implicated by authorities who said some of the discarded bodies had been on the family property 15 years, and possibly longer.

Mr. Neil Magnassen, assistant athletic director at the University of Tennessee at Chattanooga who had coached Marsh said, "He was one of those middle of the road, dependable kind of kids." We can only guess that something must have changed since his college football days.

In February of 2002, a "financially troubled" Southern California funeral home owner was accused of illegally dissecting corpses and selling the body parts to medical researchers at universities and pharmaceutical companies without the permission of family members, who believed their loved ones' remains were cremated. Michael Francis Brown, of Lake Elsinore, California, was charged with 156 felony counts for the unlawful mutilation of human remains and embezzlement. Riverside D.A. Karen Gorham said Brown had received about $400,000.00 for the body parts he sold in one year. The incident raised California awareness for the potential of this growing illegal industry.

It would be unfair to judge the funeral industry by the actions of these two radical examples. But it is safe to say that the practices of such individuals certainly contribute to a black-eye image of those who handle the dead. Of course, the up-side of these barbaric events is that at the state and national level, laws governing oversight of the funeral industry are sure to be tightened for the protection of the innocent—dead and living alike.

While Misters Marsh and Brown were busy taking the death business backward, second generation funeral director, Mr. Fred Fergerson, has been taking us all forward. Kelly Smith, of the Wisconsin-based National Funeral Directors Association said, "Death is different now than it was 50 years ago because family, friends and relatives are more scattered. The need for a different kind of service is greater." Mr. Fergerson, of Syracuse, N.Y., has proposed an answer to that challenge. His idea came out of the blue, after the death of an old high school friend's father. His friend, who lived on the West Coast, made funeral arrangements but could not come back when his dad died. Because of that incident, Ferguson began to webcast funerals on the Internet. "I went all over the internet on search engines," said the 52-year old

Fergerson, whose father started the business in 1948. "Nobody's doing it. To my knowledge, we're the only ones. I don't think there is going to be a big demand for it," he said. He is providing the service for free. "But we've got it if anybody wants it." Industry experts feel that others will follow, but just how quickly the trend might develop is unknown. It would seem that it will depend upon the reactions of the consumers, and how quickly those in the funeral business get online. Since most of the consumers who make funeral decisions are still a generation different from the computer generation, it may be that this trend-setting paradigm will be a bit behind the curve when compared with other e-commerce services.

# Epilogue

A strange thing happened one day when I was officiating at a graveside service. The family of the deceased had been delayed in getting to the cemetery which meant the service was late getting started. Our funeral director was in a tizzy. His firm had scheduled a number of services back to back, and he was supposed to be the FDIC (Funeral Director In Charge) at the next service which was to begin in a short time in one of the other chapels in their memorial park. He was in a jam. Because we were close friends, he also knew that at one time I had been a licensed funeral director. Forever to be unknown by his employers, he did the unthinkable. He asked me to wear two hats, and he left. I received the family when they came, had them all sign the registration book, presided over the service, presented them the American flag, gave them information about paying their funeral bill, took the honorarium, thanked them, and helped them into their car as they drove off. I could have jumped on the backhoe and filled the grave, but enough was enough.

I do not recommend wearing more than one hat because it greatly confuses the people, and they should always see each of the callings as distinct. They are, however, joined at the hip. Funeral directors should understand what it is to be the clergy officiant. The clergy should understand the role of the funeral director and his changing industry. Clearly, we must work in harmony if we are to serve our families well.

# CHAPTER TEN

# Helpful Aids

## HEAVENLY MUSIC

*"Malcolm W. Dunlap, violin repairs. Malcolm,
we are so pleased to see you."*

In my Father's house are many mansions: if it were not so I would have told you. I go to prepare a place for you. And if I go and prepare a place for you, I will come again, and receive you unto myself; that where I am, there ye may be also.

—John 14:2–3

Hymnody has made a great theological contribution in the realm of comfort for the suffering. The focus of every believer is that after this life we shall be with Jesus. Especially relevant are hymns that focus on that which awaits God's faithful children—heaven. Following is a sampling of lyric poetry, along with an extensive list of hymns.

## The Sands of Time Are Sinking

The sands of time are sinking, the dawn of heaven breaks
The summer morn I've sighed for, the fair, sweet morning awakes;
Dark, dark hath been the midnight; but dayspring is at hand
And glory, glory dwelleth in Immanuel's land

O Christ, He is the fountain, the deep, sweet well of love!
The streams on earth I've tasted, more deep I'll drink above:
There to an ocean fullness, His mercy doth expand
And glory, glory dwelleth in Immanuel's land.

O I am my Beloved's, and my Beloved's mine
He brings a poor vile sinner into His "house of wine."
I stand upon His merit; I know no other stand,
Not e'en where glory dwelleth, in Immanuel's land.

The Bride eyes not her garment, but her dear Bridegroom's face;
I will not gaze at glory, but on my King of grace
Not at the crown He giveth, but on His pierced hand.
The Lamb is all the glory of Immanuel's land.

—Anne Ross Cousin

## We're Marching to Zion

Come, we that love the Lord, and let our joys be known;
Join in a song with sweet accord, join in a song with sweet accord
And thus surround the throne, and thus surround the throne.

Let those refuse to sing who never knew our God;
But children of the heavenly King, but children of the heavenly King
May speak their joys abroad, may speak their joys abroad

The hill of Zion yields a thousand sacred sweets
Before we reach the heavenly fields, before we reach the heavenly fields
Or walk the golden streets, or walk the golden streets.

Then let our songs abound and every tear be dry;
We're marching through Immanuel's ground,
we're marching through Immanuel's ground
To fairer worlds on high, to fairer worlds on high.

We're marching to Zion, beautiful, beautiful Zion
We're marching upward to Zion, the beautiful city of God.

—Isaac Watts

## There Is a Land of Pure Delight

There is a land of pure delight, where saints immortal reign;
Infinite day excludes the night, and pleasures banish pain.
There everlasting spring abides, and never withering flowers;
Death, like a narrow sea, divides this heavenly land from ours.
Sweet fields beyond the swelling flood stand dressed in living green;
So to the Jews old Canaan stood, while Jordan rolled away.
O could we make our doubts remove, those gloomy doubts that rise,
And see the Canaan that we love with unbeclouded eyes;
Could we but climb where Moses stood, and view the landscape o'er,
Not Jordan's stream, nor death's cold flood, should fright us from the shore.

—Isaac Watts

## Around the Throne of God in Heaven

Around the throne of God in heaven thousands of children stand.
Children whose sins are all forgiven, a holy, happy land.
In flowing robes of spotless white see every one arrayed,
Dwelling in everlasting light and joys that never fade.
What brought them to that world above, that heaven so bright and fair
Where all is peace, and joy, and love; How came those children there?
Because the Savior shed His blood to wash away their sin;
Bathed in that pure and precious flood, behold them white and clean,
On earth they sought the Savior's grace, on earth they loved His name
So now they see His blessed face, and stand before the Lamb,
Saying, "Glory, glory, glory be to God on high."

—Anne H. Shepherd

## No Night There

In the land of fadeless day lies the city foursquare;
It shall never pass away, and there is no night there.
All the gates of pearl are made in the city foursquare;
All the streets with gold are laid, and there is no night there.
And the gates shall never close to the city foursquare;
There life's crystal river flows, and there shall be no night there.
There they need no sunshine bright, in that city foursquare;
For the Lamb is all the light, and there is no night there.
God shall wipe away all tears; there's no death, no pain, no fears;
And they count not time by years; for there is no night there.

—John R. Clements

## Beyond the Sunset

Beyond the sunset, O blissful morning, when with our Savior heaven is begun;
Earth's toiling ended, O glorious dawning, beyond the sunset, when day is done.
Beyond the sunset, no clouds will gather, no storms will threaten, no fears annoy;
O day of gladness, O day unending, beyond the sunset, eternal joy!
Beyond the sunset a hand will guide me to God, the Father, whom I adore;
His glorious presence, His words of welcome, will be my portion on that fair shore.
Beyond the sunset, O glad reunion, with our dear loved ones who've gone before;
In that fair homeland we'll know no parting, beyond the sunset for evermore!

—Virgil P. Brock

## While With Ceaseless Course The Sun

While with ceaseless course the sun hasted through the former year,
Many souls their race have run, never more to meet us here:
Fixed in an eternal state, they have done with all below;
We a little longer wait, but how little none can know.

As the winged arrow flies speedily the mark to find,
As the lightning from the skies darts, and leaves no trace behind,
Swiftly thus our fleeting days bear us down life's rapid stream;
Upward, Lord, our spirits raise, all below is but a dream.

Thanks for mercies past receive; pardon of our sins renew;
Teach us henceforth how to live with eternity in view;
Bless Thy Word to young and old; fill us with a Savior's love;
And when life's short tale is told, may we dwell with Thee above.

—John Newton

## There Is No Night in Heaven

There is no night in heaven; in that blest world above
Work never can bring weariness, for work itself is love.
There is no grief in heaven; for life is one glad day;
And tears are of those former things which all have passed away.
There is no sin in heaven; behold that blessed throng;
All holy is their spotless robe, all holy is their song.
There is no death in heaven; for they who gain that shore
Have won their immortality, and they can die no more.
Lord Jesus, be our guide; O lead us safely on,
Till night and grief and sin and death are past, and heaven is won!

—Francis M. Knollis

## When We All Get to Heaven

Sing the wondrous love of Jesus, sing His mercy and His grace;
In the mansions bright and blessed, He'll prepare for us a place.
While we walk the pilgrim pathway, clouds will overspread the sky;
But when traveling days are over, not a shadow, not a sigh.
Let us then be true and faithful, trusting serving every day;
Just one glimpse of Him in glory will the toils of life repay.
Onward to the prize before us! Soon His beauty we'll behold;
Soon the pearly gates will open, we shall tread the streets of gold.
When we all get to heaven, what a day of rejoicing that will be;
When we all see Jesus, we'll sing and shout the victory!

—E.E. Hewitt

## In Addition

Ring the Bells of Heaven . . . . . . . . . . . . . . . . . . . . . . . . . . . . . . . . .William O. Cushing
On Jordan's Stormy Banks
The Promised Land . . . . . . . . . . . . . . . . . . . . . . . . . . . . . . . . . . Dr. Samuel Stennett
Heaven . . . . . . . . . . . . . . . . . . . . . . . . . . . . . . . . . . . . . . . . . . . . . . . .J. Staphan
The Grapes of Canaan
Realms of Glory . . . . . . . . . . . . . . . . . . . . . . . . . . . . . . . . . . . . . . . . Thomas Kelly
There Is A Land of Pure Delight
When I Can Read My Title Clear
Joyful Work For You . . . . . . . . . . . . . . . . . . . . . . . . . . . . . . . . . . . Isaac Watts
Enter to Thy Rest . . . . . . . . . . . . . . . . . . . . . . . . . . . . . . . . . . . .Jane Taylor
O My Sweet Home . . . . . . . . . . . . . . . . . . . . . . . . . . . . . . . . . Francis Quarles
Where the Gates Swing Outward Never
O That Will Be Glory . . . . . . . . . . . . . . . . . . . . . . . . . . . . . Charles H. Gabriel
My Father Is Rich In Houses And Lands . . . . . . . . . . . . . . . . . . . . . . Harriet E. Buell
Jerusalem, My Happy Home . . . . . . . . . . . . . . . . . . . . . . . . . . Anonymous
I'm Just A Poor, Wayfaring Stranger . . . . . . . . . . . . . . . American Folk Hymn
Love Divine, So Great and Wondrous . . . . . . . . . . . . . . . . . . . Frederick A. Blom
I Belong to The King . . . . . . . . . . . . . . . . . . . . . . . . . . . . . . . . Ida R. Smith
Come, Come Ye Saints . . . . . . . . . . . . . . . . . . . . . . . . . . Avis B. Christiansen

Face to Face with Christ My Savior . . . . . . . . . . . . . . . . . . . . . .Carrie E. Breck

Shall We Gather at the River . . . . . . . . . . . . . . . . . . . . . . . Robert Lowry

Finally Home . . . . . . . . . . . . . . . . . . . . . . . . . . . . . . . Don Wyrtzen

My Home, Sweet Home . . . . . . . . . . . . . . . . . . . . . . . . . N.B. Vandall

Sweet By And By . . . . . . . . . . . . . . . . . . . . . . . . . . . Sanford F. Bennett

A Few More Years Shall Roll . . . . . . . . . . . . . . . . . . . . Horatius Bonar

When the Roll Is Called Up Yonder . . . . . . . . . . . . . . . . . . . . . James M. Black

Safe in the Arms Of Jesus

What a Gathering . . . . . . . . . . . . . . . . . . . . . . . . . . . . . Fannie Crosby

The Unclouded Day . . . . . . . . . . . . . . . . . . . . . . . . . . .Rev.J.K. Alwood

I Will Not Be a Stranger . . . . . . . . . . . . . . . . . . . . . . . .James B. Singleton

How Beautiful Heaven Must Be . . . . . . . . . . . . . . . . . . . . . . . . A.P. Bland

Where We'll Never Grow Old . . . . . . . . . . . . . . . . . . . . . James C. Moore

Jerusalem the Golden . . . . . . . . . . . . . . . . . . . . . . . . . Bernard of Cluny

Beulah Land . . . . . . . . . . . . . . . . . . . . . . . . . . . . . Edgar Page Stites

Meet Me There . . . . . . . . . . . . . . . . . . . . . . . . . . . . .Henrietta E. Blair

Dwelling in Beulah Land . . . . . . . . . . . . . . . . . . . . . . . . . C. Austin Miles

The Home Over There . . . . . . . . . . . . . . . . . . . . . . . . . D.W. Huntington

Heaven Is Calling Me Home . . . . . . . . . . . . . . . . . . . . . .Marion W. Easterling

I'm Going Home . . . . . . . . . . . . . . . . . . . . . . . . . . . William Hunter

Ten Thousand Times Ten Thousand . . . . . . . . . . . . . . . . . . . . . Henry Alford

In Heaven Above . . . . . . . . . . . . . . . . . . . . . . . . . Laurenitus Laurentii Laurinus

Then I Saw a New Heaven and New Earth . . . . . . . . . . . . . . . . . Christopher M. Idle

Whose Builder and Maker Is God . . . . . . . . . . . . . . . . . .John R. Clements

At Eventide . . . . . . . . . . . . . . . . . . . . . . . . . . . . . . . .B.B. McKinney

Goodnight and Good Morning . . . . . . . . . . . . . . . . . . . . . Lizzie DeArmond

Some Bright Morning . . . . . . . . . . . . . . . . . . . . . . . . . Charlotte G. Homer

Sunrise . . . . . . . . . . . . . . . . . . . . . . . . . . . . . . . . . . . . W.C.Poole

Heaven Is My Home . . . . . . . . . . . . . . . . . . . . . . . . . . . Thomas Taylor

# THE POETRY OF HEAVEN

Heaven is a place where most people want to reside at the conclusion of this present life. This section of poetry serves to demonstrate the extent to which the hope and contemplation of heaven can direct the lives of those who seek for a city whose builder and maker is God.

## Not Half Has Ever Been Told

I have read of a beautiful city, far away in the kingdom of God;
I have read how its walls are of jasper, how its streets are all golden and broad:
In the midst of the street is life's river, clear as crystal and pure to behold,
But not half of that city's bright glory to mortals has ever been told.
I have read of bright mansions in heaven, which the Saviour has gone to prepare;
And the saints who on earth have been faithful, rest forever with Christ over there;
There no sin ever enters, nor sorrow, the inhabitants never grow old;
But not half of the wonderful story to mortals has ever been told.
I have read of white robes for the righteous, of bright crowns which the glorified wear,
When our Father shall bid them "Come, enter, and My glory eternally share."
How the righteous are ever more blessed as they walk thro' the streets of pure gold;
But not half of the wonderful story to mortals has ever been told.
I have read of a Christ so forgiving, that vile sinners may ask and receive
Peace and pardon for every transgression, if one asking only believe.
I have read how He'll guide and protect us, if for safety we enter His fold;
But not half of His goodness and mercy to mortals has ever been told.
Not half has ever been told; not half has ever been told;
Not half of that city's bright glory to mortals has ever been told.

—John Burch Atchinson

## No Disappointment in Heaven

There's no disappointment in heaven, no weariness, sorrow or pain;
No hearts that are bleeding and broken, no song with a minor refrain.
The clouds of our earthly horizon will never appear in the sky,
For all will be sunshine and gladness, with never a sob nor a sigh.
We'll never pay rent for our mansion, the taxes will never come due;
Our garments will never grow threadbare, but always be fadeless and new.
We'll never be hungry nor thirsty, nor languish in poverty there,
For all the rich bounties of heaven His sanctified children will share.
There'll never be crepe on the door-knob, no funeral train in the sky;
No graves on the hillsides of glory, for there we shall never more die.
The old will be young there forever, transformed in a moment of time;
Immortal we'll stand in His likeness, the stars and the sun to outshine.
I'm bound for that beautiful city my Lord has prepared for His own;
Where all the redeemed of all ages sing "Glory!" around the white throne;
Sometimes I grow homesick for heaven, And the glories I there shall behold:
What a joy that will be when my Saviour I see, in that beautiful city of gold!

—F.M. Lehman

## I Want To Go There

They tell of a city far up in the sky, I want to go there, I do;
'Tis built in the land of "the sweet by and by," I want to go there, don't you?
There Jesus has gone to prepare us a home, I want to go there, I do;
Where sickness nor sorrow nor death ever come, I want to go there, don't you?
Its gates are all pearl, its streets are all gold, I want to go there, I do;
The Lamb is the light of that city, we're told, I want to go there, don't you?
Death robs us all here, there none ever die, I want to go there, I do;
Where loved ones will never again say goodbye, I want to go there, don't you?
When the old ship of Zion shall make her last trip, I want to be there, I do;
With heads all uncovered to greet the old ship, I want to be there, don't you?
When all the ship's company meet on the strand, I want to be there, I do;
"With songs on our lips and with harps in our hands," I want to be there, don't you?
When Jesus is crowned the Kings of all kings, I want to be there, I do;
With shouting and clapping till all heaven rings, I want to be there, don't you?
Hallelujah! we'll shout again and again, I want to be there, I do;
And close with the chorus, Amen, and Amen, I want to be there, don't you?

—Rev. D. Sullins

## Gathering Home

Up to the bountiful Giver of life, gathering home! gathering home!
Up to the dwelling where cometh no strife, The dear ones are gathering home.
Up to the city where falleth no light, gathering home! gathering home!
Up where the Savior's own face is the light, The dear ones are gathering home.
Up to the beautiful mansions above, gathering home! gathering home!
Safe in the arms of His infinite love, The dear ones are gathering home.
Gathering home! gathering home! Never to sorrow more, never to roam;
Gathering home! gathering home! God's children are gathering home!

—Mrs. Mariana B. Slade

## Rest for the Weary

In the Christian's home in glory, there remains a land of rest;
There my Savior's gone before me, to fulfill my soul's request.
He is fitting up my mansion, which eternally shall stand,
For my stay shall not be transient, In that holy, happy land.
Pain and sickness never shall enter, grief nor woe my lot shall share;
But, in that celestial center, I a crown of life shall wear.
Death itself shall then be vanquished, and his sting shall be withdrawn;
Shall for gladness, oh, ye ransomed! Hail with joy the rising morn.
There is rest for the weary, there is rest for the weary,
There is rest for the weary, there is rest for you.
On the other side of Jordan, In the sweet fields of Eden,
Where the tree of life is blooming, there is rest for you.

—William Hunter

## I Never Saw a Moor

I never saw a moor, I never saw the sea;
Yet know I how the heather looks, and what a wave must be.
I never spoke with God, nor visited in Heaven;
Yet certain am I of the spot as if the chart were given.

—Emily Dickinson

## The Father's House

No, not cold beneath the grasses, nor close-walled within the tomb;
Rather, in our Father's mansion, living in another room.
Living like the one who loves me, like my child with cheek abloom,
Out of sight, at desk or school book, busy in another room.
Nearer is my love, whom fortune beckons where the strange lands loom;
Just behind the hanging curtains, serving in another room.
Shall I doubt my Father's mercy? Shall I think of death as doom?
Or the stepping o'er the threshold to a bigger, brighter room?
Shall I blame my Father's wisdom? Shall I sit enswathed in gloom?
When I know my loves are happy, waiting in another room.

—Robert Freeman; John 14:2

## Epilogue

One who never turned his back but marched breast forward,
Never doubted clouds would break,
Never dreamed, though right were worsted, wrong would triumph,
Held we fall to rise, are baffled to fight better, sleep to wake.

—Robert Browning

At the end of his life, Robert Browning wrote *Epilogue* and asked that it conclude all his published works as a testimony to his faith.

## I'm a Pilgrim

I'm a pilgrim, and I'm a stranger; I can tarry, I can tarry but a night!
Do not detain me, for I am going to where the streamlets are ever flowing.
Of that city, to which I journey; My Redeemer; my Redeemer is the light;
There is no sorrow, nor any sighing, nor any tears there, nor any dying:
There the sunbeams are ever shining, oh, my longing heart,
my longing heart is there;
Here in this country, so dark and dreary, I long have
wandered forlorn and weary.

—Author Unknown

221

## The Things in the Cabinet Drawer

There are whips and tops and pieces of string and shoes that no little feet ever wear;
There are bits of ribbon and broken wings and tresses of golden hair;
There are dainty jackets that never are worn, there are toys and models of ships;
There are books and pictures all faded and torn, and marked by fingertips
Of dimpled hands that have fallen to dust—yet we strive to think that the Lord is just.
Yet a feeling of bitterness fills our soul; sometimes we try to pray,
That the Reaper has spared so many flowers and taken ours away.
And sometimes doubt if the Lord can know how our riven hearts did love them so.
But we think of our dear ones dead, our children who never grow old,
And how they are waiting and watching for us in the city with streets of gold;
And how they are safe through all the years from sickness and want and war.
We thank the great God, with falling tears, for the things in the cabinet drawer.

—Anonymous

## With Our Sympathy

After the tempest—calm,
After the shadow—light,
And the golden dawn breaks clearly.
After the long, long night,
After the rain, the sunshine,
After the tears, the laughter—
And when this life is over, life eternal follows after.

—Author Unknown

## Afraid?

To feel the spirit's glad release? To pass from pain to perfect peace,
The strife and strain of life to cease? Afraid? Of that?
Afraid to see the Savior's face, To hear His welcome and to trace
The glory gleam from wounds of grace? Afraid? Of what?
A flash, a crash, a pierced heart, darkness, light, O heaven's art!
A wound of His a counterpart! Afraid? Of that?
To do by death what life could not, baptize with blood a stony plot,
Till souls shall blossom from the spot—Afraid? Of THAT?

—C.H. Hamilton

## A Boy Meets God

Look God: I have never spoken to You, but now I want to say, "How do you do." You see God, they told me You did not exist: And, like a fool, I believed all this. Last night from a shell hole I saw Your sky; I figured right then they had told me a lie. Had I taken the time to see the things You made, I would know they weren't calling a spade a spade. I wonder, God, if You would shake my hand; somehow I feel that You will understand. Strange, I had to come to this hellish place before I had time to see Your face. Well, I guess there isn't much more to say, But I am sure glad, God, I met You today. I guess the zero hour will soon be here, but I am not afraid since I know You are near. The signal—well, God, I will have to go; I love you lots, this I want you to know. Looks like this will be a horrible fight; who knows, I may come to Your house tonight. Though I wasn't friendly with You before, I wonder, God, if You would wait at the door. Look, I am crying, me shedding tears! I wish I had known You these many years. Well, I will have to go now, God. Goodbye—strange, since I met you, I am not afraid to die.

—Found on the body of a nineteen-year-old American soldier in Vietnam

## Safely Home

I am home in Heaven, dear ones; all's so happy, all's so bright!
There's perfect joy and beauty in this everlasting light.
All the pain and grief are over, every restless tossing past;
I am now at peace forever, safely home in Heaven at last.
Did you wonder I so calmly trod the Valley of the shade?
Oh! But Jesus' love illumined every dark and fearful glade.
And He came Himself to meet me in that way so hard to tread;
And with Jesus' arm to lean on, could I have one doubt or dread?
Then you must not grieve so sorely, for I love you dearly still;
Try to look beyond earth's shadows, pray to trust our Father's will.
There is work still waiting for you, so you must not idle stand;
Do your work while life remaineth, You shall rest in Jesus' land.
When that work is all completed, He will gently call you home;
Oh, the rapture of the meeting! Oh, the joy to see you come!

—Author unknown

## The Christian's Good-night

Sleep on, beloved, sleep and take thy rest;
lay down thy head upon thy Savior's breast;
We love thee well, but Jesus loves thee best—Good-night!
Calm is thy slumber as an infant's sleep; but thou shalt
take no more to toil and weep;
Thine is a perfect rest secure and deep—Good night!
Until the shadows of this earth are cast; until He gathers
in His sheaves at last;
Until the twilight gloom be overpast—Good night!
Until the Easter glory lights the skies; until the dead
in Jesus shall arise;
And He shall come, but not in lowly guise—Goodnight!
Until, made beautiful by Love Divine, Thou, in the
likeness of thy Lord shall shine,
And He shall bring that golden crown of thine—Good night!
Only "Good-night," beloved, not "Farewell";
a little while and all His saints shall dwell
In hallowed union indivisible—Good night!
Until we meet again before His throne, clothed in the
spotless robe He gives His own,
Until we know even as we are known—Good night!

—Sarah Doudney

## Someday, We Shall Understand

Not now, but in the coming years, It may be in the better land,
We'll read the meaning of our tears, And there, someday, we'll understand.
We'll catch the broken threads again and finish what here we began;
Heaven shall the mysteries explain, And then, ah then, we'll understand.
God knows the way, He holds the key. He guides us with unerring hand;
Sometime, with tearless eyes, we'll see; Yes there, up there, we'll understand,
Then trust in God through all thy days. Fear not, for He doth hold thy hand
Though dark the way, still sing and pray; Sometime, someday, we'll understand.

—El Nathan

## Heaven

I sit and think, when the sunset's gold
Is flushing river and hill and shore,
I shall one day stand by the water cold
And list for the sound of the boatman's oar.
I shall watch for a gleam of the flapping sail,
I shall hear the boat as it gains the strand.
I shall pass from sight with the boatman pale,
To the better shore of the spirit land.
I shall know the loved who have gone before,
And joyfully sweet will the meeting be,
When over the river, the peaceful river,
The angel of death shall carry me.

—N.A.W. Priest

## No Night in Heaven

No night shall be in Heaven; no gathering gloom
Shall o'er that glorious landscape ever come.
No tears shall fall in sadness o'er those flowers,
That breathe their fragrance through celestial bowers.

No night shall be in Heaven, no dreadful hour
Of mental darkness, or the tempter's power.
Across those skies no envious clouds shall roll,
To dim the sunlight of the raptured soul.

No night shall be in Heaven; no sorrow's reign,
No secret anguish, no corporeal pain;
No shivering limbs, no burning fever there;
No soul's eclipse, no winter of despair.

No night shall be in Heaven, but endless noon;
No fast declining sun, no waning moon;
But there the Lamp shall yield perpetual light,
'Mid pastures green, and waters ever bright.

—Anonymous

## Heaven At Last

Angel voices sweetly singing, Echoes through the blue dome ringing,
News of wondrous gladness bringing; Ah, 'tis heaven at last!

On the jasper threshold standing; Like a pilgrim safely landing
See, the strange bright scene expanding, Ah, 'tis heaven at last!

Sin forever left behind us, Earthly visions cease to blind us,
Earthly fetters cease to bind us, Ah, 'tis heaven at last!

Not a teardrop ever falleth, Not a pleasure ever palleth,
Song to song forever calleth; Ah, 'tis heaven at last!

Christ Himself the living splendor, Christ the sunlight mild and tender;
Praises to the Lamb we render; Ah, 'tis heaven at last!

—Horatius Bonar

## Home to Glory

Jesus called her to Glory yesterday,
Bringing His daughter home, forever to stay.
The trial she has borne these several years
Brings heavenly passage, not continual tears.
The grace she received from her Sovereign Lord
Was reflected in her life pointing heavenward.
Not a sinless saint, but as one who loves Jesus,
Striving to please Him and be a witness to us.
May God bless her offspring, in grace fruit-bearing,
Then beyond the grave, heaven's home-sharing.

—Furbur Jolle

## Conviction

I believe; therefore, celebrate my journey
to be with Jesus and all the saints.
At my death, make it so.

—Request of Commander William Nicholas Morgan

## The Beautiful Land

Full oft do I dream of the Beautiful Land
That lies over the mystical river.
And my soul seems to follow the beckoning hand
That guides me along till my forehead seems fanned
By the breeze which is fragrant forever.

And the sorrows of earth, like a hideous dream,
Dissolve in the sunlight of heaven.
And I wander by many a radiant stream,
Whose musical waters flash back in the gleam
Of a day that fades not into even.

And magical blooms that are wondrously fair
Lie spread out like visions before me.
And a spell of enchantment is borne on the air
That steals from the heart every shadow of care,
And sheds sweet tranquility o'er me.

There mercy and Love wander, hand clasped in hand,
And Faith twines her wreath of 'Mortelles.
And the sky—by God's rainbow of tenderness spanned
Reflects on its bosom the Beautiful Land
Its angels and glittering portals.

—Anonymous

## A Day of Sunny Rest

There is a day of sunny rest
For every dark, and troubled night;
And grief may bide an evening quest
But joy shall come with morning light.
For God hath marked each sorrowing day
And numbered every secret tear,
And Heaven's long age of bliss shall pay
For all His children suffer here.

—William Cullen Bryant

## Little Angels

When God calls little children to dwell with Him above
We mortals sometimes question the wisdom of His love.
For no heartache compares with the death of one small child,
Who does so much to make our world seem wonderful and mild.
Perhaps God tires of calling the aged to His fold,
And so He picks a rosebud before it can grow old.
God knows how much we need them, so He takes but a few,
To make the land of Heaven more beautiful to view.
Believing this is difficult, still somehow we must try,
The saddest word mankind knows will always be, "Goodbye."
So when a little child departs, we who are left behind . . .
Must realize God loves children and angels are hard to find.

—Author unknown

## The Garden of Promise

There is a place, I have been told,
Beyond an open gate
Where all friends and loved ones wait
It holds eternal promise
Of everlasting peace
No pain or sorrow ever comes
And teardrops there have ceased
Abundant life is evident
Constant, fresh and new
A garden of provision
With eternity in view
The promise is awaiting
A place we can abide
Fulfilled for all who answer
The call to come inside

## In Another Room

No, not cold beneath the grasses,
Not close-walled within the tomb,
Rather in my Father's mansion,
Living in another room.

Living, like the one who loves me,
Like your child with cheeks abloom,
Out of sight, at desk or school-book,
Busy in another room.

Nearer than the youth whom fortune
Beckons where the strange lands loom,
Just behind the hanging curtain,
Serving in another room.

Shall I doubt my Father's mercy?
Shall I think of death as doom,
Or the stepping o'er the threshold
To a bigger, brighter room?

Shall I blame my Father's wisdom,
Shall I sit enswathed in gloom,
When I know my love is happy,
Waiting in another room?

—Robert Freeman

## When I Am Gone

Weep not for me when I am gone—life has just begun!
That which you've looked upon is just my dwelling, it is not I.
I've been but tenant, limited by slowing pace and dimming eye,
But now I see! Gloriously clear and brilliantly
No longer through a glass dimmed by sin and stubborn will,
No more the struggle with self and God's enemy.

Oh, rejoice with me for now I stand before Him who loved me eternally.
At last I am pure—holy—perfect—free;
As pure and holy as He—My Father, My Savior, My Wonderful Lord.
At last I've entered Home—no more a stranger wandering,
Intent of time with empty pleasures occupied.
At last I know full joy, perfect peace, eternal love.

Sing with gladness and rejoice for me,
Separated forever from pain and sadness,
Gathered into His wonderful presence there to sing
As I've always longed to sing.
There to praise as He deserves my praise.
There to serve as I never could have served while here.

Oh weep not for me, for I am at last with my Beloved.
Weep not when I've laid down the old to take up the New
Life everlasting, forever parted from sin.
If tears are shed let them be for those who have no hope.
If you sorrow let it be for those who recognize no need
For Jesus, God the Son, who offers such eternal life.

—Virginia Humphrey Davis

# POETRY

I wish our clever young poets would remember my homely definitions of prose and poetry; that is: prose = words in their best order; poetry = the best words in the best order.

—Samuel Taylor Coleridge

## The Day God Called You Home

We thought of you with love today, but that is nothing new
We thought about you yesterday, and the day before that too
We think of you with silence, and often speak your name
All we have now are memories, and your picture in a frame
Your memories are our keepsakes, with which we'll never part
God has you in His keeping; we have you in our hearts
It broke our hearts to lose you, but you did not go alone
A part of us went with you, the day God called you home

—Bonnie Ryerson

## A Lifetime Wish

If we could have a lifetime wish, a dream that would come true,
We'd pray to God with all our hearts for yesterday and you.
A thousand words can't bring you back, we know because we've tried
Neither will a thousand tears, we know because we've cried.
You left behind our broken hearts, and happy memories, too
But we never wanted memories, we only wanted you.

## Final Peace

When the writer of Revelation spoke of the coming of the day of shalom,
he did not say that on that day we would live at peace with death.
He said that on that day "There will be no more death or mourning
or crying or pain, for the order of things has passed away."

—Nicholas Wolterstorff; lament for a son

## Remembering A Friend

To my friend, God bless you, I'll see you in heaven anon
Where a friendship born on earth, In heaven will carry on
Until then, friend, Heaven's love, Via Con Dios from my heart
Where everything is held sacred, You'll always be a part
In a thousand ways dear friend, I'll remember through the days
The times we shared together, Then bowing down I'll pray
Giving my thanks to heaven, For a special friend and true
So once again, from my heart, Via Con Dios, to you.

## Oven-Fired Hope

Christian hope for life beyond death is a hope that has passed through
the furnace of suffering and death. Christians affirm the good news
of Easter only in the wake of Good Friday. Our hope for everlasting
life permits no evasion of death's hard reality.

—Amy Plantinga Pauw

## Funeral Wisdom

Better than baptisms or marriages, funerals press the noses
of the faithful against the windows of their faith . . .
The afterlife begins to make the most sense after life,
when someone we love is dead on the premises.

—Thomas Lynch, *The Undertaking*

## Mortal Knowledge

Everyone knows they're going to die . . . but nobody believes it.
If we did, we would do things differently. There's a better approach.
To know you're going to die, and to be prepared for it at any time.
That's better. That way you can actually be more involved
in your life while you're living.

—Morrie Schwartz; *Tuesdays with Morrie*

## Heavenly Banquet

Whoever does not have some foretaste of the heavenly banquet
will never partake of it.

—Johann Tauler

God saw her getting tired, and a cure was not to be
So He put His arms around her and whispered, "Come with me."
With tearful eyes we watched her, and saw her fade away.
Although we loved her dearly, we could not make her stay
A golden heart stopped beating, hard-working hands come to rest
God broke our hearts to prove to us, God only takes the best.

—Author Unknown

## Anonymous Confederate Soldier

I asked God for strength, that I might achieve,
I was made weak, that I might learn humbly to obey.
I asked for health, that I might do greater things,
I was given infirmity, that I might do better things.
I asked for riches, that I might be happy,
I was given poverty, that I might be wise.
I asked for power, that I might have the praise of men,
I was given weakness, that I might feel the need of God.
I asked for all things, that I might enjoy life,
I was given life, that I might enjoy all things.
I got nothing that I asked for—but everything I had hoped for.
Almost despite myself, my unspoken prayers were answered.
I am, among all men, most richly blessed.

## To Those I Love

If I should ever leave you whom I love to go along the Silent Way,
Speak of me not only with tears, but also laugh and talk of me as if I
were beside you there.
(I'd come, I'd come, could I but find a way!)
And when you hear a song or see a bird I loved,
please do not let the thought of me be sad
For I am loving you just as I always have . . . You were so good to me!
There are so many things I wanted still to do . . . so many things to say to you . . .
Remember that I did not fear . . . It was just leaving you that was so hard to face . . .
We cannot see beyond . . . but this I know, I loved you so—'twas heaven here
with you!

—Isda Paschal Richardson

## The Dash

I read of a man who stood to speak at the funeral of a friend.
He referred to the dates on her tombstone from the beginning . . . to the end.
He noted that first came the date of her birth and spoke of the following
date with tears, but he said what mattered most of all was the dash between
those years. For that dash represents all the time that she spent alive on earth . . .
and now only those who loved her know what that little line is worth. For
it matters not, how much we own; the cars . . . the house . . . the cash. What matters
most is how we live and love and how we spend our "dash." So thinking about
this long and hard . . . are there things you'd like to change? For you never know
how much time is left. (You could be at the "dash mid-range.") If we could
just slow down enough to consider what's true and real, and always try to
understand the way other people feel. And be less quick to anger, and show
appreciation more and love the people in our lives like we've never loved before.
If we treat each other with respect, and more often wear a smile . . . remembering
that this special dash might only last a little while. So, when your eulogy is
being read with your life's actions to rehash . . . would you be proud of the things
they say about how you spent your dash?

A corpse is something like the cover of an old book,
Its contents torn out, and stripped of its lettering
And gilding . . . yet the work itself shall not be lost, for
It will appear once more in a new and more beautiful edition.

—Benjamin Franklin

## Consolation

For those I love and those who love me, when I am gone,
release me, let me go. I have so many things to see and do.
You must not tie yourself to me with tears,
Be happy that we had so many beautiful years.
I gave my love, you can only guess how much you gave
to me in happiness. I thank you for the love we each have shown,
but now it's time I travel on alone. So grieve awhile for me,
if grieve you must, then let your grief be comforted by trust.
It's only for a while that we must part, so bless now, the memories
within your heart. I won't be far away, for life goes on.
So if you need me, call and I will come.
Though you can't see me, or touch me, I'll be near.
And if you listen with your heart you will hear all my love
around you, soft and clear. And then when you must come this
way alone, I'll greet you with a smile and "welcome home."

## I Remember, I Remember

In the Spring, when the first crocus pokes it's head out of the frozen ground
I think of you and I remember . . . I remember.
In the Summer, when the blaring heat wilts the rose petals
and paints unsightly cracks in the ground,
I think of you and I remember, I remember.
In the Autumn, when the trees are ablaze in the glory of Fall
and my shoes make crackling sounds as I walk,
I think of you and I remember, I remember
And in the Winter, when I stand at my window
to watch a blizzard whirl snow around my grief and loneliness
Then, too, I think of you and I remember, I remember.

—Joy Johnson

## Funeral Blues

Stop all the clocks, cut off the telephone
Prevent the dog from barking with a juicy bone
Silence the pianos, and with a muffled drum
Bring out the coffin, let the mourners come
Let the aero plane circle, morning overhead
Scribbling on the sky the message . . . he is dead
Put crepe bows around the white necks of the public doves
Let traffic policemen wear black cotton gloves
He was my north, my south, my east and west
My working week, my Sunday rest
My noon, my midnight, my talk, my song
I thought that love would last forever, I was wrong
The stars are not wanted now, put out every one
Pack up the moon and dismantle the sun
Put away the ocean and sweep up the wood
For nothing now can ever come to any good

—W.H. Auden


A good man never dies—
In worthy deed and prayer
And helpful hands, and honest eyes,
If smiles or tears be there;
Who lives for you and me—
Lives for the world he tries
To help—he lives eternally.
A good man never dies

—James Whitcomb Riley


Ah Christ, that it were possible
For one short hour to see
The souls we loved, that they might tell us
What and where they be.

—Tennyson

All mankind is of one Author, and is one volume;
when one man dies, one chapter is not torn out of
the book, but translated into a better language; and
every chapter must be so translated; God employs several
translators; some pieces are translated by age, some by sickness,
some by war, some by justice; but God's hand is in every translation,
and His hand shall bind up all our scattered leaves again for that
library where every book shall lie open to one another.

—John Donne


All our finite eyes could tell us
Was the sadness and the gloom
All the emptiness and silence
Of the sorrow stricken room;
But we could not see the welcome,
Could not hear the angels sing,
Nor the shouts of exaltation
As the pilgrims entered in.

—F. Norman Barrington


Angels, joyful to attend,
Hovering, round thy pillow bend;
Wait to catch the signal given,
And escort thee quick to heaven.
Saints in glory perfect made,
Wait thy passage through the shade;
Ardent for thy coming o'er,
See, thy throng the blissful shore.

—Augustus Toplady


Be near me, Lord, when dying;
O show thy cross to me;
And, for my succour flying,
Come, Lord to set me free;
These eyes, new faith receiving,
From thee shall never move;
For he who dies believing
Dies safely through thy love.

—Bernard of Clairvaux

Christ taught an astonishing thing about physical death:
Not merely that it is an experience robbed of its terror,
but that as an experience it does not exist at all. To "sleep
in Christ," "depart and be with Christ," "fall asleep,"—
these are the expressions the New Testament uses.
It is high time the "icy river," "the gloomy portal,"
"the bitter pains," and all the rest of the melancholy
images were brought face to face with the fact:
Jesus Christ has abolished death.

—J.B. Phillips

God calls our loved ones,
But we lose wholly
What He hath given;
They live on earth
In thought and deed
As truly in His heaven.

—John Greenleaf Whittier

Has this world been so kind to you
that you would leave it with regret?
There are better things ahead than
any we leave behind.

—C.S. Lewis

Is this the end? I know it cannot be,
Our ships shall sail upon another sea;
New islands yet shall break upon our sight,
New continents of love and truth and might.

—John White Chadwick

Jesus Christ alone is qualified to guide us into the vast unknown.
Since He is the only One who has returned from the grave,
He tells us accurately about life after death.

—Erwin W. Lutzer

Leaves have their time to fall,
And flowers to whither at the northwind's breath,
And stars to set—but all,
Thou hast all seasons for thine own,
O Death!

—Felicia Hemans


Of all the thoughts of God that are
Borne inward into souls afar,
Along the Psalmist's music deep,
Now tell me if there any is,
For gift or grace, surpassing this—
"He giveth His beloved sleep!"

—Elizabeth Barrett Browning


Shall I doubt my Father's mercy?
Shall I think of death as doom,
Or the stepping o'er the threshold
To a bigger, brighter room?

—Robert Freeman


Sleep on, beloved, sleep and take thy rest;
Lay down thy head upon thy Savior's breast;
We love thee well, but Jesus loves thee best—
Good night! Good night! Good night!

—Sarah Doudney


Someday you will read in the papers that D.L. Moody of
East Northfield is dead. Don't you believe a word of it.
At that moment I shall be more alive than now. I shall
have gone up higher, that is all—out of this old clay
tenement into a house that is immortal; a body that death
cannot touch, that sin cannot taint, a body fashioned like
unto His glorious body. That which is born of the flesh
may die. That which is born of the Spirit shall live forever.

—Dwight Lyman Moody

These eyes, new faith receiving,
From Jesus shall not move;
For he who dies believing,
Dies safely through thy love.

—Bernard of Clairvaux

When all is done, say not my day is o'er,
And that through night I seek a dimmer shore;
Say rather that my morn has just begun—
I greet the dawn and not a setting sun, when all is done.

—Paul Laurence Dunbar

When the friends we love the best
Lie in their churchyard bed,
We must not cry too bitterly
Over the happy dead.

—Cecil Frances Alexander

## Jesus of Nazareth Passeth By

Mourner, who sits in the church yard lone,
Scanning the lines on that marble stone,
Plucking the weeds from thy loved one's bed,
Planting the myrtle and the rose instead,
Look up from the tomb with thy tearful eye—
"Jesus of Nazareth" passeth by.

Stranger, afar from thy native land,
Whom no man takes with a brother's hand;
Table and hearthstone are lowing free,
Casements are sparkling, but not for thee;
There is One can tell of a home on high—
"Jesus of Nazareth" passeth by.

## I Remember

I remember coming to visit you, when I was very small
We'd give each other a hug and a kiss, and I'd go running down the hall.
I remember being at your house, sometimes staying a day or two.
You'd paint my nails, and talk of school, and I'd say, "Grandma, I love you."
I remember, as I was growing up, all the stories we would share.
If times got tough, you helped me out, for me, you were always there.
I remember, when I lived far away, how I'd call you on the phone.
We'd sit and chat for way too long, on how big the kids had grown.
I remember you asking me years ago, if I thought you were getting old.
I remember saying, "Oh, heavens no, for your hair is not yet gray, but gold."
I remember thinking way back then, "Take more time for them somehow."
And now I wish more than ever, that I knew then what I know now.
I remember though, that time did pass, and soon you were getting sick.
But you always had a smile for us, though life's timer had begun to tick.
I remember wondering where years had gone, and finally I figured out.
It's what God has planned for most of us, what growing old is all about.
I remember visiting Grandma, sitting patiently in her chair.
I held her hand and prayed to God, that she knew that I was there.
I remember saying, "Grandma, I love you," when you were ill.
I pray to God you heard me, though you laid so very still.
I remember my tears falling on your pillow, as I held your hand and cried.
God was soon to take you from us, leaving angels as your guide.
I remember hoping that over all the years, that I hadn't forgotten to say,
"You've been the most wonderful Grandma," then you began to slip away.
I remember saying goodbye to you, as I held your sleeping face.
You had quietly entered Heaven above, resting peacefully in God's place.
I remember thinking to myself, on how much I'll miss her love.
But then joyfully it dawned on me, she's now with Grandpa up above.

—Leslie Marae Skjordal

## We Are Seven

A simple child,
That lightly draws its breath,
And feels its life in every limb,
What should it know of death?

I met a little cottage girl:
She was eight years old, she said;
Her hair was thick with many a curl
That clustered round her head.

She had a rustic, woodland air,
And she was wildly clad:
Her eyes were fair, and very fair;
Her beauty made me glad.

"Sisters and brothers, little Maid,
How many may you be?"
"How many? Seven in all," she said
And wondering looked at me.

"And where are they? I pray you tell."
She answered, "Seven are we;
And two of us at Conway dwell,
And two are gone to sea.

"Two of us in the church-yard lie,
My sister and my brother;
And, in the church-yard cottage, I
Dwell near them with my mother."

"You say that two at Conway dwell,
And two are gone to sea,
Yet ye are seven!—I pray you tell,
Sweet Maid, how this may be."

Then did the little Maid reply,
"Seven boys and girls are we;
Two of us in the church-yard lie,
Beneath the church-yard tree."

"You run about, my little Maid,
Your limbs they are alive;
If two are in the church-yard laid,
Then ye are only five."

"Their graves are green, they may be seen,"
The little Maid replied,
"Twelve steps or more from my mother's door,
And they are side by side.

"My stockings there I often knit,
My kerchief there I hem;
And there upon the ground I sit,
And sing a song to them.

And often after sunset, Sir,
When it is light and fair,
I take my little porringer,
And eat my supper there."

"The first that died was sister Jane;
In bed she moaning lay,
Till God released her of her pain;
And then she went away.

"So in the church-yard she was laid;
And, when the grass was dry,
Together round her grave we played,
My brother John and I.'

"And when the ground was white with snow,
And I could run and slide,
My brother John was forced to go,
And he lies by her side."

"How many are you, then, "said I,
"If they two are in heaven?"
Quick was the little Maid's reply,
"O Master! We are seven."

But they are dead; those two are dead!
Their spirits are in heaven!"
'Twas throwing words away: for still
The little Maid would have her will,
And said, "Nay, we are seven!"

—William Wordsworth

## I Love You

I love you—not only for what you are
But for what I am when I am with you
I love you—not only for what you have made of yourself,
But what you are making of me. I love you for the part of me that you bring out.
I love you—for putting your hand into my heaped up heart,
And passing over all the weak, foolish things that you can't help dimly seeing there;
And for drawing out into the light all the beautiful belongings
That no one else had looked quite far enough to find.
I love you—because you are helping me to make of the lumber of my life
Not a tavern, but a temple out of the words of my everyday
Not a reproach, but a song.
I love you—because you have done more than any creed could have done
To make me good, and more than any fate could have done to make me happy.
You have done it without a touch, without a word, without a sign.
You have done it by being yourself. Perhaps that is what being a
friend means after all.

—Ray Croft

## When We Two Parted

When we two parted in silence and in tears,
Half broken hearted to sever for years
Pale grew thy cheek and cold, colder thy kiss;
Truly that foretold hour sorrow to this!
They name thee before me, a knell to mine ear,
A shudder comes o'er me—why wert thou so dear?
Who knew thee too well, long, long shall I rue thee,
Too deeply to tell.
In secret we met, in silence I grieve,
That my heart could forget thy spirit deceive.
If I should meet thee—after long years,
How should I greet thee? With silence and tears.

—Lord Byron

## The Chain

We knew little that morning,
God was going to call your name,
In life we loved you dearly,
In death we do the same.
It broke our hearts to lose you,
You did not go alone,
For part of us went with you
The day God called you home.
You left us beautiful memories,
Your love is still our guide,
And though we cannot see you,
You are always by our side.
Our family chain is broken
And nothing seems the same,
But as God calls us one by one,
The chain will link again.

## Fallen Asleep in Jesus

Fallen asleep in Jesus! How precious is that word!
Enjoying now forevermore the presence of the Lord.
This is not death! 'tis only sleep;
The Lord doth now thy loved one keep.

The earthen vessel's broken, the Treasure now has flown,
The Lord hath taken back again what is by right His own.
But when He takes what most we store,
It is that He may give thee more.

Thou wouldst have gladly kept her a little longer here,
To soothe, and nurse, and cherish, and make her wants thy care.
But He who doeth what is best,
Hath called her to Himself to rest.

As members of one body in sympathy we weep,
And yet rejoice, because we know in Jesus she doth sleep.
For all her pain and sufferings o'er;
And joy her portion evermore.

'Tis not "Good-bye," beloved, 'tis only just "Farewell."
A little while, a moment, we too with Christ shall dwell.
And so we dry the falling tear,
Because we know the Lord is near.

O, may the God of comfort His richest grace impart!
Himself fill up the aching void, bind up thy broken heart;
And give thee now to look above,
And rest in His unchanging love.

## Miss You, Miss You, Miss You

Miss you, miss you, miss you; everything I do
Echoes with the laughter and the voice of you.
You're on every corner, every turn and twist
Every old familiar spot whispers how you are missed.
Miss you, miss you, miss you! Everywhere I go
There are poignant memories dancing in a row.
Silhouette and shadow of your form and face,
Substance and reality everywhere displace.
Oh, I miss you, miss you Gad, I miss you, girl.
There's a strange sad silence 'mid the busy whirl.
Just as though the ordinary daily things I do
Wait with me, expectant, for a word from you.
Miss you, miss you, miss you, nothing now seems true.
Only that 'twas heaven just to be with you.

## Take Time

If I knew it would be the last time that I see you walk out the door
I would give you a hug and a kiss and call you back for one more
And just in case I might be wrong, and today is all I get
I'd like to say how much I love you and I hope we never forget
Tomorrow is not promised to anyone, young or old alike
And today may be the last chance you get to hold your loved one tight
So if you're waiting for tomorrow, why not do it today?
For if tomorrow never comes, you'll surely regret the day
That you didn't take that extra time for a smile, a hug, or a kiss
And you were too busy to grant someone what turned out to be their one last wish
So hold your loved ones close today, whisper in their ear
Tell them how much you love them and that you'll always hold them dear
Take time to say, "I'm sorry," "Please forgive me," "Thank you," or "It's okay."
And if tomorrow never comes, you'll have no regrets about today

## To a Friend

You entered my life in a casual way, and saw at a glance what I needed;
There were others who passed me or met me each day,
but never a one of them heeded.
Perhaps you were thinking of other folks more, or chance simply seemed to decree it;
I know there were many such chances before, but the others—well they didn't see it.
You said just the thing that I wished you would say, and you made
me believe that you meant it;
I held up my head in the old gallant way, and resolved you should never repent it.
There are times when encouragement means such a lot, and a
word is enough to convey it;
There are others who could have, as easy as not, but, just the same, they didn't say it.
There may have been someone who could have done more
to help me along, though I doubt it.
What I needed was cheering, and always before they had let me plod
onward without it.
You helped me to refashion the dream of my heart, and made me turn eagerly to it;
There were others who might have (I question that part)—
but after all, they didn't do it.

—Grace S. Dawson

## Friend

Many know the word of "Friend," but it is given to few.
To know and have the kind of friend that I have found in you.
Friendship needs no symbol, or vow to make it whole;
It's just a sacred covenant that's locked within the soul;
It knows no creed or station or thought of gain or fame,
For what it does is sacred and is done in Friendship's name.

## Honor

No man was ever honored for what he received.
Honor has been the reward for what he gave.

—Calvin Coolidge

## The Best is Yet to Come

There was a woman who had been diagnosed with a terminal illness and was given three months to live. As she was "getting her things in order," she had her pastor come to her house to discuss certain aspects of her final wishes. She told him which songs she wanted at her service, what Scriptures she wanted to be read, and what outfit she wanted to be buried in. She also requested to be buried with her favorite Bible. Everything was in order and the pastor was preparing to leave when the woman remembered something very important. "This is very important," the woman continued. "I want to be buried with a fork in my right hand." The pastor looked at the woman, not knowing what to say. "That surprises you, doesn't it?" the woman asked. "I'm puzzled by the request," said the pastor. The woman explained, "In all my years of attending church socials and potluck dinners, I always remember that when the dishes of the main course were being cleared, someone would inevitably lean over and say, "Keep your fork." It was my favorite part because I knew that something better was coming . . . like velvety chocolate cake or deep-dish apple pie. Something wonderful and with substance! So I just want people to see me there in the casket with a fork in my hand and I want them to wonder "What's with the fork?" Then I want you to tell them: "Keep the fork . . . the best is yet to come." The pastor's eyes welled up with tears of joy as he hugged the woman good-bye. He knew this would be one of the last times he would see her before her death. But he also knew that the woman had a better grasp of heaven than he did. She knew that something better was coming. At the funeral people were walking by the woman's casket and they saw the pretty dress she was wearing and her favorite Bible and the fork placed in her right hand. Over and over, the pastor heard the question "What's with the fork?" And over and over he smiled. During his message, the pastor told the people of the conversation he had with the woman shortly before she died. He also told them about the fork and what it symbolized to her. The pastor told the people how he could not stop thinking about it either. He was right. So the next time you reach down for your fork, let it remind you oh so gently, that "THE BEST IS YET TO COME."

## Think

of stepping on shore, and finding it heaven!
of taking hold of a hand, and finding it God's hand,
of breathing a new air, and finding it celestial air
of feeling invigorated, and finding it immortality,
of passing from storm and tempest to an unbroken calm,
of waking up, and finding it Home

## Untitled

One ship sails east and one sails west, with the very same wind that blows
It's the set of the sail and not of the gale that determines the way it goes.
And as the waves of the sea . . . so are the waves of fate,
as you journey along through life
It's the set of the soul that determines the goal,
not the storms and the strife

## And Your Praise Goes On

And when my final breath you lend
I'll thank you for the life you gave
But that won't mean the praises end
'Cause I won't be silenced by the grave
And your praise goes on
I'll be running to your throne
With every nation tribe and tongue
To your arms I'll fly
I'll gaze into your eyes
Then I'll know as I am known
And Your praise goes on!

—Chris Rice

## The Ship

I am standing upon the seashore. A ship at my side spreads her white sails in the morning breeze and starts for the blue ocean. She is an object of strength and beauty, and I stand and watch her until she is only a ribbon of white cloud where the sea and the sky seem to mingle with each other. Then someone at my side says, "There, she's gone!" Gone? Gone where? Gone from my sight, that's all. She is just as complete in mast and hull and spar as she was when she left my side, and just as able to bear her precious freight to the place of destination. Her diminished appearance is in me—not in her. And at the very moment when someone at my side says, "There, she's gone!" other voices shout with gladness, "Here she comes!" And that is death. Death is only a horizon, and a horizon is the limit of our sight.

## Untitled

Life is but a stopping place, a pause in what is to be
A resting place along the road to sweet eternity
We all have different journeys, different paths along the way
We all were meant to learn some things, but never meant to stay
Our destination is a place far greater than we know
For some the journey is quicker, For some the journey is slow
And when the journey finally ends we'll claim a great reward
And find an everlasting peace . . . together with the Lord

## Miss Me, But Let Me Go

When I come to the end of the day and the sun has set for me
I want no rites in a gloom-filled room, why cry for a soul set free?
Miss me a little, but not too long, and not with your head bowed low
Remember the love we once shared—Miss me, but let me go
For this is a journey we all must take, and each must go it alone
It's all a part of the Maker's plan, a step on the road to home
When you are lonely and sick at heart, go to the friends we know
And bury your sorrows in doing good deeds—Miss me, but let me go

## Now the Laborer's Task Is Over

Now our friend's task is over, now the busy day is past
Upon the farther shore lands _____ at last
There the tears of earth are dried, there the hidden things are clear
There the work of life is tried, by a juster judge than here
Father in Thy gracious keeping leave we now_____ sleeping
There no more the power of hell to mar their peace
Christ the Lord shall guard them well, He who died for their peace,
Christ the Lord shall guard them well, He who died for their release,
Father in Thy gracious keeping, leave we now _____ sleeping
Ashes to ashes, dust to dust, calmly now words we say
Leaving _____ to sleep in trust, 'til the resurrection day
Father in Thy gracious keeping, leave we now _____ sleeping

## First Christmas In Heaven

I see the countless Christmas trees around the world below
With tiny lights like heaven's stars reflecting on the snow
The sight is so spectacular, please wipe away the tear
For I am spending Christmas with Jesus Christ this year

I hear the many Christmas songs that people hold so dear
But the sounds of music can't compare with the Christmas choir up here
I have no words to tell you the joy their voices bring
For it is beyond description to hear the Angels sing

I know how much you miss me, I see the pain inside your heart
But I am not so far away, we really aren't apart
So be happy for me dear one, you know I hold you dear
And be glad I'm spending Christmas with Jesus Christ this year

I send you a special gift from my heavenly home above
I send you a dear memory of my true undying love
After all, "love" is the gift more precious than pure gold
It was always most important in the stories Jesus told

Please love and keep each other as my Father said to do
For I can't count the blessings or love He has for you
So have a Merry Christmas and wipe away that tear
Remember I am spending Christmas with Jesus Christ this year

## Untitled

God gives us each a gift of life, to cherish from our birth
He gives us friends and those we love, to share our days on earth
He watches us with loving care and takes us by the hand
He blesses us with countless joys and guides the lives we've planned
And when our work on earth is done, He calls us to His side
To live with Him in happiness, where peace and love abide

## You Will Fly

He knows you're weary but you've got to play your part
And though thin may be your soles and endless seems the trail
When nothing's left to lose, when you think you've failed
Seek the beauty you possess and let God do the rest
He'll get you there and see you through, He'll be the wings upon your shoes
So leave your burdens in the sky, and triumphantly you will fly

## A Dream

High o'er the city in a tiny cell
My view is entrancing—water and isle
Here in my dotage I chose to dwell
A fine place for dreaming—to rest awhile
Yearning again for those beautiful things
A hot summer morning
To hear a meadow lark sing
Hushed so soon by a hawk's harsh warning
Small trout flipping—shining
In a tree darkened pool
Low hills carpeted in autumn glow
Scent of mown grass in evening cool
Honeysuckle fragrance on soft twilight breeze
Sail and sweep of gulls a-wing
Sleepy cheeps from nests in trees
Soft stringed music all lilt and swing
If then I'm faithful these things that I love
Will be all around me in some space far above—

## Worth

We can curse the fate that made us or love each living hour
If we do the job God gave us be we humble weed or flower
For each of us is needed, and each of us has worth
Or He never would have bothered to honor us with birth

## Please

Please, don't ask me if I'm over it yet . . . I'll never be over it
Please, don't tell me she's in a better place . . . she isn't here with me
Please, don't say at least she isn't suffering . . . I haven't come to
terms with why she had to suffer
Please, don't tell me you know how I feel, unless you have lost a child
Please, don't ask me if I feel better . . . Bereavement isn't a condition that clears up
Please, don't tell me at least you had her for so many years . . .
What year would you choose for your child to die?
Please, don't tell me God never gives us more than we can bear . . .
Please, just say you're sorry
Please, just say you remember my child, if you do
Please, just let me talk about my child
Please, mention my child's name
Please, just let me cry

—Rita Moran

## An Irish Melody

I wish I was in Carrick Fergus only for nights in Bally Grand
I would swim all over the deepest ocean, the deepest ocean to be by your side
Well I'm drunk today and I'm seldom sober, a handsome rover from town to town
But I am sick now, my days are numbered, So come all ye young men and
lay me down
So come all ye young men and lay me down

## An Irish Blessing

May the road rise to meet you,
May the wind be always at your back,
May the sun shine warm upon your face,
And the rains fall soft upon your fields.
And, until we meet again, may God
Hold you in the palm of His hand.

## When Life's Cut Short

Our life of service to the Lord
Bears fruit long after we are gone
So even if our life's cut short
Our work for Christ will carry on

—David Sper

## God Hath Not Promised

God hath not promised skies always blue
Flower-strewn pathways all our lives through
God hath not promised sun without rain
Joy without sorrow, peace without pain
But God hath promised strength for the day
Rest for the labor, Light for the day
Grace for the trials, Help from above
Unfailing sympathy, Undying love

## Untitled

Yesterday is but a memory and tomorrow only a vision.
But today well lived makes every yesterday a memory
of happiness, and every tomorrow a vision of hope.
Some people come into our lives and quickly go
Some stay for a while and leave footprints on our hearts . . .
We are never the same

## Afterglow

I'd like the memory of me to be a happy one
I'd like to leave an after glow of smiles when life is done
I'd like to leave an echo whispering softly down the ways,
Of happy times and laughing times and bright and sunny days
I'd like the tears of those who grieve to dry before the sun
Of happy memories that I . . . leave when life is done

## Footprints

One night a man had a dream. He was walking along the beach with the Lord, and across the sky flashed scenes from his life. In each scene, he noticed two sets of footprints in the sand; one made by him, and the other by the Lord. When the last scene of his life flashed before him, he looked at the footprints in the sand, and noticed that many times along the path of his life there was only one set of footprints. He also noticed that it happened at the worst times of his life. This bothered him, so he asked the Lord about it.

"Lord, You said that once I decided to follow You, You'd walk with me all the way. But I've noticed that during times of trouble there is only one set of footprints. I don't understand why you left me when I needed You most." The Lord replied, "My precious child, I love you and would never leave you. During your times of trouble where you see only one set of footprints, I was carrying you."

—Margaret Powers

## All Is Well

Death is nothing at all
I have only slipped away into the next room
I am I and you are you
Whatever we were to each other
That we still are
Call me by my old familiar name
Speak to me in the easy way which you always used
Put no difference into your tone
Wear no forced air of solemnity or sorrow
Laugh as we always laughed at the little jokes we enjoyed together
Play, smile, think of me, pray for me
Let my name be ever the household word that it always was
Let it be spoken without effect
Without the trace of a shadow on it
Life means all that it ever meant
It is just the same as it ever was
There is absolutely unbroken continuity
Why should I be out of mind because I am out of sight?
I am but waiting for you . . . for an interval
Somewhere very near . . . just around the corner
All is well

—Canon Henry Scott Holland, of St. Paul's Cathedral

## Untitled

Those who have passed from this world die
only when we, whom they loved, forget them

What a wee little part of a person's life are his acts and his words! His real life is led in his head, and is known to none but himself. All day long, the mill of his brain is grinding, and his thoughts, not those other things, are his history. These are his life, and they are not written, and cannot be written. Every day would make a whole book of 80,000 words—365 books a year. Biographies are but the clothes and buttons of the man—the biography of the man himself cannot be written.

—Mark Twain

## A Soldier's Prayer

Lord, bless the wives who grieve alone
And comfort the mothers who mourn their own
Give solace to the fathers who lost their sons
On foreign shores and in places unknown
Lord, strengthen the resolve of we who remain
To see that they did not die in vain

—Major General James B. Middleton

## Surprise in Heaven

I dreamed I went to heaven
And the pearly gates did open wide
An angel with a halo bright . . . ushered me inside
And there to my astonishment
Stood folks I had labeled as "quite unfit"
And of "little worth" and spiritually disabled
Indignant words rose to my lips
But never were set free
For every face showed stunned surprise
No one expected me!

—Harriet Kirby

## Ode to Fred Bennett

An Irish head quite old and grey, is sent to the pulpit most Lord's days
The body is weak and the flesh trembles so, a trial from God for
this journey below
A box is set up to raise up nigh, those precious words, to read he'll try
The Scriptures are opened, enlivened and clear, as the prophets of old
resound quite near
The body is blessed coming face to face, with the Word of Jehovah
for a chosen race
Bennett's that man so often seen, proclaiming the path to our Sovereign King
The text is closed, the eye looks around for a tormented sinner now cast down
A brother edified might be seen in that place, to whom the spirit
manifested Holy grace
The aged man used of God, to direct His Kingdom, a voice His rod
A brother assists Bennett back down the stair, the two together, a red-haired pair
His beloved Hazel awaits in the pew, a more serving wife is known by few
We are grateful to God for the breath of the man, He's equipped him
well to work in "His land"

—Lorie Ann Glover

## Be Still and Know

Be still, and know that I am God, where you now tread, I too have trod
I know your griefs—I have a part, I know the anguish of your heart
Did I not walk the toilsome road, a wanderer, without abode?
Did I not stand in Pilate's hall, though innocent, hear judgment fall?
Did I not hang on yonder tree at Golgotha, to die for Thee?
Did I not break the bars away, on that first Resurrection Day?
Ah, yes, my friend, I've journeyed far, to break the might of death's cold bar
'Twas all for you I paid the price, for you, I made such sacrifice
In me, you'll find your source of power, to gird you in this trying hour
Let not your heart then troubled be, believe in God, and so in Me
Where you now tread, I too have trod, be still and know that I am God

## The Perfect Passing

If I should leave this world without a warning
And not even whisper a fond farewell
Grieve not for one more message
From the lips that God has stilled
But just remember me with love
And prayers for my soul's journey
To that fair land beyond life's tears
For I have believed with all my heart
In its existence and I know
That God is good, for He has come to me
Through the life of Him whose very garment I have sought to touch
It may be lonely and I hope you miss me
Just a little, because I have loved so deeply
My own family and faithful friends
Forgive if I have ever hurt you
And remember me for what I longed to be
Have faith that I am nearer than your dreams and fondest longings
For the God of love shall keep all kindred spirits
Close together, though the misty vale between
This world and that to come
Keep us from each other's sight for a few precious moments
Whisper softly that you love me
And it shall linger on within my soul until you come
Say not goodbye, for on some bright tomorrow we shall meet again

## Untitled

Lonely is the home without you
Life to us is not the same
All the world would be like heaven
If we could have you back again

—Anonymous

## Mother I Miss You

Is it me, or have I deceived myself
I thought I heard you call my name out in the pouring rain
I really thought . . . I thought I saw your face
But after a second look I saw
I made a clear mistake
Mother I miss you
And nights I just wish you were here with me
So we can laugh and talk again
Mother I miss you
But I'll just kiss you and send it on the wind
'Cause you know I plan to see you again
So much I wanted to show you
So much I wanted to give
I thought our time would be much longer
I miss my best friend
Mother I miss you
And nights I just wish you were here with me
So we can laugh and talk again
Mother I miss you
But I'll just kiss you and send it on the wind
'Cause you know I plan to see you again

## Meditation

I would do well not to think of the Red Sea of difficulties
that lie ahead. I am sure that when I come to the Red Sea,
the waters will part and I will be given all the power I need to
face and overcome many difficulties and meet what is in store
for me with courage. I believe that I will pass through the
Red Sea to the Promised Land, the land of the spirit where many
souls meet in perfect comradeship. I believe that when that time
comes I will be freed of all dross of material things and find peace.

## Who Will Take Grandma?

Who will take grandma? Who will it be?
All of us want her, I'm sure you agree
Let's call a meeting; let's gather the clan
Let's get it settled as fast as we can
In such a big family, there's certainly one
Willing to give her a place in the sun
Strange how we thought she'd never wear out
But see how she walks, It's arthritis no doubt
Her eyesight is faded, her memory is dim
She's apt to insist on the silliest whim
When people get older, they become such a care
She must have a home, but the question is where?
Remember the days when she used to be spry?
Baked her own cookies and made her own pies
Helped with lessons, mended our seams
Kissed away our troubles and tended our dreams
Wonderful Grandma, we all loved her so
Isn't it dreadful, she's no place to go?
One little corner is all she would need
A shoulder to cry on, her Bible to read
A chair by the window, with sun coming through
Some pretty spring flowers still covered with dew
Who'll warm her with love, so she won't mind the cold
Oh who will take Grandmother, now that she's old?
What: nobody wants her? Oh yes there is one
Willing to give her a place in the sun,
Where she won't be our problem to worry about
Pretty soon now, God will give her a bed
But who'll dry our tears, when dear Grandma is dead?

I'm leaving here a name, I trust,
That will not perish in the dust

—Robert Southey

## Mother

You painted no Madonnas
On chapel walls in Rome;
But, with a touch diviner,
Upon the walls of home.
You wrote no lofty poems
The world pronounces art;
But, with a nobler genius,
You put poems in my heart.
You carved no shapeless marble
To symmetry divine;
But, with a finer sculpture,
You shaped this soul of mine.
Had I the gift of Raphael,
Or Michaelangelo,
Ah, what a rare Madonna
My Mother's life should show!

—T.W. Fessenden

## The Burial of Sir John Moore

Not a drum was heard, not a funeral note
As his corpse to the rampart we hurried
We buried him darkly at dead of night
The sod with our bayonets turning
But he lay like a warrior taking his rest
With his martial cloak around him
Few and short were the prayers we said
And we spoke not a word of sorrow
But we steadfastly gazed on the face that was dead
And we bitterly thought of the morrow
We carved not a line, and we raised not a stone
But we left him alone with his glory

—Charles Wolfe

# A Loaf of Mother's Bread

I have heard them speak of biscuits,
"Like my mother used to bake."
I have heard them tell of cookies,
Apple pie and angel cake;
But for good old joy of eating
When the hungry must be fed,
I'll just take some homemade butter
And a loaf of Mother's bread.

There was love that went in the mixing
And the kneading of the dough.
There was care that went in the watching,
That the fire burned just so.
There was hearty satisfaction,
When she took them, golden brown,
From the oven to the table
And there turned them upside down.

There she greased them well with butter,
Bottom, sides and tops and ends;
And to see them there a-cooling,
Was like greeting old time friends.
I'd give a baker's dozen
Of loaves which now I spread,
For a bit of homemade butter
And a loaf of Mother's bread

—W. Earlington Whitney

# Death of Sir Albertus Moreton's Wife

He, first deceased; she for a little tried
To live without him: liked it not, and died

—Sir Henry Wotton

## Mother

When I think of the childhood days
I can see you there
Doing all those many things
With tender love and care
You treated me so special
Taught me values true
I am glad God gave to me a
Mother such as you.

## Untitled

I lost a grandma with a heart of gold
Who was more to me than wealth untold
Without farewell she fell asleep
With only memories for me to keep
I have lost, but God has gained
One of the best grandmas the world contained
Her heart was the truest in all the world
Her love the best to recall
For none on earth can take her place
She is still the dearest grandma of all
If she could have spoken before she died,
These are the words she would have replied
This life for me has truly passed
I've loved you to the very last
Weep not for me, but courage take
And love one another for my sake

## Prayer for the Day

I pray that I may face the future with courage
I pray that I may be given strength to face both life and death fearlessly

## A Poem by Scotty

Thanks for letting me visit your world
Walk on your lawn, play in your fields
Your world is a private place I know
Where the big crowds fade and spirits grow
So mine was a treat, a rare delight
A chance to escape, to spend the night
To share your warmth and friendly smile
To hike your hills and ski a mile

## Their Journey's Just Begun

Don't think of them as gone away—their journey's just begun
Life holds so many facets—this earth is only one
Just think of them as resting from the sorrows and the tears
In a place of warmth and comfort where there are no days or years
Think how they must be wishing that we could know, today,
How nothing but our sadness can really pass away
And think of them as living in the hearts of those they touched . . .
For nothing loved is ever lost—and they were loved so much

## Untitled

Not for him but for us should our tears be shed,
Mourn, mourn, for the living, but not for the dead.
Let the dirge be unsung, and awaken the psalm,
No cypress for him who lies crowned with the palm.

That which we call death is like the going down into a great ship
to sail away to some rich and historic clime.
But the Divine stands upon the prow, the Divine hand holds the helm,
the Divine chart marks the voyage, the Divine mind knows where the
distant harbor is!

—Anonymous

## The Day God Called You Home

God looked around His garden and found an empty place.
He then looked down upon earth and saw your tired face.
He put His arms around you, and lifted you to rest.
God's garden must be beautiful, for He always takes the best.
He knew that you were suffering; He knew you were in pain,
He knew that you would never get well on earth again.
He saw the road was getting rough, and the hills were hard to climb.
So He closed your weary eyelids, and whispered, "Peace be Thine."
It broke our hearts to lose you, but you didn't go alone,
For part of us went with you the day God called you home.

## Choose Thou Not for Me

I dare not choose my lot, I would not if I might
Choose Thou for me, my God, so shall I walk upright
The Kingdom that I seek is Thine; so let the way
That leads to it be Thine, else surely I might stray
Take Thou my cup and it with joy or sorrow fill
As best to Thee may seem, choose Thou my good and ill
Choose Thou for me my friends, my sickness or my health
Choose Thou my cares for me, my poverty or wealth
Not mine—not mine the choice, in things both great and small
Be Thou my guide, my strength, my wisdom and my all

—Horatius Bonar

## The Future

There's an unknown path before me, and yet I fear it not
I know through all the years gone by, what e'er has been my lot
That a kind and Heavenly Father planned out the way for me
And I know that in the future, watched over I shall be
Yes, I know God's care and kindness will ever with me stay
To assist me on life's journey, and brighten up my way
So then, welcome, unknown future, bring me whate'er you will
With God's loving hand to guide me, I shall be cared for still!

—Cora Baker Hall

## Progress

Until I learned to trust, I did not learn to pray
And I did not learn to fully trust, Till sorrows came my way
Until I felt my weakness, His strength I never knew
Nor dreamed till I was stricken, that He would see me through
Who deepest drinks of sorrow, drinks deepest too of grace
He sends the storm so He Himself, can be our hiding place
His heart that seeks our highest good knows well when things annoy
We would not long for heaven, If earth held only joy

—Anonymous

## God's Unchanging Word

For feelings come and feelings go, and feelings are deceiving
My warrant is the Word of God, naught else is worth believing
Though all my heart should feel condemned for want of some sweet token
There is one greater than my heart, whose Word cannot be broken
I'll trust in God's unchanging Word till soul and body sever
For, though all things shall pass away, His Word shall stand forever

—Martin Luther

## Untitled

I would rather have a little rose from the garden of a friend
Than flowers strewn around my casket when my days on earth must end
I would rather have a living smile from one I know is true
Than tears shed 'round my casket when this world I bid adieu
Bring me all the flowers today, whether pink or white or red
I would rather have one blossom now than a truckload when I am dead

## The Dissolution of Mr. Fox

A power is passing from the earth, to breathless nature's dark abyss
But when the great and good depart, what is it more than this . . .
That man, who is from God sent forth, doth yet again to God return?
Such ebb and flow must ever be, then wherefore should we mourn?

—William Wordsworth

## The King of Love

The King of love my shepherd is, whose goodness faileth never
I nothing lack if I am His and He is mine forever
Where streams of living water flow, my ransomed soul He leadeth
And where the verdant pastures grow, with food celestial feedeth
Perverse and foolish oft I strayed, but yet in love He sought me
And on His shoulder gently laid, and home, rejoicing, brought me
In death's dark vale I feel no ill, with Thee, dear Lord, beside me
Thy rod and staff they comfort sill, Thy cross before to guide me
And so through all the length of days, Thy goodness faileth never;
Good Shepherd, may I sing Thy praise, within Thy house forever

—Henry W. Baker

## Adonais

It might make one in love with death,
To think that one should be buried in so sweet a place.

—Percy Bysse Shelley

## Goodby, Till Morning

"Goodby, till morning come again."
We part, if part we must, with pain,
But night is short, and hope is sweet,
Faith fills our hearts, and wings our feet;
And so we sing the old refrain,
"Goodby, till morning come again."

"Goodby, till morning come again,"
The thought of death brings weight of pain.
But could we know how short the night
That falls, and hides them from our sight,
Our hearts would sing the old refrain,
"Goodby, till morning come again."

## He Takes My Hand

She's just a little kiddie who walks by her mother's side,
And she'd rather go out walking than to take a little ride
She likes to skip and hop along, to run ahead and wait
For mother to catch up to her down by the garden gate
But sometimes when they go walking it gets hard for her to stand
And when the road gets rocky, she says, "Mother, take my hand."
It's all right when paths are easy, for her to skip along
But when it's getting hard to walk she wants a hand so strong
To reach down and take hold of hers, to help her find the way
"Mother, mother, hold my hand," is what you'll hear her say
I guess that we're all children, sometimes the way is bright
Then we like to run along; but when the day grows night
When the shadows lengthen, when the sky is overcast
Or when we walk the valley, when the day is done at last
I think that we shall reach right up, I know He'll understand
And we'll cry like weary children, "Lord Jesus, take my hand."
I know that He will reach right down to help us in our need
For when we cannot help ourselves He'll always intercede
Then when the journey's over and we stand on yonder strand
Methinks that we shall ask again, "Lord Jesus, take my hand."

—Louis Paul Lehman, Jr.

## Crossing the Bar

Sunset and evening star, and one clear call for me
And may there be no moaning of the bar, when I put out to sea
But such a tide as moving seems asleep, too full for sound and foam
When that which drew from out the boundless deep, turns again home
Twilight and evening bell, and after that the dark
And may there be no sadness of farewell, when I embark
For tho' from out our bourne of time and place, the flood may bear me far
I hope to see my Pilot face to face . . . when I have crossed the bar!

—Alfred Tennyson

## He Looked at Me with Love

I sat lonesome and forlorn, weary and without hope
Jesus walked by and He looked at me with love
I stood tired and worn crying before His cross
He looked down at me and smiled through His pain
I lay tossing and turning unable to fall asleep
He said, "Call out my name and I will give you rest."
I walked a far distance and my body ached with pain
He saw me as I faltered and fell and He reached out a gentle hand
I lay dying on my bed, His angels came and bore me up
They carried me with gentle hands into the presence of My Lord and
laid me at His feet

—John Baird

## Two Precious Boxes

I have in my hand two boxes, which God gave me to hold
He said, "Put all your sorrows in the black, and all your joys in the gold."
I heeded His words, and in the two boxes both my joys and sorrows I store
But though the gold became heavier each day, the black was as light as before
With curiosity, I opened the black, I wanted to find out why
And I saw, in the base of the box, a hole which my sorrows had fallen out by
I showed the hole to God, and mused aloud, "I wonder where my sorrows could be."
He smiled a gentle smile at me, "My child, they're all here with me."
I asked, "God, why give me the boxes, why the gold, and the black with the hole?"
"My child, the gold is for you to count your blessings . . . the black is for you to let go."

—Anonymous

Under the wide and starry sky, dig the grave and let me lie
Glad did I live and gladly die, and I laid me down with a will
This be the verse you gave for me, "Here he lies where he longed to be
Home is the sailor, home from the sea, and the hunter home from the hill"

—Robert Louis Stevenson

## To My Sons

They say when you love someone . . . set them free
And if they love you enough, they will come back
I raised you to be free, so I'd never have to let you go
Which ever way you travel, whatever path you take
However you should choose to go . . . my love is always with you
But that you surely know.
Then as your journey's ebbing or your goal is finally near;
Just turn and look behind you, and know you started here
And when my time is over, and I have ceased to be
Please know I'll live forever . . . 'Cause part of you is me!

—Crystal Pelleg

## When I Am Dead

When I am dead, my dearest
Sing no sad songs for me
Plant thou no roses at my head
Nor shady cypress tree
Be the green grass above me
With showers and dewdrops wet
And if thou wilt, remember
And if thou wilt, forget

—Christina Georgina Rossetti

## The Death of a Physician

Who feels not thoughts within him rise,
At some beloved physician's name,
Which fill with brimming tears the eyes,
And waken memory's warmest claim?
In tenderest hours of life and death,
That healing friend is by our side,
Perhaps the last to catch our breath,
And whisper, "Jesus died."

## I'm Free

Don't grieve for me, for now I'm free, I'm following the path God has laid you see
I took His hand when I heard His call; I turned my back and left it all
I could not stay another day, to laugh, to love, to work or play
Tasks left undone must stay that way; I found the peace at the close of the day
If my parting has left a void, then fill it with remembered joys
A friendship shared, a laugh, a kiss . . . oh yes, these things I too will miss
Be not burdened with times of sorrow, I wish you the sunshine of tomorrow
My life's been full, I savored much, Good friends, good times, a loved one's touch
Perhaps my time seemed all too brief, don't lengthen it now with undue grief
Lift up your hearts, and peace to thee, God wanted me now; He set me free

## Ode on the Death of the Duke of Wellington

Bury the great Duke, with an empire's lamentation
Let us bury the great Duke to the noise of the mourning of a mighty nation

## The Promise of Resurrection

I went to a graveyard one day in late autumn
For the last loving rites of a friend who had gone
In the city of God was his spirit now singing
What triumph for him in eternity's dawn
There was many a tree in that place called "God's acre"
But motionless, gaunt and forbidding were they
Yes, lifeless and leafless those trees were appearing
As lifeless as those who not far from them lay
And I said to myself, "but the springtime is coming,
How glorious then these trees will appear,
Bejeweled with splendor in emerald verdure
To demonstrate God's living hope has come near"
And so it shall be this day with our brother
Whose body today to the grave we must bring
Resurrection's bright promise he'll surely be knowing
Through Christ, the life-giver . . . the maker of spring

272

## Litany of Remembrance

In the rising of the sun and it's going down . . . we remember them

In the blowing of the wind and in the chill of the winter . . . we remember them

In the opening of the buds and in the warmth of the summer . . . we remember them

In the rustling of the leaves and in the beauty of the autumn . . . we remember them

In the beginning of the year and when it ends . . . we remember them

When we are weary and in need of strength . . . we remember them

When we are lost and sick at heart . . . we remember them

When we have joys we yearn to share . . . we remember them

So long as we live, they too will live for they are now a part of us as . . .
we remember them

—From *The Gates of Prayer*

My prime of youth is but a frost of cares

My feast of joy is but a dish of pain

My crop of corn is but a field of tares

And all my good is but vain hope of gain

The day is past, and yet I saw no sun

And now I live, and now my life is done

—Chidiock Tichborne, written in the tower before his execution

## On His Brother's Death—Catullus

By ways remote and distant waters sped,

Brother, to thy sad grave-side am I come,

That I may give the last gifts to the dead,

And vainly parley with thine ashes dumb;

Since she who now bestows and now denies

Hath ta'en thee, hapless brother, from mine eyes.

But lo! These gifts, the heirlooms of past years,

Are made sad things to grace thy coffin shell;

Take them, all drenched with a brother's tears,

And, brother, for all time, hail and farewell!

## On Eternal Life

Whether we be young or old
Our destiny, our being's heart and home
Is with infinitude and only there;
With hope it is, hope that can never die,
Effort, and expectation, and desire,
And something evermore about to be

Sickness and sorrow come to us all
But through it we grow and learn to stand tall
For trouble is part and parcel of life
And no man can learn without struggle and strife
The more we endure with patience and grace
The stronger we grow and the more we can face

—Anonymous

## The Death of a Young Man

What though you grieve for him who passed today,
Untouched, in his young life, by sin or shame
Not yours the sorrow that one may not name,
The grief that eats so many hearts away,
The secret shame that makes a whole life gray,
The craves the sympathy it may not claim,
And sears the soul, as with a hidden flame!
No, you have clean sweet grief who mourn today!
How quickly blasted by life's flame are we
But death was kind to him—and tenderly
It kept him scatheless from the flame—he knew
Only the dawn! The freshness of the dew
Still lay upon the roses of his youth—
Aye, you know splendid sorrow here in truth!

—Roselle Mercier Montgomery

## If We Could Only Know

We are so prone to see only what souls (mankind) go from.
When our loved one dies we think of all delights of life.
All the sweet friendships, all the splendor of the sunlight . . .
if we could only know . . . the presence of God into which our friend
enters on the other side, the higher standards, the larger fellowship,
the new assurance of personal immortality in God; if we could only
know all this, how our poor comfortless effort of comfort when our
friends depart, our feeble raking over the ashes of memory, our
desperate struggles to think that the inevitable must be right;
how all this would give way to something almost like a burst of triumph,
as the soul we loved went forth to such vast enlargement, to such
glorious consummation of its life!

## The Open Door

You, my son have shown me God
Your kiss upon my cheek has made me feel
the gentle touch of Him who leads us on
The memory of your smile, when young,
reveals His face as mellowing years come apace.
And when you went before, You left the gates
of Heaven ajar that I might glimpse,
Approaching from afar . . . the glories of His grace.
Hold, son, my hand, Guide me along the path
That, coming, I may stumble not, nor roam,
nor fail to show the way . . . which leads us . . . Home.

—Grace Coolidge


Out of the dusk a shadow, Then a spark;
Out of the cloud a silence, Then, a lark;
Out of the heart a rapture, Then, a pain;
Out of the dead, cold ashes, Life again.

—John B. Tabb

## Days End

As I sat in the evening twilight
A wonderful dream I dreamed
I saw many angels in heaven
And old friends were there, too, it seemed
I saw there a beautiful garden
As I walked in the cool evening air
And there amidst all the flowers
Loved ones were waiting there
They turned as I drew nearer
As the breeze softly ruffled their hair
With a smile they came toward me
To greet and welcome me there
We all dream of bright tomorrows
And may all these dreams come true
For there will always be angels in heaven
And loved ones waiting there, too

Swing softly, beauteous gates of death,
To let a waiting soul pass on,
Achievement crowns life's purposes
And victory is forever won.
Swing softly, softly, heavenly gate,
Thy portal passed, no more to roam;
Our traveler finds her journey o'er,
And rest at last in "Home Sweet Home."
Even for the dead I will not bind
My soul to grief-death cannot long divide:
For is it not as if the rose that climbed
My garden wall had blossomed on the other side?
Death doth hide but not divide;
Beloved, thou art on Christ's other side.

—Alice B. How

Lord of all Light and Darkness
Lord of all Life and Death,
Behold, we lay in earth today
The flesh that perisheth.
Take to Thyself whatever may
Be not as dust and breath—
Lord of all Light and Darkness,
Lord of all Life and Death

—William Watson


Warm summer sun, shine kindly here
Warm southern wind, blow softly here.
Green sod above, lie light, lie light
Good night, dear heart, good night good night.

—Robert Richardson


## Beyond the Horizon

When men go down to the sea in ships,
'Tis not to the sea they go;
Some isle or pole the mariner's goal.
And thither they sail through calm and gale,
When down to the sea they go.
When souls go down to the sea by ship,
And the dark ship's name is Death,
Why mourn and wail at the vanishing sail?
Though outward bound, God's world is round,
And only a ship is Death.
When I go down to the sea by ship,
And Death unfurls her sail,
Weep not for me, for there will be
A living host on another coast
To beckon and give "All Hail!"

—Robert Freeman

## There Is No Death

There is no death! The stars go down
To rise upon some other shore,
And bright in heaven's jeweled crown
They shine forevermore.

There is no death! The forest leaves
Convert to life the viewless air;
The rocks disorganize to feed
The hungry moss they bear.

There is no death! the dust we tread
Shall change, beneath the summer showers,
To golden grain, or mellow fruit,
Or rainbow-tinted flowers.

And ever near us though unseen,
The dear immortal spirits tread,
For all the boundless universe
Is life—"there is no death."

—John Luckey McCreery

## The Monument

God before He sent His children to earth
gave each one of them a very carefully selected package of problems.
These, he promised, smiling, are yours alone.
No one else may have the blessings these problems will bring you,
and only you have the special talents and abilities that will be needed
to make these problems your servants.
Now go down to your birth and to your forgetfulness.
Know that I love you beyond measure.
These problems that I give you are a symbol of that love.
The monument you make of your life will be a symbol of
your love for Me.

—Anonymous

## The Victors

They have triumphed who have died;
They have passed the porches wide,
Leading from the House of Night
To the splendid lawns of light.
They have gone on that far road
Leading up to their abode,
And from curtained casements we
Watch their going wistfully.
They have won, for they have read
The bright secrets of the dead;
And they gain the deep unknown,
Hearing Life's strange undertone,
In the race across the days
They are victors; theirs the praise,
Theirs the glory and the pride
They have triumphed, having died!

—Charles Hanson Towne

# QUIPS AND ANECDOTES

Salt your food with humor, pepper it
with with wit and sprinkle over it the
charm of fellowship . . .
    —Samuel Butler the Younger

*"His underwear was spotless."*

## Obituary—The Pillsbury Doughboy

Veteran Pillsbury spokesperson Pop N.
Fresh died yesterday of a severe yeast
infection. Known to his friends
as Brown-N-Serve, Fresh was an avid
gardener and tennis player.

Fresh was buried in one of the largest funeral ceremonies in
recent years. Dozens of celebrities turned out including Mrs.
Butterworth, the California Raisins, Hungry Jack, Aunt Jemima,
Betty Crocker, the Hostess Twinkies, and Skippy.

The grave side was piled high with flours as longtime friend
Aunt Jemima delivered the eulogy, describing Fresh as a man
who "never knew how much he was kneaded."

Fresh rose quickly in show business, but his later life was filled
with many turnovers. He was not considered a very smart cookie,
wasting much of his dough on half-baked schemes-conned by
those who buttered him up. Still, even as a crusty old man,
he was a role model for millions.

Fresh is survived by his second wife. They have two children
and another bun in the oven. The funeral was held at 3:50 for about 20 minutes.

## Untitled

There is so much good in the worst of us
And so much bad in the best of us
That it hardly behooves any of us
To talk about the rest of us.

Here lies Lester Moore
Four shots from a forty-four
No less, no more.

—From the movie, *Tombstone*

## Fitz-Greene Halleck

Green be the turf above thee,
Friend of my better days!
None knew thee but to love thee
None named thee, but to praise.

## Obituary Notice

An actual obituary which appeared in a local newspaper; a photo of
the individual accompanied the notice. It is unique and demonstrates
an honest expression by the family to represent the individual's
life. The name and facts have been changed to protect anonymity.

Bob, 84, died July 16, 1998 in Orlando, Florida. Because of his
high school grades, he won a four-year scholarship to Smith College
in Kansas. He got his Master's in Sociology from Mississippi
State College. He was employed at the University of Brownsville,
one semester, but was fired because he wouldn't sign the loyalty
oath. Even then, he had fallen prey to the scourge of alcoholism
which had already snared his brother. By the time he finally went
on the wagon (stopped drinking), his life was a shambles and the pieces
were never successfully put back together. He is survived by . . .

This is an unusual obituary. It was written expressly for Jim's
youthful companions. After such a promising start on the road
to success, it explains why Bob could not live up to the hopes
and expectations of those around him.

## Enjoying Life

If the things for which we hunger with our age should interfere
Why not die a little younger and enjoy our life while we're here

## Untitled

To get the most out of life, think about your eulogy and work backward!

—Anonymous

## The Undertaker

Our undertaker is very smart
He doesn't need a dole
'Cause he is making money fast
When other folks are going in the hole

The death of a parent is the one misfortune for which there is no compensation.
—From the movie, *A Thousand Acres*

Q. What is the difference between an Irish wedding and an Irish wake?
A. One less celebrant

—Irish proverb

## The Hearse Song

Don't ever laugh as the hearse goes by
for you may be the next to die
They wrap you up in a big white sheet
from your head down to your feet
They put you in a big black box
and cover you up with dirt and rocks
All goes well for about a week,
and then your coffin begins to leak
The worms crawl in, the worms crawl out,
the worms play pinochle on your snout
They eat your eyes, they eat your nose,
they eat the jelly between your toes
A big green worm with rolling eyes
crawls in your tummy and out your eyes
Your stomach turns a slimy green,
and pus pours out like whipping cream
You spread it on a slice of bread,
and that's what you eat . . .
when you are dead.

—Unclaimed

# Notes

## CHAPTER 1 - DEATH

1. Bill & Teresa Syrios, Ecclesiastes: Chasing After Meaning (Downers Grove, IL: IVP, 1992), 37.
2. Derek Kidner, *A Time To Mourn And A Time To Dance: The Message of Ecclesiastes* (Downers Grove, IL: IVP, 1976).
3. Walter C. Kaiser, Jr., *Ecclesiastes: Total Life* (Chicago: Moody, 1979).

## CHAPTER 2 - THEODICY

1. R. C. Sproul, *The Invisible Hand: Do All Things Really Work For Good?* (Dallas: Word, 1997), 159–168.
2. Harold Kushner, *When Bad Things Happen To Good People* (New York: Shocken, 1981).
3. A. S. Peake, *Job: The Problem of the Book—Theodicy in the Old Testament*, ed. James L. Crenshaw (Philadelphia: Fortress, 1983).
4. Walter C. Kaiser, Jr., *A Biblical Approach to Personal Suffering* (Chicago: Moody, 1982) 121–129.
5. Paul Tournier, *Creative Suffering* (New York: Harper and Row, 1982).

6. Viktor E. Frankl, *Man's Search For Meaning: An Introduction To Logotherapy,* (New York: Simon and Schuster, 1984).

7. Philip Yancey, *Where Is God When It Hurts?* (Grand Rapids: Zondervan, 1977).

8. Oliver, Earl. *"Antidote For Suffering," Acquainted With Grief* (Quarterly Newsletter, Buckley-King Funeral Homes Inc., Tacoma, WA, 1984).

# CHAPTER 3 - THE BIBLE AND MOURNING

1. George B. Eager, *International Standard Bible Encyclopedia: Burial* (Grand Rapids: Eerdmans, 1939), Volume I, 529–532.

2. Glen W. Davidson, *Understanding Mourning: A Guide For Those Who Grieve* (Minneapolis: Augsburg, 1984), 24–37.

3. Ibid. (quoting J. William Worden), 31.

4. Elizabeth Kubler-Ross, Preface, *On Death And Dying* (New York: MacMillan, 1969).

# CHAPTER 4 - OPPORTUNITY

1. David Wesley Reid, *"Generic Funerals," Ministry Magazine* (Jan. 1999), 24.

2. William Hendriksen, *New Testament Commentary: Exposition of Philippians* (Grand Rapids: Baker, 1962).

3. Thomas Lynch, *"A Serious Undertaking," The Washington Post* (August 3, 2001).

# CHAPTER 6 - THE MESSAGE

1. Mark Coppenger, *"Funerals For Those You Barely Know," Leadership Magazine* (Carol Stream, IL: Christianity Today, Spring 1987).

2. E.M Blaicklock, *The Acts of the Apostles—Tyndale New Testament Commentaries,* gen. ed., R.V.G. Tasker (Grand Rapids: Eerdmans, 1979).

3. William M. Ramsay, *St. Paul the Traveller and Roman Citizen* (Nashville, TN: Broadman, 1979).

4. John Calvin, *Sermons from Job* (Grand Rapids: Baker, 1979).

5. Matthew Henry, *Matthew Henry's Commentary On The Whole Bible* (Old Tappan, NJ: Revell), Volume III, 110.

6. F.F. Bruce, *The Epistle To The Hebrews* (Grand Rapids: Eerdmans, 1964), 311.

7. John G. Mitchell, *An Everlasting Love: A Devotional Study of the Gospel of John* (Portland, Oregon: Multnomah, 1982).

8. Henry, Volume VI, 594.

9. Del Tarr, "*Making Truth Memorable,*" *Leadership Magazine* (Carol Stream, IL: Christianity Today Spring 1983), 66–67.

10. James Montgomery Boice, *Foundations Of The Christian Faith: A Comprehensive and Readable Theology* (Downers Grove, IL: IVP, 1986), 341.

11. John Updike, "Seven Stanzas at Easter," *Telephone Poles and Other Poems* (New York: Knopf, 1961) from Boice, Foundations (1971), 710.

# CHAPTER 7 - MEMORIAL TEXTS

1. James Randolph Hobbs, *The Pastor's Manual* (Nashville: Broadman, 1962).

2. Arthur W Pink, *The Life of David* (Grand Rapids: Baker Book, 1981).

3. Matthew Henry, Volume VI, 597.

4. William Barclay, *The Gospel of John* (Philadelphia: Westminster, 1975), 155.

# CHAPTER 8 - DIFFICULT SERVICES

1. "Difficult," *Thorndike-Barnhart Comprehensive Desk Dictionary* (New York: Doubleday, 1951).

# CHAPTER 9 - CLERGY AND FUNERAL DIRECTORS

1. "Dear Abby," *Tacoma News Tribune* (Tacoma, WA).

2. Thomas Lynch, "A Serious Undertaking," *The Washington Post* (August 3, 2001).

To order additional copies of

# MEMORIALIZING the DEAD
# PREACHING to the LIVING

Have your credit card ready and call:

1-877-421-READ (7323)

or please visit our web site at
www.pleasantword.com

Also available at: www.amazon.com
and www.barnesandnoble.com.

Printed in the United States
35199LVS00005B/19-20

9 781414 100128